Ancient Indian Historiography

Sources and Interpretations

Reconstructing Indian History & Culture
(ISSN 0971-3824)

1. Society in Ancient India; by Sures Chandra Banerji
2. Political Thought in Ancient India; by G.P. Singh
3. Early Indian Historical Tradition and Archaeology; by G.P. Singh
4. Vasantotsava: The Spring Festivals of India; by Leona M. Anderson
5. Ecological Readings in the Veda; by M. Vannucci
6. Vṛndāvana in Vaiṣṇava Literature; by Maura Corcoran
7. Social History of the Tamils (1707-1947); by P. Subramanian
8. Ancient Indian Coinage; by Rekha Jain
9. Buddhism and Socio-Economic Life of Eastern India; by Bimal Chandra Mohapatra
10. Chandragupta Maurya; by P.L. Bhargava
11. Mṛtyu: Concept of Death in Indian Traditions; by Gian Giuseppe Filippi
12. Yama: The Glorious Lord of the Other World; by Kusum P. Merh
13. Sacred Complex of Ujjain; by D.K. Samanta
14. Vedic View of the Earth; by S.R.N. Murthy
15. Society in the Atharvaveda; by B.S. Kharade
16. Orissan History, Culture and Archaeology; by S. Pradhan
17. Education in Ancient India; by Mitali Chatterjee.
18. Surā: The Liquor and the Vedic Sacrifice; by M.B. Kolhatkar
19. Human Ecology in the Vedas; by Marta Vannucci
20. Governance in Ancient India; by Anupa Chandra Pandey
21. The Cultural Glory of Ancient India: A Literary Overview; by Sures Chandra Banerji
22. Kauṭilya's Arthaśāstra in the Light of Modern Science & Technology; by Sunil Sen Sarma
23. History of Jainism : With Special Reference to Mathurā; by V.K. Sharma
24. Cultural Tourism in India: Museums, Monuments & Arts : Theory and Practice; by S.P. Gupta; Krishna Lal; Mahua Bhattacharya
26. Republics, Kingdoms, Towns and Cities in Ancient India; by G.P. Singh
27. Facets of Ancient Indian History and Culture : New Perception; by G.P. Singh
28. Kamakhya : A Socio-cultural Study; by Nihar Ranjan Mishra
29. History and Culture of Tamil Nadu as Gleaned from the Sanskrit Inscriptions Vol. 1 (up to c. AD 1310); by Chithra Madhavan
30. Lifestyle of the Vedic People; by Pranati Ghosal
31. History and Culture of Tamil Nadu as Gleaned from the Sanskrit Inscriptions Vol. 2 (up to c. AD 1310 - c. AD 1885); by Chithra Madhavan
32. Matrimonial Alliances and Ancient Indian Polity (c. 600 BCE to c. 650); by Preeti Prabhat
33. Artisans and Craftsmen of Northern India; by Kuldeep Singh Thind
34. The Evolution of Historiographical Tradition in Ancient and Medieval India; by G.P. Singh
35. Warfare in Ancient India: In Historical outline; by Soma Basu
36. Sanskrit Education and Literature in Ancient India; by Chitra Madhavan
37. Rājadharma in Mahābhārata; by Priyanka Pandey
38. Interstate Relations in Northern India – Circa 800–1200 CE; by Shiva Gopal Bajpai

Reconstructing Indian History & Culture, no. 25

Ancient Indian Historiography
Sources and Interpretations

by
G.P. Singh

PRINTWORLD
Publishers of Indian Traditions

Cataloging in Publication Data — DK
[Courtesy: D.K. Agencies (P) Ltd. <docinfo@dkagencies.com>]

Singh, G.P., author.
Ancient Indian historiography : sources and interpretations / by G.P. Singh.
pages cm. – (Reconstructing Indian history & culture ; no. 25)
"First published in India in 2003" – Title page verso.
Includes bibliographical references and index.
ISBN 9788124602287 (HB)

1. India – History – To 324 B.C. – Historiography. 2. India – History – 324 B.C.-1000 A.D. – Historiography. 3. India – History – 1000-1526 – Historiography. 4. Literature and history – India.
I. Title. II. Series: Reconstructing Indian history & culture ; no. 25.

LCC DS451.S56928 2024 | DDC 954.0072 23

ISBN 978-81-246-0228-7
First published in India in 2003
Reissued in 2017
Third impression printed in 2024

Printed and published by:
D.K. Printworld (P) Ltd.
Regd. Office: "Vedaśrī", F-395, Sudarshan Park
ESI Hospital Metro Station, New Delhi – 110015
Phones: (011) 4172 2626, 98713 94815
e-mail: indology@dkprintworld.com
Website: www.dkprintworld.com

Preface

The primary objective of writing this book is to dispel the hitherto existing impression created by some Indian and foreign scholars that the ancient Indians (the Hindus, Buddhists and Jains) had no sense of history and chronology, and to prove on the basis of my researches carried out over the past two decades that they made substantial contributions to the evolution of historiography in ancient India. A number of important works were produced by the ancient historians of India. The Muslim historian (author of the chronicle "*Chachnama*") of Sindh of early medieval period has also been brought within the preview of the treatment of the subject.

This book is intended for post-graduate students of Indian Universities, research scholars, historians of ancient India and those who are interested in making further study of historiography in ancient India.

I would like to extend my grateful thanks to all those scholars whose I have utilized for writing this book.

The author craves the indulgence of readers for all the errors and misprints that may have crept into the volume.

G.P. Singh

Contents

Abbreviations

AAR	*Annals and Antiquities of Rajasthan.*
ABORI	*Annals of the Bhandarkar Oriental Resarch Institute*, Poona.
Agn.	*Agni Purāṇa.*
AICL	*Ancient India as Described in Classical Literature.*
AIHA	*Aspects of Indian History and Archaeology.*
AIHT	*Ancient Indian Historical Tradition.*
AIIC	*Ancient India and Indian Civilization.*
AIMA	*Ancient India as Described by Megasthenes and Arrian.*
AISH	*Ancient Indian Social History.*
Ait.Br.	*Aitareya Brāhmaṇa.*
AN	*Aṅguttara Nikāya.*
Arth.	*Arthaśāstra of Kauṭilya.*
ASB	Asiatic Society of Bengal, Calcutta.
A.S.Res.	*Asiatic Researches* (*Comprising History and Antiquities, the Arts, Sciences, Ethnology and Literature of Asia*).
ASWI (or *Arch.SWI*)	*Archaeological Survey of Western India, Reports.*
AV	*Atharvaveda.*
BDCRS	*Bulletin of the Deccan College Research Society,* Poona.
BGP	Bhāratiya Jñānapīṭha, Kāśī.
Bhāg.	*Bhāgavata Purāṇa.*
BIS	*Bibliotheca Indica Series* (a Collection of Oriental Works), Asiatic

	Society, Calcutta.
Bmd.	*Brahmāṇḍa Purāṇa.*
Bmv.	*Brahmavaivartta Purāṇa.*
BORI	Bhandarkar Oriental Research Institute, Poona.
Br. (or *Brh*)	*Brahma Purāṇa.*
BRWW	*Buddhist Records of the Western World.*
CAI	Classical Accounts of India (a compilation of the English translations of the Early Greek and Roman Writers' accounts of India), by R.C. Majumdar.
CCBM	*Catalogue of the Indian Coins in the British Museum, Ancient India.*
CCIM	*Catalogue of the Coins in the Indian Museum,* Calcutta, *Coins of Ancient India.*
CHI	Cambridge History of India, vol. I, *Ancient India.*
Chro.Anct.Ind.	*Chronology of Ancient India.*
CII (or *Corp. Ins. Ind.*)	*Corpus Inscriptionum Indicarum.*
CMI	*Coins of Medieval India,* by A. Cunningham, Landon, 1893.
Co.An.Ind.	*Coins of Ancient India from the Earliest times down to the Seventh Century* AD.
Com.Hist.Ind.	*Comprehensive History of India.*
CSARM	*Classical Studies in Ancient Races and Myths.*
Cul. Her. Ind.	*Cultural Heritage of India,* Published by The Ramakrishna Mission Institute of Culture, Calcutta.
DDEI	*Dates and Dynasties in Earliest India.*
DIP	*Dipavaṁsa* (An Ancient Buddhist Historical Record).
DN	*Dīgha Nikāya.*
EAB	*Ethnology of Ancient Bhārata.*

EB (or *En. Br.*)	*Encyclopaedia Britannica.*
EHI	*Early History of India.*
EHIDS	*Early Hindu India : A Dynastic Study.*
EIHTA	*Early Indian Historical Tradition and Archaeology.*
EP.Ind.	*Epigraphia Indica,* Delhi.
ERE	*Encyclopaedia of Religion and Ethics*, New York.
GDEP	*A Critical Study of the Geographical Data in the Early Pirāṇas.*
GEI	*Great Epic of India.*
Geographical Eassys	*Geographical Eassys Relating to Ancient Geography of India.*
Grd. (or *Gar.*)	*Garuḍa Purāṇa.*
HAI	*History of Ancient India.*
HASL	*History of Ancient Sanskrit Literature.*
HCSL	*History of Classical Sanskrit Literature.*
HIL	*History of Indian Literature.*
HOS	Harvard Oriental Series.
HPL	*History of Pāli Literature.*
HSL	*History of Sanskrit Literature.*
Hv.	*Harivaṁśa Purāṇa.*
IETBJ	*India as Described in Early Texts of Buddhism and Jainism.*
IGI (or *Imp. Gaz. Ind*)	*Imperial Gazetteer of India.*
IHC	Indian History Congress.
IHQ	*Indian Historical Quarterly*, Calcutta, new rpt., Delhi.
IIA	*Invasion of India by Alexander the Great as Described* by Arrian, Q. Curtius, Diodoros, Plutarch and Justin.
Ind. Ant.	*Indian Antiquary* (*Journal of Oriental Research in Archaeology,*

	History, Literature, Language, Folklor, etc.), Bombay.
Ind. Co.	*Indian Coins.*
Ind.Stud.	*Indische Studien.*
JAOS	*Journal of the American Oriental Society.*
JAS	*Journal of the Asiatic Society,* Calcutta.
JASB	*Journal of the Asiatic Society of Bengal,* Calcutta.
JBBRAS	*Journal of the Bombay Branch of the Royal Asiatic Society,* Bombay.
JBHU	*Journal of the Benares Hindu University,* Benares.
JBIAS	*Journal of the Bhāratīya Itihāsa Adhyayan Saṁsthān,* Allahabad.
JBORS	*Journal of the Bihar and Orissa Research Society*, Patna.
JIH	*Journal of Indian History*, Trivandrum.
JNSI	*Journal of the Numismatic Society of India*, Vārāṇasī.
JRAS	*Journal of the Royal Asiatic Society of Great Britain and Ireland,* London.
JRASB	*Journal of the Royal Asiatic Society of Bengal*, Calcutta.
JRASB(L)	*Journal of the Royal Asiatic Society of Bengal, Letters*, Calcutta.
JSS	*Jaina Sāhitya Sāṁśodhaka*, Ahmedabad.
Km. (or *Krm*)	*Kūrma Purāṇa.*
LAIJC	*Life in Ancient India as Depicted in the Jaina Canon and Commentaries.*
Lg.	*Liṅga Purāna.*
Mahā.	*Mahāpurāṇa.*
Manu.	*Manu-Smṛti.*
Mass.	Massachusetts, USA.
Mat (or *Mts.*)	*Matsya Purāṇa.*

Mbh.	*Mahābhārata.*
Mbh.Ko.	*Mahābhārata Kośa (A Descriptive Index to the Names and Subjects in the Mahābhārata).*
MDJG	Manikchand Digambara Jaina Granthamālā Series, Bombay.
ME	Mahāvīra Era.
Mhv.	*Mahāvaṁsa.*
Mhv.Comm.	*Mahāvaṁsa Commentary.*
Mkd.	*Mārkaṇḍeya Purāṇa.*
MN	*Majjhima Nikāya.*
Nat. Hist. (or Hist. Nat.)	*Naturalis Historia (Natural History) or Historia Naturalis (History Natural)*, by Pliny.
PDKA	*Purāṇa Text of the Dynasties of the Kali Age.*
Pdm.	*Padma Purāṇa.*
PHAI	*Political History of Ancient India.*
PIHC	*Proceedings of the Indian History Congress.*
PK	*Paurāṇic Kośa.*
POC	*Proceedings of the All India Oriental Conference.*
PTS	Pāli Text Society, London.
Purāṇa	Half yearly Bulletin of the Purāṇa Department, All India Kāśīrāj Trust, Rāmnagar, Vārāṇasī.
QRHS	*Quarterly Review of Historical Studies*, Calcutta.
RPVU	*Religion and Philosophy of the Veda and Upanishads.*
R̥V	*R̥gveda.*
Śat. Br.	*Śatapatha Brāhmaṇa.*
SBA	*Sacred Books of the Aryan Series*, Delhi.
SBB	*Secred Books of the Buddhist.*
SBE	*Secred Books of the East*, Oxford.

SBLN	*Sanskrit Buddhist Literature of Nepal.*
SGAMI	*Studies in the Geography of Ancient and Medieval India.*
SI	*Select Inscriptions Bearing on Indian History and Civilization.*
SN	*Saṁyutta Nikāya.*
Tai. Aran.	*Taittirīya Āraṇyaka.*
v	Verse.
Vāl. Rām.	*Vālmīki-Rāmāyaṇa.*
Vāl. Rām.Ko.	*Vālmīki-Rāmāyaṇa Kośa* (Descriptive Index to the Names and Subjects of *Rāmāyaṇa*).
VE	Vikrama Era.
VI	*Vedic Index of Names and Subjects.*
Vmn.	*Vāmana Purāṇa.*
VOJ	*Vienna Oriental Journal.*
Vrh.	*Varāha Purāṇa.*
VS	Vikrama Samvat.
Vṣṇ	*Viṣṇu Purāṇa.*
Vṣṇ. Dh. (or *VSh.Dh.*)	*Viṣṇudharmottara Mahāpurāṇa.*
vv.	verses
Vy	*Vāyu Purāṇa.*
YCTI	*Yuan Chwang's Travels in India.*

1

Introductory

'HISTORIOGRAPHY is a progressive science, in the sense that it seeks to provide constantly expanding and deepening insights into a course of events which is itself progressive.'[1] The history of historical writing in ancient India has not been studied to the extent it needs. We need "a constructive outlook over the past".[2]

In this book an attempt has been made, as far as possible, to trace the evolution of historiographical tradition in ancient India from the Vedic age down to the twelfth century AD. Ancient India had a very rich tradition of historiography. The tradition of presenting history through literature was constantly maintained by the ancient Indians during the aforesaid period. The Vedic, epic and Purāṇic literature embodying the historical tradition, some Buddhist and Jain works of historical importance, the historical literature of the post-Gupta period, including biographical literature (historical biographies), royal chronicles and historical narratives, and other literary works dealing with contemporary civilization bear eloquent testimony to the fact. The history and culture of ancient India have been recorded in different classes of literary works. But only those works can be considered as historical documents or historical treatises which bear the character of a true history. The different traditions of historiography evolved in different parts of India in different ages. Ancient Indian historiography in perspective of its relative value as well as from chronological point of view can be divided into two distinct phases: (1) from Vedic antiquity to the sixth century AD, and (2) from the seventh to the twelfth centuries AD. There were various schools of historical writing during those periods. The schools which flourished during the latter period made significant contributions to historiography by giving fillip to the production of historical works which are relatively of greater importance. It is hard to believe that the age in which such works were produced was without an historian. The historical data contained in different categories of sources

---

1. E.H. Carr, *What is History*?, p. 124.
2. F. Powicke, *Modern Historians and the Study of History* (London, 1955), p. 174.

falling in between the period under review have been critically analysed and scientifically interpreted. The study of the subject is largely based on original sources: texts and translations.

India, without entertaining the mythical concept of '*Clio* — the Muse of History' from whom the ancient Greeks are traditionally believed to have derived the inspiration to learn history, made a beginning in the field of historiography which was fundamentally based on the literary tradition. It will not be correct to say that the first lesson of history was taught in the school of Greece. The hitherto existing belief, that before the dawn of the modern age historiography whatsoever was unknown in India, can be dismissed without any hitch and hesitation.

The ancient Indians had a clear conception and perception of history. They took history as the soul of the nation. They being conscious of the fact that the culture and civilization of any country get reflected through its history took all possible pains to preserve the historical records of the past. They were not ignorant of an art which has been cultivated in other countries from almost the earliest ages. They like their counterparts or contemporaries in Egypt, Assyria, Babylonia, Greece, Rome, China and Persia left no stone unturned to acquire the knowledge of the past. They were also aware of the fact that it is the past which determines the future of a country, and those who do not have knowledge of the past have neither present nor future. It has been rightly pointed out by E.H. Carr that "Past, present and future are linked together in the endless chain of history."[3] It is an acknowledged fact that one of the chief functions of a historian is to discover the past and the documents it left behind or to study the facts relating to the society and culture of the past so as to provide the key to the understanding of the present.[4]

With the foundation of modern historiography in the eighteenth century various schools of historical thought started emerging. Hume, Voltaire and Gibbon belonging to the school of Enlightenment historians, and Macaulay and Carlyle took the past ages as unworthy of historical study, but we must look at them sympathetically and find in them the expression of genuine and valuble human achievements. G. Barraclough correctly observed that there is nothing wrong in the realm of historiography to discover the past even on the basis of "imperfect and fragmentary evidence".[5] History in the

3. E.H. Carr, *op. cit.*, p. 134.
4. See Carr, *op. cit.*, pp. 21-22, 26, 30, 55; R.G. Collingwood, *The Idea of History*, p. 282.
5. *History in a Changing World*, pp. 29-30.

words of J. Burckhardt is "the record of what one age finds worthy of note in another".[6]

The ancient Indians did keep records of those aspects which they felt were significant and worth preserving[7] "A sense of history can be defined as a consciousness of past events, which events are relevant to a particular society, seen in a chronological framework and expressed in a from which meets the needs of that society . . . the historical tradition can be culled from existing literature, whether specifically historical or not. Every society has a concept of its past and therefore no society can be called a-historical. Furthermore, historical memory is frequently recorded in a chronological order".[8]

It is said that "Whether or not India had a sense of history, she had a lively sense of the past, though this past was generally visualised in legendary terms".[9] It can scarcely be believed that the Indians, who applied their literary genius to almost all conceivable branches of study, failed to pay their attention to chronicling of contemporary events and socio-economic, political, religious and cultural life of the people. In the words of James Tod: "Is it to be imagined that a nation so highly civilised as the Hindus, amongst whom the exact sciences flourished in perfection, by whom the fine arts, architecture, sculpture, poetry and music were not only cultivated, but taught and defined by the nicest and most elaborate rules, were totally unacquainted with the simple art of recording the events of their history, the character of their princes, and the acts of their reigns? Where such traces of mind exist, we can hardly believe that there was a want of competent recorders of events, which synchronical authorities tell us, were worthy of commemoration."[10]

There are so many attestations of the same fact. M. Elphinstone also observes that "As the rudest nations are seldom destitute of some account of the transactions of their ancestors it is a natural subject of surprise that the Hindus should have attained to a high pitch of civilization without any work that at all approaches to the character of a history".[11] However, it cannot be denied that only few of them attained perfection in the art of writing history or seriously took to it. One of the notable deficiencies in their

6. *Judgements on History and on Historians*, p. 158.
7. Romila Thapar, *The Past and Prejudice*, pp. 2-3.
8. Thapar, "The Tradition of Historical Writng in early India", in her *AISH*, pp. 268-69.
9. A.L. Basham cf. V.S. Pathak, *Ancient Historians of India*, Foreword.
10. *AAR*, vol. I, introduction, p. xiv.
11. Quoted in A.K. Majmudar, *Early Hindu India: A Dynastic Study*, vol. I, p. 41.

writings is the conspicuous absence of the details of political achievements of the kings and that of the rise and fall of kingdoms or states with few exceptions.

It is striking to note that ancient India did not witness the compartmentalisation of knowledge. It was looked at in totality and presented in its entirety. History did not emerge as a separate discipline. It rather continued to flourish as a branch of literature until the dawn of modern age. It was unlike today not a subject of specialised knowledge. Nevertheless, its study and writing was never neglected. The writing of history was not a profession but a choice. There was no class of professional historians like today. There are some instances to show that the same writer combined in himself the qualities of a historian, geographer, grammarian, dramatist, poet and so on.

In all ancient countries, including India, where historical tradition was maintained, history developed more as an art (or literature) than as a science.[12] The historiographers of ancient times usually adopted the artistic style of writing. They were least bothered about the creation of real, regular and scientific history. Almost all ancient historical works are more literary in nature than scientfic. It is said that the historical writing up to the seventeenth century (in global context) was regarded predominantly as literature.[13] A.L. Rowse has gone to the extent of saying that "Herodotus and Thucydides, Tacitus and Livy, Clarendon, Hume and Gibbon, Macaulay and Carlyle, were all great artists and among the greatest writers of their time . . . there will always remain history as an art".[14]

This statement is obviously in defence of the artistic role of a historiographer. In ancient Greece and Rome (which were the two main centres of productions of historical works), history was considered a branch of literature as it was in ancient India, and historical works were judged as much on their artistic merits as on their accuracy. It was from early nineteenth century onwards that the professional historians and other academicians with few exceptions started attaching greater importance to scientific history from the standpoints of careful or meticulous regard for the truth, exactness, accuracy and objectivity. It was J.B. Bury who in his lecture at Cambridge University in 1903 for the first time emphatically asserted that "history is not a branch of literature"

---

12. For general idea about importance of history both as a science and an art see A.L. Rowse, *The Use of History*, pp. 86-113.
13. J.W. Thompson, *A History of Historical Writing*, vol. I, preface, p. viii.
14. A.L. Rowse, *op. cit.*, pp. 112-13.

but "a science, no less and no more".[15] But G.M. Trevelyan, the famous British historian, on the other hand, stood for literary history which, acording to him, is not unscientific as it also presents the accounts of the past events in the form of narrative. According to him, the scientific and literary history are of equal importance.[16] B. Croce,[17] Lord Acton,[18] Renan and others also laid strees on both scientific and artistic presentation of truth. Hisory is not bunk in ancient Indian literature. It has only coalesced with myths or legends. But one can be easily distinguished from the other. The evolution of historiography took place in both the East and the West in a literary tradition.

Before we straightway proceed to examine the relevance or correctness of the statements of some Indian and foreign scholars that the ancient Indians lacked the historical sense; they were ignorant of the art of writing history; ancient India was barren of historical writings and it did not produce historians like Herodotus (*c.* 484-425 BC) and Thucydides (*c.* 456-396 BC) of Greece and Livy (*c.* 59 BC - AD 17) and Tacitus (*c.* AD 55-120) of Rome, we shall throw some light on the antiquity of Indian historical tradition with special reference to the *itihāsa-purāṇa* tradition, nature and types of history, traditional concepts of history and chronology, ancient historians and their works, and make a general survey of the progress achieved in the field of writing of history generally called by the Western scholars "literary history of the East".

---

15. *Selected Essays*, ed. by H.W.V. Temperley, pp. 4, 6, 9, 19, 22.

16. *Clio: A Muse and other Essays*, pp. 141ff. The views of both Bury and Trevelyan have been reproduced in F. Stem (ed.), *The Varieties of History: From Voltaire to the Present*, pp. 209-23 and 227-45.

17. *The Theory and History of Historiography*, pp. 20-26; *History as the Story of Liberty*, pp. 19ff.

18. *Lectures on Modern History*, p. 51f.

2

The Itihāsa-Purāṇa Tradition and its Impact on Historiography

IN fact, it was the *itihāsa-purāṇa* tradition which marked the beginning of ancient Indian historical tradition. The three main constituent elements of the historical tradition were *ākhyāna* (narratives), *itihāsa* (past events) and *Purāṇa* (any old tale or ancient lore). These three constitute rudimentary specimens of history. In fact, they contained the seeds of history. *Ākhyāna* signifies presentation of history in a narrative style. *Itihāsa* in real sense of the term signifies history which appears in ancient Indian literature not only as a record of the past but also as a trustworthy guide to contemporary cultures and civilization. In its broader sense it comprises ancient events arranged in the form of story based on historical truth. The writers of the *itihāsa* tradition took history in a very comprehensive sense and attached more importance to the delineation of contemporary social, economic, political, religious and cultural life of the people than to the mere description of wars and battles, political conflicts and discords, etc., Purāṇa is generally applied to tales of primeval antiquity or ancient stories whether quasi-historical, mythological or fanciful. *Itihāsa* or Purāṇa in the widest application of the term denotes actual traditional history. Various legendary and historical accounts of the events of the past or primordial events of mankind have been incoroporated in the *itihāsa*s and Purāṇas. The earliest form of *itihāsa* based on oral tradition emerged in the early Vedic age. The written records of the tradition appeared much later. The written from of history began with written tradition. The literature of both Vedic and post-Vedic times contains the rudiments of history.

The antiquity of *itihāsa-Purāṇa* tradition can be traced back to the Vedic age. The earliest reference to the word Purāṇa occurs in the *Ṛgveda Saṁhitā*, the oldest Vedic text. The sense of ancientness of anything is implied in the word.[1] In the same text, it

1. *ṚV*, 3, 5, 54, 9; 3, 5, 58, 6; 10, 11, 130, 6.

has been used in the form of a tale of hoary antiquity, *gāthā,* etc.[2] Yāska (who may be tentatively placed between *c.* 800-700 BC) also refers to Purāṇa and *itihāsa*. He cites the Kuru dynasty as an example of *itihāsa*, which according to him, may be distinguished from the gāthās.[3] He uses *aitihāsika* for those who interpreted the Veda with reference to traditional history which can also be supported by the statement of Durgācārya (AD 1300-50), a commentator on his work.[4] The Purāṇic *ākhyānas* in the Vedas were purely based on contemporary tradition.[5] *Itihāsa* as a kind of literature is repeatedly mentioned along with Purāṇa in the later texts of the Vedic period as well as in the texts of the post-Vedic times. In the *Atharvaveda Saṁhitā,* the Purāṇa has been mentioned first singularly along with three other Vedas[6] and then conjointly with *itihāsa.* And in this connection we are further told that *itihāsa*, Purāṇa, *gāthā*s (hero-lauds) and *nārāśaṁśī*s (eulogies of the warriors and princes of the past) were known to the people. They being repositories of age-old traditions were seriously studied by scholars and elites of the day.[7] The *Gopatha Brāhmaṇa* mentions not only Purāṇa[8] but also the *itihāsa*-Veda and the Purāṇa-Veda.[9] In the *Śatapatha Brāhmaṇa*, the *itihāsa* and Purāṇa have been identified with the Veda.[10] The compound word *itihāsa*-Purāṇa also figures in it.[11] In one passage, *anvākhyāna* and *itihāsa*[12] are distinguished as different classes of works, but the exact point of distinction is obscure. The former was probably supplementary to the latter. The stories narrated in the Brāhmaṇical texts were also based on *itihāsa-purāṇa* tradition. In the *Taittirīya Āraṇyaka, itihāsa* and Purāṇa have been mentioned together with *gāthā*, *nārāśaṁśī* and *kalpa*.[13] The combination of *itihāsa* and Purāṇa appears in the *Bṛhadāraṇyaka Upaniṣad*.[14]

2. *ṚV*, 9, 6, 99, 4.
3. *Nirukta* (ed. and tr. by Uma Shankar Sharma, Vārāṇasī, 1966), 2, 10; 3, 19; 3, 27; 4, 6.
4. *Nirukta* (ed. with Durgā-cārya's comm. by V.K. Rajavade, Poona, 1921-26), 2, 10; 2, 16; 12, 1-2; 12-10.
5. See S.N. Ray, *Historical and Cultural Studies in the Purāṇas*, p.5.
6. *AV*, 11, 4, 7, 24.
7. *Ibid*., 15, 1, 6, 11-12.
8. *Gopatha Brāhmaṇa*, 1, 2, 10.
9. *Ibid*., 1, 1, 10.
10. *Śat. Br*., xiii, 4, 3, 12-13.
11. *Ibid*., xi, 5, 6, 8.
12. *Ibid*., xi, 1, 6, 9.
13. *Taittirīya Āraṇyaka*, 2, 9.
14. *Bṛhadāraṇyaka Upaniṣad*, 2, 4, 10; 4, 1, 2.

In the *Chāndogya Upaniṣad* also *itihāsa* finds mention in combination with Purāṇa.[15] This is the text which specifically refers to *itihāsa*-Purāṇa as the fifth Veda (*itihāsa-purānaṁ pañcaṁ vedānāṁ vedaṁ*), the four Vedas being the *Ṛk*, *Yajur*, *Sāma* and *Atharva*.[16] From the Upaniṣads it distinctly appears that *itihāsa*, *Purāṇa* and the Vedas were important subjects of study. The *Sāṅkhāyana Śrauta Sūtra* mentions the *itihāsa* as well as the Purāṇa as a Veda.[17] In two *Gṛhya Sūtras* also *itihāsa* and Purāṇa have been mentioned which stand for stories and legends.[18] In one of the early Pāli texts, *itihāsa* is called the fifth Veda.[19] Kauṭilya, who flourished in the fourth century BC, also calls the *itihāsa* a Veda (*Arth.*, 1, 3). Sāyaṇa (AD 1300-80), a commentator on the Vedas, while examining the relationship between the *itihāsa* and Purāṇa tried to distinguish one from the other which yields no consistent result. We find that by the former he means the *Mahābhārata* and by the latter the *brahmāṇḍa*. They, according to him, form parts of the sacred literature which 'consists of either stories of gods or men, or cosmogonic traditions'.[20] In fact, the general use of the compound word *itihāsa*-Purāṇa indicates the close relation between the two.

> In the later Vedic age the three families of the Aṅgirasas, the Atharvans and the Bhṛgus (the families of priest-poets) merged and the resultant composite family of the Bhṛgvāṅgirases successfully carried on the tradition of the *itihāsa*, Purāṇa, *ākhyāna*, *ākhyāyikā*, etc.

There is no denying the fact that in the later Vedic age *itihāsa* assumed greater importance than Purāṇa. However, the fact remains that both were equally popular and remained indistinguishable. In later times, of course, some distinction was made between the two.[21] The connotation of *itihāsa* gradually changed. *Itihāsa* was often used as a general term as it embraced all the old historical and related traditions and also the Purāṇas.

---

15. *Chāndogya Upaniṣad*, 3, 4, 1 & 2.
16. *Chāndogya Upaniṣad*, 7, 1, 2 & 4.
17. *Sāṅkhāyana Śrauta Sūtra*, xvi, 2, 21, 27.
18. *Sāṅkhāyana Gṛhya Sūtra*, I, 24, 8; *Gobhila Gṛhya Sūtra*, 1, 6, 6.
19. *Sutta Nipāta*, III, 7 (Selasutta).
20. Sāyaṇa, *An Introduction to the Ṛgveda Saṁhitā*, pp. 12, 23, cf F. Max Müller, *HASL*, p. 37 note 1 and p. 38; see also *Ṛgveda Saṁhitā*, ed. and trans. with Sāyaṇa's comm. by Max Müller, vol. I.
21. For details see A.D. Pusalker, *Studies in the Epics and Purāṇas*, pp. 44-45; Baldeva Upādhyāya, *Purāṇa Vimarśa*, pp. 6, 11.

The question as to which *itihāsa*-Purāṇa or *itihāsa* has been called the fifth Veda in the Sanskrit and Buddhist texts concerned still remains to be answered. K.F. Geldner on the basis of the evidences whatsoever available in ancient Indian literary texts has reasonably concluded that there existed a single work called *itihāsaveda* or *itihāsa*-Purāṇa.[22] But he has not spelt out the name of the work. His view has been contradicted by Maurice Winternitz[23] and A.A. Macdonell and A.B. Keith.[24] According to them, the *Itihāsaveda* is not any particular book but that branch of learning which consists of stories, legends, etc. They simply state that the *itihāsa-Purāṇa* representing the great body of mythology, legendary history, etc., may roughly be classed as fifth Veda. Emil Sieg, while dealing with ancient Indian *itihāsa* tradition, pointed out that there existed a collection of *itihāsa*s, or *purāṇa*s under the title *Itihāsappurāṇaveda*. He has called the *Mahābhārata* the fifth Veda contending that this great epic possesses all the elements of *itihāsa* and *purāṇa*.[25] J. Hertel has also dealt with the subject but without drawing any positive conclusion.[26] However, the so-called fifth Veda is no other than the *Itihāsa Saṁhitā* or *Purāṇa Saṁhitā* of Vyāsa which has been interchangeably called the *itihāsa-Purāṇa* and the *Purāṇa-itihāsa*. This can irrefutably be proved on the combined testimony of the Purāṇic texts themselves.[27] The details of the subject have been furnished in a separate section dealing with the antiquity and history of the Purāṇa as a single text. Here suffice it to say that ancient traditions preserved in the so-called *itihāsa-Purāṇa* (Purāṇas) about kings of various dynasties, their genealogies and famous deeds, etc., are of great historical importance. The Purāṇic texts deal with various aspects of ancient Indian history which are the glaring examples of *itihāsa*s. The Purāṇas appeared as writ-large (or in the enlarged from) of the Vedas. That is why the *itihāsa-Purāṇa* has been mentioned in the Vedic and Purāṇic literature as the fifth Veda along with other four Vedas. The *itihāsa-Purāṇa* and the Vedas were closely related and equally important. The Purāṇas

22. *Vedische Studien*, I, p. 290f cf. A.A. Macdonell and A.B. Keith, VI, vol. I, pp. 76-78; Maurice Winternitz, *HIL*, vol. I, pp. 312-14.

23. *Op. cit.*

24. *Op. cit.*

25. *Die Sagenstoffe des Ṛgveda und die Indische Itihāsa tradition*, I, pp. 22, 24ff cf. J. Hastings (ed.) *ERE*, Vol. VII (1914), pp. 461-62.

26. J. Hertel, *VOJ*, XVIII, p. 59; XXIII, p. 273.

27. *Bhāg.*, I, 4, 20; 3, 12, 39; *Km.*, 1, 1, 3 and 5; 1, 50, 13-14; *Vy.*, 103, 48, 51, 55-8; *Bmd.*, 1,1, 173; 4,4, 47, 50, 54-58; *Vmn.*, 12,3; *Vṣṇ. Dh.*, 3, 15, 1; *Pdm.*, 5, 2, 53 (all for *Purāṇa Saṁhitā*, *Itihāsa-Purāṇa* or *Purāṇa-Itihāsa*); *Bmv.*, 133, 5 (for *Itihāsa Saṁhitā*); see also Radha Kamal Mukherjee, *The Culture and Art of India*, pp. 24-25.

were considered relatively more important than the Vedas. For achieving proficiency in the correct interpretation, explantion and analysis of the data contained in the Vedas, the sound knowledge of the *itihāsa* and Purāṇa was essential for the brāhmaṇas as evidenced by the *Mahābhārata*,[28] the Purāṇas[29] and one of the Smṛtis.[30] The Purāṇa (in the sense of *itihāsa-Purāṇa*) was one of the main fourteen branches of learning.[31] According to well-established tradition, the *itihāsa* and Purāṇa were regularly studied by the learned members of the society.[32]

The value of *itihāsa-Purāṇa* tradition is fairly illustrated in some of the Purāṇic texts. In some of the Purāṇas, *itihāsa*, Purāṇa and *ākhyāna* have been treated as almost identical. The texts call themselves by all these terms. No clear-cut distinction has been made between them. However, as collective terms *itihāsa* and Purāṇa are often mentioned as distinct.[33] They actually became separate from each other much later. The Purāṇic evidence in this regard is more explicit than the Vedic and Brāhmaṇic ones.

The two epics, the *Rāmāyaṇa* and the *Mahābhārata,* include almost all the elements of historical tradition. The texts themselves bespeak the truth concerned. Vālmīki himself calls his *Rāmāyaṇa* a *purātana* (ancient) *itihāsa*[34] whose justification lies in the historical data contained in the next. The *Mahābhārata* is called *itihāsa*, Purāṇa and *ākhyāna.* Actually, it embodies several *ākhyānas*, *upākhyānas* (short narratives or episodes), etc.[35] It is also called *Arthaśāstra* and *Dharmaśāstra*.[36] It is further said in the text that it is well supproted by the Vedic and Purāṇic evidences.[37] The word *itihāsa* occurs several times in this epic along with *purāvṛtta*, *ākhyāna*, *purāṇa*, *kathā*, etc., which are all synonymous. According to E.W. Hopkins, the *Mahābhārata* (great epic of the Bharatas)

---

28. *Ādi Parva*, I, 204.
29. *Vy.*, I, 200-3; *Pdm.*, V, 2, 50-2; *Nārada Purāṇa*, 2, 24, 17-18.
30. *Vasiṣṭha-Smṛti*, I, 362 (cf. Twenty *Smṛtis*, ed. with Hindi trans. by Shri Rāma Sharma Ācārya, 2 vols., Bareilly, 1979-80).
31. For details see *Vṣṇ.*, 3, 6, 28-29; *Yājñavalkya-Smṛti*, 1, 3.
32. *Yājñavalkya-Smṛti*, I, 101.
33. *Vy.*, 54, 1-3, 115; 103, 48, 51, 55-58; *Bmd.*, IV, 4, 47, 50, 54-58; *Br.*, 131, 2; 161, 27; 234, 4; 245, 27, 30; *Mat.*, 69, 55; *Pdm.*, V, 32, 8-9; VI, 29, 1-3; 192,16; 193, 90-1; *Lg.*, 1, 39, 61.
34. *Vāl. Rām*; *Yuddha (Laṅkā) Kāṇḍa*, 131, 116.
35. *Ādi Parva*, I, 17-19, 24-25, 48-52, 61-63; 56, 18.
36. *Ibid.*, 56, 21.
37. *Ādi Parva*, 56, 15-16.

indifferently called the *itihāsa* and Purāṇa also claims the title of the fifth Veda. The epic accounts in the present form is based upon that of the Purāṇa.[38] He further states that the "historical tales embedded in this epic is not wholly without scholastic affinities".[39] The *Mahābhārata* is relatively more important than the *Rāmāyaṇa* from the historical point of view. It is no doubt a semi-historical work. It is encyclopaedic in nature containing a plethora of materials relating to some conceivable aspects of ancient Indian history and culture. F.E. Pargiter has correctly observed that 'The Purāṇas, the *Mahābhārata* and in a minor degree the *Rāmāyaṇa* profess to give acounts from tradition about the earliest occurrences.'[40] The former two constitute main pillars of the edifice of early Indian historical tradition. In literature of the later period, names like *itihāsa*, *ākhyāna* and Purāṇa are by no means restricted to the *Mahābhārata*, *Rāmāyaṇa* and the Purāṇas. some Buddhist and Jain works are also based on *itihāsa*-Purāṇa tradition to a considerable extent.

The historical data contained in the *R̥gveda*, the epics, the Purāṇas and the Buddhist and Jain works have been highlighted here separately along with other historical works.

Kauṭilya had a comprehensive idea of history. According to him, *itihāsa* is not a single work but a class of literature consisting of the *Purāṇa*, *itivr̥tta* (an account of past events, a narrative or story), *ākhyāyikā* (biographices of kings or princes and important historical personages), *udāharaṇa* (an illustration), the *Dharmaśāstra* (law) and the *Arthaśāstra* (science of polity or state and government).[41] These were the six constituent elements of history. Purāṇa here means Purāṇas which, according to him, were most important of all component parts of *itihāsa*. His description of the *itihāsa* goes well in accord with what we find in one of the Jain Purāṇas of the ninth century AD.[42]

The *itihāsa*, *Purāṇa*, *ākhyāna* and *ākhyāyikā* also received the notices of Kātyāyana (second half of the fourth century BC)[43] and Patañjali as different literary works.[44] Manu

38. *GEI*, pp. 47f, 50, 53; see also E.J. Rapson (ed.), *CHI*, vol. I, p. 224.
39. *CHI*, I, p. 225.
40. *AIHT*, p. 1.
41. *Arth*., I, 5, 13-14.
42. *Mahāpurāṇa* (*Ādi Purāṇa* of Jinasena and *Uttara Purāṇa* of Guṇabhadra, Indore, VE 1973-75), I, 24-25.
43. *Vārttika* (on Pāṇini's *Aṣṭādhyāyī*), 4, 2, 60; also Weber, *Indische Studien*, I, p. 147.
44. *Mahābhāṣya*, ed. by F. Kielhorn (Bombay, 1892-1909), vol. 2, p. 284.

also refers to *ākhyāna*, *itihāsa* and *Purāṇa* (*ākhyānānitihāsāṁś ca purānāṇi*) which were learnt and taught.[45] The *itihāsa* or history mentioned in this text, according to some scholars, include also the two epics. But here it does not refer to any particular book. This is just a traditional way of looking at various form of *itihāsa*. However, works on history embodying ancient traditions, stories, *gāthās*, etc., did exist.[46]Amara Siṁha (fifth or sixth century AD), in his *Amarakoṣa* defines *itihāsa* as *purāvṛtta* (accounts of past events). The commentator on this work includes the *Mahābhārata* in it.[47] Further, *akhyāyikā* (a biographical work dealing with historical subject) has also been referred to therein along with the Purāṇa characterised by its five sections (including dynastic generalogies based on traditions) which it comprises.[48] Rājaśekhara (who belonged to the last quarter of the ninth and first quarter of the tenth century AD) calls the *itihāsa* a Veda. He identifies the Purāṇa (with eighteen divisions) with *itihāsa*. According to him, there are two different kinds of *itihāsa*, viz., *parakriyā* and *purākalpa*. The former focuses on only one hero such as in the *Rāmāyaṇa* and the latter on several heroes such as in the *Mahābhārata*.[49]

The ancient Indian writers do not appear to be consistent in their use of the expression *ākhyāna, itihāsa* and *Purāṇa*, for they sometimes use them as synonymous and sometimes describe them as various kinds of narrative. As a matter of fact, it was not always possible for them to draw any hard and line fast of distinction between them. For a considerable period of time they were treated as intertwined or interrelated. They were actually complementary to each other.

The *itihāsa-Purāṇa* tradition finds reflection not only in Vedas, the epics and Purāṇas but also in the writings of the Buddhist and Jain scholars. The historical writings in ancient India at least to the end of the Gupta period were broadly based on this tradition. The three legitimate constituents of this tradition were myth, genealogy and historical narrative. In the post-Gupta period, there was no doubt slight departure from the earlier tradition. However, the impact of *itihāsa-Purāṇa* tradition is discernible on the historical literature of that period too. The concept or idea of history started changing to a reasonable extent from the seventh century onwards. The *itihāsa* and Purāṇa developed as two

45. *Manu.*, III, 232.
46. See V.S. Agrawala, *India as Described by Manu*, pp. 2 & 9.
47. *Amarakoṣa*, I, 6, 4.
48. *Amarakoṣa*, I, 6, 5.
49. *Kāvyamīmāṁsā*, pp. 5-8.

distinct subjects of study. But the older tradition did not completely die down. Even the writings of Kalhaṇa, the best of all ancient historians of India, bear the stamp of the *itihāsa* and Purāṇa tradition. The statement of V.S. Agrawala, that in ancient India a clear-cut demarcation line between the two was never drawn, is absolutely justified.[50] From the time of Vyāsa to Kalhaṇa various traditions of historiography, including the Vedic, epic, Purāṇic, Buddhist and Jain, flourished one after another.

> Traditions, whether epic or puranic, Jain or Buddhist or purely local, have an important role to play in helping unravel our past cultures and civilization.[51]

Our knowledge of the most ancient past rests mainly on tradition. The tradition is human testimony concerning the long past, and hence it is not to be discarded simply because it contains discrepancies. Ancient Indian historical tradition cannot be put aside as wholly unworthy of credence. Its general trustworthiness can be tested by the results of discoveries and excavations. It may be examined and weighed with the aid of all information available to us. The reasons why some historians are not inclined to accept the forms of ancient Indian *itihāsa* as historical find reflection in the following statement of V.S. Pathak: ". . . conditioned by the language and ideas of modern historiography, historians viewed them rather as the monsters of the fable, who callously turtured and disfigured the fairy princesses of history, and from whose clutches the historians as gallant kings were duty-bound to liberate them; at the best these texts were thought to be full of irrational accretions which should be removed before the pure gold of history could be seen."[52]

The ancient Indian historians have bequeathed to us various types of historical works which include dynastic annals, genealogical records, historical biographies, local chronicles, historical narratives, regional histories, etc. The historical sense of ancient Indian writers is eloquently reflected in the works they have left behind.

---

50. *Itihāsa-Darśana*, pp. 21-22.
51. H.D. Sankalia, "Archaeology and Tradition" in S.P. Gupta and K.S. Ramachandran (ed.), *AIHA* (Delhi, 1977), p. 281.
52. *Ancient Historians of India*, p. 138.

3

The Vedic Tradition

THE earliest literary work of some historical value which the Āryans have left to posterity is the *Ṛgveda*. It is a Saṁhitā or collection of total 1028 (1017 + 11) hymns composed by various priest-poets or sages of great antiquity and arranged into ten *maṇḍala*s or books. The hymns containing historical information reflect the historical sense of those who composed them. They were carefully preserved by the brāhmaṇas and handed down from generation to generation. The knowledge of the past was originally transmitted from one to other through the oral tradition. After the introduction of writing the tradition connected with men and events of bygone times, contemporary persons, the culture and civilization of the Āryans and other subjects was recorded by the brāhmaṇas. They were actually the keepers or preservers of the records of the past. Here it is worthwhile to mention that the Vedic hymns on the whole composed by various authors were collected, compiled, properly arranged and divided or classified into four Saṁhitās by the great sage, Kṛṣṇa Dvaipāyana Vyāsa (the son of Parāśara), in the beginning of the *Dvāpara* age. And thereafter he became popularly known as Veda-Vyāsa. It is believed that Vasukra, a famous Kaśmīrī Brāhmaṇa, undertook the task of explaining the Veda and committing it to writing.

The *Ṛgveda* contains a lot of historical data about the life and culture of the Āryans. The data contained in the text about their original homeland within the geographical boundary of India and their settlement patterns are of exceptional value. It is this text from which we learn that the Āryans were originally settled in the territory lying along the rivers, Kubhā (Kābul), Suvāstu (Swāt), Krumu (Kurram), Gomatī (Gomal) and Hariyupiā (Hariruda of Herat) in Afghanistan,[1] and the Sindhu (Indus) and its principal tributaries, Vitastā (Jhelum), Asikni (Cenāb), Paruṣṇi (Rāvī), Vipāśā (Vyāsa) and Śutudri (Sutlej) — the five rivers of the Punjab on the west — and the Sarasvatī on the east

1. *ṚV*, 5, 53, 9; 5, 61, 19; 6, 27, 5; 8, 19, 37; 10, 75, 6; see also 10, 64, 8-9.

called the Sapta-Sindhu region (the land of seven rivers).[2] There are some indications in the text about their original settlements in Bālhika or Bāhlika region (the Vaṁkṣu Valley) also.[3] The allusions to the rivers — the Gaṅgā and the Yamunā — in the text[4] indicate that they were partly settled in the Gangetic doab. In early Vedic times, the Gaṅgā-Yamunā doab and "the territory between the rivers, Sarasvatī and Dṛṣadvatī, were occupied by the Bharatas" (3, 23, 4). The areas inhabited by the Āryans in the Ṛgvedic age extended from Afghanistan to the Gangetic valley. The information contained in the text about the social system, economic condition, political organisation and religious and cultural life of the Āryans, their internal divisions, mutual hostility and conflicts with the non-Āryans, inter-tribal warfare, the Dāsas or Dasyus, the expansion of Āryan culture by the Paṇis (a trading class) outside India, etc., are of great historical value.

There are incidental allusions in the *Ṛgveda* to the five allied Āryan peoples, viz., Anus, Druhyus, Yadus, Turvasas and Purus[5] who were the dwellers of the Sapta-Sindhu region. Besides these, the Bharatas (who later merged into the Kurus), Tritṣus, Śṛñjayas, Krivis, and other minor groupes are also mentioned in the text. One of the notable events of the Ṛgvedic age known as the Battle of ten kings also finds mention in the text (7,18; 7,83, 1-8). This great battle was fought on the river Paruṣṇi or Rāvī in which Sudās, king of the Bharatas, defeated with the help of Indra the confederate peoples led by ten kings (five of whom were heads of the above-mentioned allied Āryan groups and remaining five were the chiefs of non-Āryan tribal groups, viz., Alinas, Pakthas, Śivas, Bhalānases and the Viṣāṇins of the north-west) and established the political supremacy of the former over the latter. This event constitutes one of the significant aspects of the Ṛgvedic history dealing with political life of the Āryans.

The *Ṛgveda* refers to some important kings like Manu, the son of Vivasvāna (10, 63, 1), Ikṣvāku (10, 60, 4), the dynastic history of which is available in the *Rāmāyaṇa* and Purāṇa, Purūravā (10, 95, 11), Kuruśravaṇa (10, 33, 4), who is identical with Saṁvaraṇa's

---

2. *ṚV*, 10, 75, 1-8; 2, 12, 12; 2, 41, 16-17; 3, 33, 1-3; 4, 30, 11; 5, 52, 9; 5, 53, 9; 6, 61, 1-14; 7, 36, 6; 7, 95, 1-6; 7, 96, 1-5; 7, 185, 89, 8, 24, 27; 8, 28, 25; 10, 43, 3; 10, 49, 9; see also A.C. Das, *Ṛgvedic India — Cultural History of India as depicted in the Ṛgveda*, vol. I, pp. 8ff, 19-67, 122f; J. Muir, *Original Sanskrit Texts*, vol. II, p. 322; Z.A. Ragozin, *History of Vedic India*, p. 63f.
3. Das, *op. cit.* vol. I, p. 72.
4. *ṚV*, 10, 75, 5.
5. *ṚV*, I, 108, 8; 7, 18, 6, 12-14; 10, 62, 10; see also A.A. Macdonell and A.B. Keith, VI, I, pp. 466-67; II, pp. 11-13; R.C. Jain, *EAB*, pp. 70-92; Hopkins, *JAOS*, XV, p. 260.

son Kuru mentioned in the *Mahābhārata* and Purāṇas, Nahuṣa (1, 122, 8; 7, 95, 2; 9, 91, 2) and his son and successor, Yayāti (10, 63, 1). Their dynasties and genealogies are not given in the text, but their historicity is beyond doubt. The text also metions the names of Divodāsa, Mudgala, Śṛñjaya, Cyavana and his son Sudāsa and one of his descendants named Somaka[6] who were the rulers of North Pañcāla kingdom north of the Gaṅgā. The historical credibility of the Ṛgvedic references to these kings can be confirmed by the Purāṇic genealogy of North Pañcāla dynasty. However, it cannot be denied that the contemporary historical notices in the *Ṛgveda* in spite of having all the trustworthiness of first-hand evidence have no chronological setting, and by themselves yield little information that can be co-ordinated for historical purposes.

Louis Renou has correctly stated that some of the Ṛgvedic hymns are "historical". They contain the "rudiments of history".[7] Adolf Kaegi also observes that these hymns were composed "with the intention of protecting the heritage of ancestral times from further corruption, and from destruction"; and the "*Ṛgveda* is therefore, to an extent, a scientific, historical collection".[8] "We have in these hymns", writes L. Geiger, "the picture of an original, primitive life of mankind, free from foreign influences. . . ."[9] "They are not narration of events, but provide incidental evidence on the life of the Aryans. They can be treated as being historically fairly authentic, since their composition was contemporary with the period described".[10]

R.P. Chanda says : "The dawn of history is heralded in India by the hymns sung by the Ṛṣis and enshrined in the *Ṛgveda Saṁhitā*". (*The Indo-Aryan Races*, p.1)

Muir calls the *Ṛgveda* a "historic Veda".[11] Its historical value as the most ancient record of the Āryans has been acknowledged by a number of scholars.[12] A.A. Macdonell

---

6. See also C. Chakraberti, *CSARM*, pp. 26-27 for the kings mentioned in the *Ṛgveda*.
7. *Vedic India*, p. 6.
8. *Life in Ancient India* (Studies in Rigvedic India), pp. 11-12.
9. Quoted in *ibid.*, p. 37.
10. Romila Thapar, *A History of India*, vol. I, p. 30, note.
11. *Op. cit.*, p. 201.
12. Ragozin, *op. cit.*, pp. 274ff, 335; A. Weber, *HIL*, pp. 5-8; Winternitz, *HIL*, pp. 119f. 169, 290; A.B. Keith, *HSL*, p. 3f; *RPVU*, *HOS*, vol. XXXI, pt. 1, p. 15; *The Hymns of the Atharvaveda*, Eng. trans. with comm. by R.T.H. Griffith, vol. I, Preface, pp. IV-V; W.D. Whitney, *On the Vedas* (trans. of the *Atharvaveda Saṁhitā*), vol. I, pp. 10 & 21; H. Baveridge, *A Comprehensive History of India*, vol. I, p. 19; R.C. Dutt, *A History of Civilisation in Ancient India based on Sanskrit Literature*, vol. I, *c.* 2000-320 BC, pp. 2, 4-5, 9-12, 30-32, 109-11; Radha Kumud Mookerji, *Ancient India*, p. 5; Pt. Viśveśvaranāth Reu, *Ṛgveda Par Ek Aitihāsik Dṛṣṭi*, pp. 119ff.

describes it as a "unique monument of a long vanished age" and further adds that it contains some materials of historical interest.[13] "The Indian conception of history is skilfully embodied in one of the early extant Vedic Aryan culture."[14]

According to F. Max Müller, the Veda is the earliest history of the Āryan family. It is the safe basis of Indian history. It has importance not only in the history of India but also in the history of the world.[15] He writes in one of his essays that "For a study of man, or . . . for a study of Aryan humanity, there is nothing in the world equal in importance to the Veda. I maintain that to everybody who cares for himself, for his ancestors, for his history or for his intellectual development, a study of the Vedic literature is indispensable . . . it is far more improving than the reigns of Babylonian and Persian kings, even than the dates and deeds of many of the kings of Judah and Israel."[16]

U.N. Ghoshal has clearly stated that the oldest Indian historical tradition is preserved in the Vedic literature. The historical sense, according to him, had dawned upon the Indians at the beginning of their history.[17] This can more or less be corroborated by the statements of A.K. Warder.[18]

F.E. Pargiter admits that the *Ṛgveda*, which is the oldest and the greatest Brāhmaṇical book, "contains historical allusions, of which some record contemporary persons and events, but more refer to bygone times and persons and are obviously based on tradition".[19] He further observes that "the historical tradition preserved in the Vedic literature has one great merit over that in the epics and Purāṇas that that literature has been very carefully preserved and what it contains now is the statements of the contemporary age". Its statements "being ancient are nearer accuracy than statements in the epics and Purāṇas which were not so scrupulously preserved".[20] But, on the other hand, he contradicts his own statement by saying that "Vedic literature is not authoritative in historical matters ("except where it notices contemporary matters"), and conclusions

13. *HSL*, pp. 140-41.
14. Radha Kamal Mukerjee, *op. cit.*, p. 37.
15. *HASL*, pp. 11, 57-59; see also M. Krishnamachariar, *HCSL*, introduction, p. VII; Maurice Phillips, *The Teaching of the Vedas*, pp. 26-27.
16. *The Vedas*, introduction, p. ix.
17. *The Beginnings of Indian Historiography and other Essays*, pp. 22-23.
18. *An Introduction to Indian Historiography*, pp. 15-16.
19. *AIHT*, p.1.
20. *Ibid.*, p. 10.

drawn from it are not criteria for estimating the results yielded by historical tradition in the epics and Purāṇas".[21] He has repeatedly mentioned that the Vedic texts are not books of historical purpose nor do they deal with history.[22] But such view is no longer tenable. A.B. Keith while dealing with the nature of Vedic *itihāsa* has attached considerable importance to the Ṛgvedic history.[23] He says: "That the Vedic texts, the Saṁhitās and the Brāhmaṇas, are not books of historical purpopse is notorious."[24]

The Vedic historical tradition cannot be brushed aside as wholly unworthy of attention. It has been truly said that "The evidences derived from the Vedic literature are indeed very strong and generally carry more authority inasmuch as many of them are either directly contemporary records or are traditions derived from contemporary evidences".[25]

In fact, It is only the *Ṛgveda* which deals with history and culture of the early Vedic period. L.J. Trotter observes: "The history of that olden (Āryan) civilization has been written for us, not in chronicles like those which form the boast of Muhammadan India, but in the sacred writings of Saskrit-speaking Hindus, and in poems which portray the social life of pre-historic India as vividly as Homer portryed the social life of pre-historic Greece."[26]

---

21. *Ibid.*, p.14.
22. *Ibid.*, pp. 2, 9, 10-12, 61.
23. *JRAS*, 1911, pp. 979-95; 1912, pp. 429-38.
24. *Ibid.*, 1914, pp. 739, 1031 note; 1915, p. 143, note.
25. S.N. Pradhan, *Chro. Anct. Ind.*, Preface, p. XI.
26. *History of India from the Earliest Times to the Present day*, pp. 2-3.

4

The Epic and Purāṇic Tradition

The Epic Tradition

THE epic tradition of presenting the history was completely different from that of the Vedic, as it appears from the *Rāmāyaṇa* and the *Mahābhārata*. Both the epics have considerable historical value.

The *Rāmāyaṇa* of Vālmīki has been rightly called a historical epic.[1] As already stated, the author himself calls it a *purātana itihāsa* (ancient history) which gets vindicated by his incorporation of dynastic history of the Solar and Lunar families and other historical details of various kingdoms and principalities, towns and cities, polity and administration, the condition of the Āryan society in the time of the *Rāmāyaṇa*, life and culture of some tribal people, etc., in it. The historicity of *Rāmāyaṇa* can no doubt be proved to a certain extent.[2] But K.K. Dasgupta's view, that it is "the first historical biography produced in India",[3] cannot be accepted.

The genealogy of the kings of Ayodhyā (the capital of Kośala kingdom) from Ikṣvāku down to Rāma of the Solar family is preserved in Vālmīki's *Rāmāyaṇa*. The genealogy is no doubt systematically arranged. But it is incomplete as it contains only some 35 kings.[4] As a matter of fact, there were 64 kings in the pre-Rāma period as it appears from the Purāṇic records. A brief history of two other dynasties (the Videha dynasty and the

---

1. *Vāl. Rām.*, *Bāla Kāṇḍa*, ed. with Hindi tr. of Pt. Yudhiṣṭhira Mimāṁsaka by Pt. Akhilānanda, p. 13 note 2.
2. See S.C. De, *Historicity of Rāmāyaṇa and the Indo-Aryan Society in India & Ceylon*, pp. 37ff.
3. "Historical Biography in Sanskrit Literature" in S.P. Sen (ed.), *Historical Biography in Indian Literature*, p. 6.
4. *Bāla Kāṇḍa* 70, 21-44; *Ayodhyā Kāṇḍa*, ed. with Hindi tr. by Pt. Akhilānanda, 110, 6-35; see also *Vāl. Rām. Ko.*, p. 136 (for genealogical list).

Vaiśāla dynasty) of the same Solar family is also given in the text. The Videha dynasty sprang from Ikṣvāku's son Nimi who is also called Videha. He was the founder of the royal family of Mithilā. He was succeeded by his son Mithi whose son was Janaka I who was further succeeded by several kings down to the time of Śiradhvaja (identical with Janaka II). From the genealogical order of the kings of this dynasty it appears that in the line of Nimi there were fifty-two kings after him who ruled over the kingdom of Videha with its capital at Mithilā (Janakapura, which now lies just with in the border of Nepal).[5] The text is replete with some valuable information about the history and antiquity of the Vaiśāla dynasty. The king Viśāla was the founder of this dynasty or kingdom with its capital at Vaiśālī also called Viśālā. From the genealogical list of the kings of this dynasty as given in the text it appears that he was succeeded by nine kings down to Sumati.[6]

The *Rāmāyaṇa* furnishes us with the history of the Lunar family also. We are told that Purūravā ruled at Pratiṣṭhāna (modern Jhūnsī opposite Allahabad), the capital city of Madhyadeśa.[7] Nahuṣa[8] was succeeded by his son, Yayāti, whose five sons, Yadu,Turvasa or Turvasu, Druhyu, Anu and Puru[9] ruled over different kingdoms. Brahmadatta, the king of Kāmpilipurī (Kāmpilya), the capital of south Pañcāla kingdom, also finds mention in the text.[10] The information supplied in it about the Haihaya dynasty is of paramount historical importance. The Haihayas constitute one of the branches of the Yādavas in Yadu's line. The king Haihaya and his successors are generally called the Haihayas. Their genealogy is also partly given in the text. The Haihayas extended their rule to the Narmadā Valley during the time of Kṛtavīrya's son Arjuna. The latter is said to have conquered Māhiṣmatī, situated on the banks of the Narmadā, by defeating Karkoṭaka, a Nāga chief who had settled over there and subsequently made it his fortress capital. The Haihayas established themselves in that part of India by overthrowing the Nāgas of the Narmadā region.[11] The hostile relations of the Haihayas and Tālajaṅghas with the Kośala kingdom during the time of one of its king, Asita, also finds reflection in the text.[12] Some

5. *Bāla Kāṇḍa*, 71, 3-20; see also *Vāl. Rām. Ko.*, pp. 114-16, 171.
6. *Ibid.*, 47, 11-17; also 45, 8-12.
7. *Uttara Kāṇḍa*, 56, 26; also 90, 22.
8. *Ibid.*, 56, 27-28.
9. *Ibid.*, 58, 8-13.
10. *Bālakāṇḍa*, 33, 19; *Vāl. Rām. Ko.*, p. 57.
11. *Uttara Kāṇḍa*, 31, 7-10; 32, 1-7.
12. *Bāla Kāṇḍa*, 70, 28-29.

fragments of information about the Kāśī dynasty are also found there in.[13]

Vasu (Uparicara Vasu, fourth in succession from Kuru's son, Sudhanvan) and his five sons, including Bṛhadratha who was the founder of the kingdom of Magadha with its capital at Girivraja and Kuśa or Kuśāmba who founded Kauśāmbī (the capital of Vatsa kingdom), also find mention in the *Rāmāyaṇa*.[14]

A number of towns and cities like Pratiṣṭhāna, Prāgjyotiṣapura, Ayodhyā, Mithilā, Vaiśālī, Mathurā, Hastināpura, Girivraja (Rājagṛha), Māhiṣmatī, Kāmpilya and Kuśāvatī also figure in the *Rāmāyaṇa*. The text not only deals with the history of their foundations but also gives their vivid description and provides a glimpse into an urban life. It also abounds in information about the rights and duties of a king, nature and funçtioning of the state, administration of justice, war and politics, the social and religious life of the Āryans, etc.

The *Rāmāyaṇa* throws a good deal of light on the historical geography also with regard to various kingdoms, principalities, *janapada*s and urban centres and various races and tribes existing in different parts of India in those days.[15] Monier-Williams (*Indian Epic poetry*, London, 1863, p. 8) H. Jacobi (*Das Rāmāyana,* Bonn,1893) and R.C. Dutt (*A History of Civilisation in Ancient India*, Calcutta, 1899, p. 211) have also acknowledged the historical value of this epic.

The *Mahābhārata* was originally composed by Vyāsa exactly three years after the Great Bhārata battle came to an end.[16] It was first named *Jaya Itihāsa*. In the text itself it has been repeatedly called an *itihāsa* (history).[17] It is further said that this *Bhārat Itihāsa*, full of the details of valuable subjects, is the best of the *itihāsas*.[18] It was also called *Bhārata Saṁhitā* because of being a history of Bharat dynasty. It consisted of 24,000 verses.[19] Further, many stories and contemporary events were incorporated and many additions were made in it which led to the increase in the number of its verses to 100,000. And thereafter it became popularly known as the *Mahābhārata*. The text in the present enlarged form (divided into eighteen *parvan*s or books) consists of exactly the

13. *Uttara Kāṇḍa*, 38, 15-20.
14. *Bāla Kāṇḍa*, 32, 1-9; also *Vāl. Rām. Ko*., pp. 71, 73, 83, 103, 315.
15. See *Kiṣkindhā Kāṇḍa*, ed. with Hindi tr. by Pt. Akhilānanda, Chs. 37-50.
16. *Ādi Parva*, 56, 32.
17. *Ibid*., I, 24-25, 48, 52; 56, 18-20, 25-27; *Svargārohaṇa Parva*, 5, 39, 43; also *Bh. Sv*., vol. 3, p. 230.
18. *Ibid*., 2, 31-33; also 56, 15-16.
19. *Ibid*., 1, 61.

same number of verses. It is believed to have been redacted twice, once in the Śuṅga period and then in the Gupta period.

Some scholars are of the view that the *Mahābhārata* is "a work of history",[20] which is not unworthy of acceptance. C.V. Vaidya considers it both an epic and a history.[21] He further writes: ". . . . Works known as Histories or *Itihāsas* were known even in Vedic times. The *Mahābhārata* itself was originally a history. . . ."[22] V.S. Agrawala opines that it is not that type of history in which historical events are chronologically arranged. It has its own historical value.[23] It is no doubt an encyclopaedia of historical knowledge. It sheds light on different aspects of ancient Indian history.

The *Mahābhārata* as a whole contains valuable historical information about the dynastic history and genealogies of the Lunar race of both pre- and post-Bhārata war period, towns and cities, kingdoms and republics, kingship and state, polity and adminstration, Āryans and non-Āryans, the contemporary social and religious conditions of the people, etc.

The genealogies of the kings of the Lunar dynasty of the pre-war period given in the *Mahābhārata* include that of Purūravā, of the five sons Yayāti, Aṇu, Druhyu, Turvasu, Yadu and Puru, of the kings of Puru's descendants called Pauravas, the kings of Bharata and Kuru dynasties in the line of the Pauravas and the kings of the Pañcāla dynasty.[24] The histories of the kingdoms and dynasties of the Āṇavas (descendants of Aṇu),[25] The Yādavas in general including the Andhaka-Vṛṣṇīs,[26] the Bhojas[27] and the Haihayas,[28] the

20. K.K. Dasgupta, *op. cit.*, p. 6; Umāśaṅkar Dīkṣita, *Maharṣi Vedavyāsa* (A Historical & Cultural Biography), p. 13.

21. *The Mahābhārata : A Criticism*, pp. 37ff, 50ff.

22. *Ibid.*, p. 59.

23. *Bh. Sv.*, vol. 1, pp. 27-30; vol. 3, pp. 235-39, 262-64.

24. *Ādi Parva*, 1, 44-45, 138; 69, 49; 70, 11-45; ch. 71; 80, 26; 82, 5; 89, 5-55; 90, 7-96; also *Bh. Sv.*, vol. 1, pp. 83-87, 150-72.

25. *Ādi Parva*, 88, 6, 17-19; also 1, 172-75; 207, 9-10; *Sabhā Parva*, 29, 5-6; *Droṇa Parva*, 6, 2-7; *Bhīṣma Parva*, 10, 7.

26. *Ādi Parva*, 210, 15-20; 213, 23-55; *Sabhā Parva*, 13, 3-55; *Śānti Parva*, 82, 8-29.

27. *Sabhā Parva*, 13, 4-7, 24-25; 28, 1-15, 37-43.

28. *Ādi Parva*, 31, 5-8; 98, 1; *Anuśāsana Parva*, 152, 3-4; *Udyoga Parva*, 19, 22-23; *Sabhā Parva*, 28, 17 & 24; see also Sorensen, *Index to the Names in the Mahābhārata*, I, p. 458; II, p. 457.

Yādavas from Mathurā to Dvārakā (which include the details of the reasons of shifting the capital from the former place to the latter, their fratricidal war and destruction and sinking of Dvārakā city in the sea),[29] the Pauravas, Bhāratas, Kurus and Pañcālas,[30] etc., are also depicted therein. The dynastic history of the Kāśī[31] and Magadha kingdoms[32] described in the text is of equal historical value. The details provided therein about the Kuru kingdom of Hastināpura ruled by the successors of Parīkṣit II in the post-war period are also of considerable historical importance.[33] There are also some fragments of information about the Nāga dynasty.[34] However, the dynastic genealogies are not mutually consistent, and the chronological sequence of events is broken to a certain extent. These are the two deficiencies which are noticeable in the presentation of the historical accounts of the kingdoms and dynasties in this epic.

The *Mahābhārata* also throws light on early phase of urban settlements in the Gangetic valley as well as in other parts of India. It contains information about the foundations and growth and some urban features of some towns and cities like Hastināpura, Indraprastha, Kauśāmbī, Ahicchatrā, Kāmpilya, Girivraja (Rājagṛha), Campā, Kāśī (Vārāṇasī) and Māhiṣmatīpur. Their existence have already been archaeologically proved. The history of Dvārakā city in Gujarat in particular from its foundation to its submerging into the sea exactly thirty-six years after the war or Great Bhārata battle is recorded in the epic. The information provided in it about the seals made out of shell bearing the engravings of *padma* (lotus) symbol (*Āraṇyaka Parva*, 80, 83) is quite consistent with the findings of distinguished marine archaeologist, S.R. Rao. He discovered exactly the same seals from Bet-Dvārakā sometime between November 1987 and February 1988. It is striking to note that the political importance and economic

29. *Ādi Parva*, 210, 15-20; 213, 23-55; *Sabhā Parva* 13, 5-55; *Āraṇyaka Parva*, 16, 5-23; 17, 1-33; *Mūsala Parva*, 2, 1-20; 3, 1-22; 4, 32-41; 6, 1-15; 7, 9-22; 8, 4-10, 32-74; *Mahāprasthānika Parva*, 1, 43 (for Sunken Dvārakā city in the sea as beheld by the Pāṇḍavas with their own eyes during the course of their wanderings); see also *Bh. Sv*; vol. I, pp. 143-44; vol. 3. pp. 221-23; *Mbh. Ko.*, p. 100.

30. For all see *Ādi Parva*, 89, 5-90; 90, 10-96; also 1, 44-45; 55, 22-25; 105, 17-22; 214, 13, 22-35; 3, 144-46; 37, 9; *Sabhā Parva*, Ch. 48; *Virāṭa Parva*, 1, 9-14; *Bh. Sv.*, vol. 1, pp. 84-85, 99; *Mbh. Ko.*, pp. 199-200.

31. *Anuśāsana Parva*, 31, 10-26.

32. *Ādi Parva*, 57, 1-2, 7-12, 27-30; *Sabhā Parva*, 17, 4-9, 21-23; 18, 21-30; 19, 1-18; 13, 29-32; *Bh. Sv.*, vol. 1, pp. 143, 146-47.

33. *Ādi Parva*, 3, 10-18, 144-46, 179-80; 40, 6-8, Ch. 94; *Bh. Sv.*, vol. I, p. 53; *Mbh. Ko.*, p, 293.

34. *Ādi Parva*, 3, 119-22, 140, 144-46, 166-69; 31, 5-18; 52, 5-19; *Bh. Sv.*, vol. 1, pp. 128-29.

value of the seals of Dvārakā in Kṛṣṇa's time have also been highlighted respectively in the above Parva of the *Mahābhārata* (16, 19) and the *Harivaṁśa* (Viṣṇu Parva, 58, 57-66). The archaeological discovery of the remains of sunken Dvārakā city from the Arabian Sea and that of the said seals by Shri Rao proves not only the historicity of Kṛṣṇa but also the historical authenticity of the epic account of the city. Some other urban centres like Tāmralipti, Bharukaccha Śūrpāraka, Virāṭanagar, Madra's capital Śākala, Daśapura, Tripurī, Prāgjyotiṣapur, Bhojakatapura, Kuṇḍinapura, Sūktimatipura, Uragapura (one of the early capitals of Coḷa kingdom), Rājapura, the capital of Kāmboja, and Maśaka (Massaga in the Swāt Valley which was in a flourishing condition at the time of Alexander's invasion of north-west India) also find mention in the Great epic.

A long list of kingdoms (states) and *janapadas* (territorial units and peoples) existing in different parts of India[35] and that of republican communities, notably the Andhaka-Vṛṣṇīs, the confederate Yādava tribes of Mathurā,[36] and the Śivis, Kuṇindas, Trigartas, Ambaṣṭhas, Oḍambaras, Yaudheyas and Kṣudraka- Mālavas of the Punjab[37] are furnished in the *Mahābhārata*. The details of the evolution of institution of kingship, the origin or formation of the state and its seven constituents (based on *saptāṅga* theory), nature and types, aims and functions and growth and decline, inter-state relations, etc., have also been provided in this work.[38] The monarchical and republican forms of government are said to have prevailed. The information contained in it about the administrative system followed in a monarchical state, the powers and functions of the king and his *mantrīpariṣad*, councillors, subordinate rulers and officers, military administration, judicial administration, village and city administration, *gaṇa* form of government, i.e., the rule of the many, etc., are of great value.

---

35. *Sabhā Parva*, 23, 13-26; 24, 1-27; 25, 1-18; 26, 1-16; 27, 1-28; 28, 1-50; 29, 1-19; 31, 6-25; 47, 10-16; 48, 3-42; *Bhīṣma Parva*, 10, 37-68; 12, 33-35; *Droṇa Parva*, 4, 4-5; 6, 2-7, 10, 15-16; Chs. 17-19, 22-28, 31 & 114; *Karṇa Parva*, 27, 71-91; 30, 9-81; *Udyoga Parva*, 19, 7-32; *Virāṭa Parva*, I, 9-14; 5, 3-21; 29, 1-28; ch. 30; 31, 1-24; 32, 3-12; *Āśvamedhika Parva*, 84, 1-19; *Bh. Sv.*, vol. I, pp. 150-53; vol. 2, pp. 121-47, 159, 169-72, 247-76; *Mbh. Ko.*, pp. 14ff; see also S.N. Pande, *Geographical Horizon of the Mahābhārata*, pp. 119-43.

36. *Śānti Parva*, 82, 8-29; 108, 8-31; see also K.P. Jayaswal, *Hindu Polity*, App. A, pp. 355-60.

37. *Sabhā Parva*, 23, 13-15; 29, 1-8; 48, 12-14; *Droṇa Parva*, 6, 2-7; 10, 16; *Bh. Sv.*, vol. 3, pp. 89-95, 259-60; see also B.P. Roy, *Political Ideas and Institutions in the Mahābhārata*, pp. 166-88.

38. *Śānti Parva*, 56, 2-36; 57, 4-42; 58, 1-24; 59, 13-18; 67, 2-14; chs. 69, 81, 84, 87, 91-95, 162; 104, 11-30; 108, 8-31; ch. 308; *Bh. Sv.*, vol. 3, pp. 23, 41-58, 67-69; see also Roy, *op. cit.*, pp. 88-165, 335-82; G.P. Singh, *Political Thought in Ancient India*, pp. 21-130.

The original settlements of the Āryans in the region extending from the western bank of the Yamunā to Kurukṣetra on the bank of the Sarasvatī (which formed a part of the Sārasvata region) are also described in the Great epic.[39] Kurukṣetra was situated to the south of the Sarasvatī and the north of the Dṛṣadvatī. Several non-Āryan races and tribes and foreign invaders like Śakas, Pahalvas (Pārthians), Yavanas (Bactrian Greeks) and Hūṇas also find mention in it.

The picture of contemporary social life with details of caste system, the position of nobles, the brāhmaṇas, slaves and women, the custom of *satī*, the practice of polygamy, marriage system and the religious beliefs, etc., is vividly portrayed in the Great epic.

The Purāṇic Tradition

The Purāṇic tradition of historigraphy deserves our special attention. The Purāṇas have their own history. There was originally a single text called *Purāṇa Saṁhitā* (or *Itihāsa Saṁhitā*) whose authorship has been ascribed to the great sage, Veda-Vyāsa, twenty-eighth in the line of Vyāsas who were known by different names. He inherited the tradition of perserving and compiling the Purāṇic data from his predecessors. It is categorically stated in the Purāṇic texts that after having classified the single Veda into four Saṁhitās, he first composed the Purāṇa divided into eighteen parts consisting of *ākhyānas*, *upākhyānas*, *gāthās*, etc., and then a *itihāsa* (history) named the *Mahābhārata* (*Bhārata Saṁhitā*) incorporating in it some Purāṇic data in the *Dvāpara* age itself.[40] The said eighteen Purāṇas contain among other things historical tradition of the Āryans. A.K. Warder's view, that the original Purāṇa was composed in the eighth century BC during the reign of Adhisīmakṛṣṇa of the *Kali* age (sixth in the succession from Abhimanyu) or may have existed in some form ealier,[41] appears to be confusing. In fact, the Purāṇa was narrated and not composed during the reign of the said king. In reality, it was the *Dvāpara* age which marked the beginning of the tradition of historical writing in early India.

It is significant to note that Maharṣi Veda-Vyāsa in his Purāṇas and the *Mahābhārata*

---

39. *Āraṇyaka Parva*, 81, 1-7; also *Bh. Sv*., vol. I, pp. 255-56.

40. *Mts*., 53. 68-69; also 3, 3-4; 53, 3-11; *Vṣṇ*., 3, 3, 2-21; 3, 4, 1-10; 3, 6, 15; *Km*., I, 50, 10-11 and 20-21, also 2, 44, 145; *Devī Bhāgavat*, I, 3, 17, 25-33; *Vy*., 103, 48-51. The eighteen Purāṇas consisting of four lakh verses are listed in order of their antiquity in some of the Purāṇic texts like *Mts* (53, 12-66), *Vṣṇ*. (3, 6, 20- 24) and *Bhāg*. (XII, 7, 22-24; also XII, 13, 3-9). For historical significance of the words like *ākhyāna*, *gāthā*, *nārāśaṁsī*, *vaṁśa*, etc., see Pathak, *Ancient Historians of India*, pp. 1-21.

41. *An Introduction to Indian Historiography*, pp. 17-18.

also included some important historical subjects like dynastic genealogies of pre-Bhārata war period, contemporary events, etc. And it is perhaps on this ground that Umāśaṅkara Dīkṣita has called him *itihāsakarttā* (composer of historical work) and "a great historian".[42] N.S. Rajaram also observes: "In ancient times Veda Vyāsa was considered a great historian. Tradition credits him with the authorship of the historical epic *Mahābhārata* and also with the responsibility for preserving ancient records found in the *Purāṇas*."[43] It is practically not possible to chronologically arrange his all works. Nor can he be placed in a chronological framework. He was not a mythical figure but a historical personage. In fact, it were *ṛṣis* and *maharṣis* who built up the tradition of preserving the historical records of the past.

It was Veda-Vyāsa who taught the first lesson of history to his pupils. There are some concrete evidences in the Purāṇic records to show that he taught the *itihāsa-Purāṇa* to his famous disciple, Romaharṣaṇa (called *sūta*), who further taught it to his son, Ugraśravā, and six disciples at least five of whom were brāhmaṇas.[44] The Purāṇic brāhmaṇas belonging to a class of *sūta* had developed historical sense. Their concept of history was fundamentally based on the precepts of said Vyāsa. In all probability, the work begun by Vyāsa might have been completed by Romaharṣaṇa and his disciples. The tradition of studying, teaching and interpreting the *itihāsa* and Purāṇa set by Vyāsa and followed by his disciples was handed down from generation to generation.

The original Purāṇa contained the details of the kingdoms and dynasties with genealogies of only the pre-Bhārata war period. It saw several recensions with additions sometime between *c*. 500 BC and AD 500. The *purāṇakāra*s applying their historical sense time to time incorporated the historical events of the past along with other subjects in it during the aforesaid period.

The Purāṇic *sūta*s played very important role in the preservation of ancient Indian historical tradition. According to some Purāṇic texts, their special duty was to compose, arrange and preserve the genealogies (*vaṁśāvalīs*) of the kings of various dynasties which constituted the source material for the *itihāsa*s and Purāṇas.[45] They used to

42. *Op. cit.*, p. 13.

43. "Distortions of Indian History from Harappa to Ayodhya", in B.V. Raman (ed.), *The Astrological Magazine*, vol. 87, No. 1 (Bangalore, Jan. 1998), p. 75.

44. *Vṣṇ.*, 3, 4, 8-10; 3, 6, 16-19; *Bhāg.*, I, 4, 22; XII, 7, 5-7; *Vy.*, 61, 55-58; *Km.*, 1, 1, 2-7; 1, 50, 12-14; *Bmd.*, iv, 4, 67f; *Pdm.*, V, I, 2, 11-14.

45. *Vy.*, 1,31-32; *Pdm.*, V, 1, 27-28; see also Pargiter, *AIHT*, p. 15.

compile the royal genealogies on the basis of the information collected from the royal families and the families of the priests and others. The material collected by them were incorporated in the Purāṇic texts. They were also employed by the kings in their courts to record the events of their reigns as well as that of their ancestors. Thus they were preservers of historical tradition (both Brāhmaṇical and kṣatriya), custodians of genealogical records and chroniclers of events of the past. We are also informed by Kautilya that "the *paurāṇika*, the *sūta* and the *māgadha*" were three officials of salaried class retained by a king or prince for listening to the *itihāsa* and Purāṇa. The former two are said to have been well conversant with their subjects.[46] Maurice Winternitz also admits that the *paurāṇika*s and *aitihāsika*s were professional story-tellers in very ancient time.[47] According to V.S. Pathak, the *sūta*s belonged to brāhmaṇa class. He has connected them with the Bhr̥gu (Bhārgava), Aṅgiras (Bhāradvāja) and Kaśyapa clans of priests of whom the first two were associated with historiography or writing of history (*itihāsa*, Purāṇa and later some other texts).[48] The *sūta*s were also the warrior or kṣatriya class or of mixed parentage. The Bhr̥gu partly merged with Aṅgiras to form a Bhr̥gvāṅgiras tradition. There is evidence to show that from the end of the Paurava period to the foundation of the Magadha empire a school of Bhr̥gvāṅgiras historians revised the *itihāsa*-Purāṇa tradition.[49] The contributions made by the *sūta*s in the field of historiography was no less significant than that of any historiographer (or *itihāsakāra*) of the contemporary age.

The *sūta*s are often equated with bards[50] as they used to bestow extravagant praise on great kings and heroes of the past while writing or singing about their deeds. But the bards as such did not get official recognition in the royal courts before the dawn of the seventh century AD. Nor did their office become professional or hereditary before that period. The *sūta*s gradually lost their importance. "In the early Mediaeval age when the heroic tradition of history changed into the courtly one, the wandering Sutas and the Bhrigvangirases were replaced by salaried court-poets. . . ." [51]

---

46. *Arth.*, 1, 5 (line 15); V, 3; XIII,1.
47. *Op. cit.*, p. 313; see also B.P. Sinha, "Race, Region, Religion and Ideology", in Devahuti (ed.), *Bias in Indian Historiography*, p. 37.
48. *Op. cit.*, p. 21f; see also Warder, *op. cit.*, pp. 18-25.
49. Warder, *op. cit.*
50. Thapar, *AISH*, pp. 270-72; see also her *From Lineage to State*, p. 130; Pargiter, *AIHT*, p. 13.
51. Pathak, *op. cit.*, p. 21.

Ancient Indian historical tradition has been classified by Pargiter broadly into two groups, the brāhmaṇic and the kṣatriya, for judging their comparative historical value. The events described in brāhmaṇic tradition, according to him, do not bear historicity. Kṣatriya tradition, on the other hand, professes to deal with history. He further states that the Vedic and other brāhmaṇic literature give us notices of ancient times from purely the brāhmaṇical point of view and they do not deal with history, while kṣatriya tradition preserved in the Purāṇas enables us to have a picture of ancient India and its political conditions from the kṣatriya standpoint. He continues to maintain that before the introduction of writing the brāhmaṇas had to rely on tradition when referring to men and events of the bygone age as well as to contemporaneous occurrences, and even after writing was introduced they discountenanced it so far as their religious books were concerned. There was a total lack of the historical sense among the brāhmaṇas who composed the brāhmaṇical literature. They failed to compose genuine history. They hardly maintained distinction between history and mythology. And there was a constant tendency on their part to confuse the two by mythologising history, on the one hand, and historifying the mythology, on the other. They have been also charged by him with fabricating incorrect stories and fables. They often neglected to revise or harmonise historical tradition. The Purāṇic brāhmaṇas are said to have preserved a large mass of kṣatriya and popular tradition which was inconsistent with brāhmaṇic stories and tenets. He further adds that kṣatriya tradition preserved in the Purāṇas is not deficient in the historical sense. This tradition is concerned chiefly with kings and heroes and their great deeds, genealogies, etc. Kṣatriya tales and ballads have some historical consistency. Royal genealogies certainly do not betray the lack of historical sense. The Purāṇic "genealogies are essentially chronological; and the old tales, especially those narrated in the course of the best versions of the genealogies, have also an historical character".[52] The above observations amount to exaltation of the kṣatriya tradition and depreciation of the brāhmaṇic tradition. But the fact remains that the Vedic texts and the Purāṇas constitute joint testimony for writing traditional history.[53] This is erroneous opinion about the ancient Indians that they had neither history nor did possess any historical instinct. The historical treasures burried in the Purāṇas are of great value. "The literature of the Brāhmaṇa was always supplemented from the earliest times by the literature of

52. *Op. cit.*, pp. 58-63.

53. See *Cul. Her. Ind.*, vol. V (1978), p. 284 (for A.D. Pusalker's view).

the Kṣatriya kings."[54] As a matter of fact, the Vedic, epic and Purāṇic traditions are supplementary to each other, and no coherent picture of early India can be presented without placing our reliance on the combined testimony of all the three. It is altogether different thing that the Purāṇic account of the subject are more elaborated and amplified than the Vedic and epic ones.

The Purāṇas deal with five subjects or topics, viz., (a) *sarga* (original creation), (b) *pratisarga* (dissolution and recreation), (c) *vaṁśa* (genealogies), (d) *manvantara* (an epoch of each Manu) and (e) *vaṁśānucarita* (histories of dynasties of kings mentioned in the genealogies).[55] These are the five attributes (called *pañcalakṣaṇa*) of a Purāṇa. Out of these five, the two, *vaṁśa* and *vaṁśānucarita*, are purely historical subjects. The *purāṇakāras* had no doubt clear conception of history.[56] The dynastic genealogies in particular constitute nucleus of the political history in the Purāṇas. V.A. Smith says: ". . . the most systematic record of the Indian historical tradition is that preserved in the dynastic lists of the Purāṇas . . . modern European writers have been inclined to dispaarage unduly the authority of the Purāṇic lists, but closer study finds in them much genuine and valuable historical tradition."[57]

About the historical value of Purāṇic genealogies of the royal families, Pargiter observes: "Though historical works about ancient India are wanting, yet tradition has handed down fairly copious genealogies of the ancient dynasties. These state the succession of kings, and in that way are historical. They are almost the only historical data found in Sanskrit books as regards ancient political development; and the list of teachers in professed chronological order set out in some brahmanical books supply evidence as regards brahmanical succession. The genealogies form the basis by which the investigation of tradition for historical ends may be tested. They supply the best chronological clue, for the Vedic literature . . . is not a sure guide in historical matters."[58]

Tod also writes: "In the absence of regular and legitimate historical records, there

---

54. S.C. Vidyarnava, "Pauranik Chronology", in *The Matsya Purāṇa*, vol. I, ed. with Eng. trans. and notes of B.C. Majmudar, S.C. Vasu, H.H. Wilson, Bentley, Wilford and others by J.D. Akhtar, *SBA* (Delhi, 1972), App. VIII, LXX-XCIII.
55. *Mts*., 53, 64; *Vṣṇ*., 3, 6, 25 & 27; *Bmv*., 133, 6; *Km*. 1, 1, 12; also *Bhāg*., XII, 7, 9-10.
56. See also Pusalker, "Conception of History in Ancient Indian Literature", *Our Heritage*, XII, 2 (Calcutta, 1964), pp. 35-46.
57. *EHI*, rev. 4th edn., p. 11.
58. *Op. cit*., p. 11.

are, however, other native works, which in the hands of a skilful and patient investigator, would afford no despicable materials for the history of India. The first of these are the Purāṇas and genealogical legends of the princes, which, obscured as they are by mythological details, allegory; . . . contain many facts that serve as beacons to direct the research of the historian."[59]

The Purāṇas in general are partly legendary and partly historical. Out of eighteen main Purāṇas, the six — *Matsya*, *Vāyu*, *Viṣṇu*, *Brahmāṇḍa*, *Bhāgavata* and *Bhaviṣya* — are very important from a historical point of view. The first two have been called by their authors *purātana itihāsa* (ancient history)[60] in support of their historicity as they (like other four Purāṇas) deal with historical events of the past. These six Purāṇas really constitute very faithful historical records. They have preserved highly valuable accounts of different dynasties of both pre- and post-Bhārata war period with the help of which we can throw some new light on the dark or obscure aspects of ancient Indian political history of those periods. They have great historical value from dynastic, genealogical and chronological points of view. A. Weber has also admitted that some of the old Purāṇas contain historical portions with kings, dynasties, genealogies and chronology.[61] The observation made by J.F. Fleet is worth-quoting here: "the ancient Hindus could write short historical compositions concise and to the point but limited in extent. The historical chapters of the Purāṇas do certainly indicate a desire on the part of the ancient Hindus not to ignore general history altogether and are clearly based on ancient archives which had survived in a more or less complete shape and were somehow accessible to the composers of those works. . . ."[62]

The Purāṇas are not the productions of one age or of one brain. As stated earlier, the original Purāṇa was composed by Vyāsa sometime before the Great Bhārata battle began. And then time to time several additions were made in it by the *purāṇakāras*. The process of incorporating the past events in some of the Purāṇas began as early as the sixth or fifth century BC and generally continued till the fourth or fifth century AD but in some cases even beyond that period.

---

59. *AAR*, introduction, p. XV.
60. *Mts.*, 72, 6; *Vy.*, 103, 48; see also *Pdm.*, VI, 77, 30; 243, 3.
61. *HIL*, pp. 213-15.
62. *IGI* (new edn.) vol. II, p. 17.

Since the *Vāyu* and *Viṣṇu* provide dynastic history up to the beginning of the Gupta rule, they in the present form must have existed about the middle of the fourth century AD. The *Matsya* (one of the early Purāṇas) was compiled with new additions towards the end of the reign of king Yajña Śrī Śātakarṇi (*c.* AD. 165-95) of the Āndhra or Sātavāhana dynasty. Its compilation was further carried up to AD 236. It was finally completed before the end of the third century AD as it covers the dynastic accounts only up to the end of the rule of the Āndhras or Sātavāhanas. The *Brahmāṇḍa* in the present form existed in or about AD 400.

The *Bhaviṣya Purāṇa* existed before *c.* 500 BC as appears from the *Āpastamba Dharmasūtra*. The *Kaliyugarājavṛttānta* (details of the dynasties of the *Kali* age) given in this Purāṇa appear to be the oldest of all other Purāṇic details thereof. The dynastic accounts of the rulers of the *Kali* age was first included in it towards the end of the second century AD. The text in the revised form very much existed in the middle of the theird century AD which is supported by the fact that the *Matsya* borrowed its account of the dynasties of the *Kali* age from it before the end of that century, and the *Vāyu* and *Brahmāṇḍa* borrowed their accounts of the same dynasties from it in the next century as the internal evidence therein indicates. The *Bhaviṣya Purāṇa* contains the accounts up to the times of the famous Rājpūt ruler, Pṛthvīrāja Cauhān (AD 1179-92), so far as the ancient period is concerned. The events of the subsequent periods also appear to have been recorded in it. Therefore, no definite date can be assigned to it in the present form.

The *Bhāgavata Purāṇa* existed in the middle of the third century AD. Some additions were, of course, made in it sometime between AD 600 and 800 as appears from the text itself. Some other important Purāṇas like the *Brahma* (the oldest of all), and *Padma* (next to it in order of antiquity) must have existed at least as early as the beginning of the fifth century BC.

> "Verses praising gifts of land are quoted in various land-grants, that are dated; and some of those are found only in the *Padma*, *Bhaviṣya* and *Brahma* Purāṇas and thus indicate that those Purāṇas were in existence before AD 500 and even long before that time. Some of those verses, which occur in grants of the years 475-6 and 482-3, are declared in some grants to have been enunciated by Vyāsa in the *Mahābhārata*."[63]

The *Agni Purāṇa* in its original form can be placed much earlier than the fourth century

63. Pargiter, *op. cit.*, p. 49.

AD. However, some additions were made in it between *c.* AD 500 and 900. The *Kūrma*, *Mārkaṇḍeya*, *Brahmavaivartta*, *Liṅga*, *Vāmana* and other Purāṇas were also in existence before AD. 500.

The Purāṇic literature contains a lot of valuable historical data about the life and achievements of the kings of Solar and Lunar dynasties of both pre- and post-Bhārata war period and of some other important dynasties.

The historical reliability of the Purāṇic accounts of the kingdoms and dynasties with genealogies of the Ikṣvāku rulers of Kośala with its capital at Ayodhyā [64] and that of the rulers of Videha with its capital at Mithilā (Janakapur),[65] of Vaiśālī which was itself the capital (in north Bihar)[66] and of the Śaryātas in the line of Śaryāti (who reigned at Kuśasthalī, the ancient name of Dvārakā or Dvāravatī in Gujarat, which was named Ānarta after king Ānarta)[67] of the Solar family of the pre-Bhārata war period is beyond doubt. Likewise, the details provided in some of the Purāṇas of the kingdoms and dynasties with genealogies of the lineal descendants of Purūravā, the progenitor of the Lunar family and ruler of Pratiṣṭhānapur on the confluence of the Gaṅgā and the Yamunā in Prayāg, of the same period are of great historical value. The Purāṇic description of Purus of Madhyadeśa or Gaṅgā-Yumunā doab, the Yādavas in Yadu's line including the Haihayas of northern, western, central and southern India, the Āṇavas of north, Druhyus of north-west and Turvasus of south-east — all five branches which sprang up from Yayāti — and that of Kāśī and Kānyakubja dynasties, of Kurus in the main Paurava line, of Pañcālas, and of five kingdoms, notably Magadha founded by Bṛhadratha (who was succeeded by another nine rulers during the period concerned) and Kauśāmbī founded by Kośāmba — two of the five descendants of Vasu-Uparicara of Cedideśa in Kuru's line[68] — are historically and archaeologically well-tested.

64. *Vy.*, 88, 3-212; *Vṣṇ.*, IV, 2, 34-70; IV, 3, 1-28; IV, 4, 5-40, 75-112; *Mts.*, 12, 34-35, 42-57; *Bmd.*, III, 63, 115, 120-41, 186-91; *Bhāg.*, IX, 6, 20-39; IX, 8, 17-19; IX, 13, 1-16; Pargiter, *op. cit.*, pp. 90-94.

65. *Vy.*, 89, 1-23; *Vṣṇ.*, IV, 5, 1-34; *Bmd.*, III, 74, 1-19; *Bhāg.*, IX, 13, 1, 11-27; Pargiter, *op. cit.*, pp. 95-96.

66. *Vy.*, 86, 14-22; *Vṣṇ.*, IV, 1, 43-61; *Bmd.*, III, 61, 12-17; *Bhāg.*, IX, 2, 33-36; *PK*, p. 481; Pargiter, *op. cit.*, pp. 96-97.

67. *Vy.*, 86, 22-28; *Mts.*, 12, 21-24; *Vṣṇ.*, IV, I, 62-64; *Bmd.*, III, 61, 18-24; *Bhāg.*, IX, 3,1-2, 27-36; *Br.*, 7, 27-29; *Agn.*, 273, 12-16; Pargiter, *op. cit.*, 97-98.

68. For details see *Vy.*, 91, 1-103; 92, 1-75; 93, 26-27, 87-92; 94, 1-54; 95, 14-47; 96, 1-160; 99, 6-12, 25-28, 167-70, 194-249; D.R. Patil, *Cultural History from the Vāyu Purāṇa*, pp. 8-13; *Vṣṇ.*, IV, 8, 1-21; IV, 10, 1-32; IV, 11, 1-30; IV, 12, 2-45; IV, 13, 1-20, 35-70, 108-61; IV, 15, 1-45; IV, 17, 1-5; IV, 18, 1-30; IV, 19, 1-85; IV, 20, 1-53; *Mts.*, 43, 7-52; 44, 14-36, 45-85; 45, 1-34; 46, 1-29; 48, 6-9, 22-

→

The first phase of Pauravas' settlements in the Sārasvatī region and upper doab and Yādavas' settlements in Narmadā, Mālwā, Gujarat and Gaṅgā-Yamunā doab are archaeologically associated with Ochre-Coloured Pottery (OCP) of late Harappan period (*c.* 2200-1700 BC) and Chalcolithic Black and Red Ware (BRW) ascribed to *c.* 2000 BC respectively. The Kurus of upper Sarasvatī and upper doab and the Pañcālas of Gangetic doab belonged to PGW period.[69]

The Purāṇic history of the Āryas is also worthy of our notice. The Purāṇic data about the origin and expansion of the Āryans is of unique importance. According to some Purāṇas, their original homeland was Pratiṣṭhāna from where they expanded all over the Gangetic doab.[70] This information provides some clues about their indigenous origin in contradistinction to their foreign origin.

> "The Purāṇas profess to give us the ancient history of Āryan India. In doing so they begin from the earliest Ṛgvedic period describing genealogies of kings who established kingdoms and principalities and thus parcelled out and ruled ancient India. Occasionally the feats and achievements of kings . . . are related, battles mentioned and described, noticeable incidents and happenings recorded and very valuable synchronisms noted down."[71]

A.S. Altekar has rightly pointed out that the history of India of pre-Bhārata war period can be reconstructed with the help of epic and Purāṇic evidences. He further says that the pre-Bhārata war dynasties mentioned in the Purāṇas are as historical as the dynasties of *Kali* age like Maurya, Sātavāhana, etc.[72]

→ 29; 49, 1-59; 50, 26-33; *Bmd.*, III, 65, 45-46; III, 66, 1-75; III, 67, 1-79; III, 68, 27, 90-92; III, 69, 3-55; III, 70, 14-48; III, 71, 1-144; III, 74, 7-12; *Bhāg.*, IX, 14, 1ff; IX, 15, 1-36; IX, 17, 2-10; IX, 20, 1-39; IX, 21, 1-35, IX, 22, 1-18; IX, 23, 1-39; IX, 24, 6-45; *Br.*, 10, 13-68; 12, 18-19; 13, 154-207, 14, 14-25; 15, 30-45; 16, 9-49; *Agn.*, 274, 1-23; 275, 1-51; 277, 4-4; 278, 27-41; Pargiter, *op. cit.*, pp. 99-119 and Ch XXIV ('Ancient History from Tradition'), pp. 258-84; A.D. Pusalker, "Traditional History from the Earliest Time to the Accession of Parikshit", in R.C. Majumdar (ed.), *The Vedic Age*, pp. 277ff; G.P. Singh, *EIHTA*, pp. 50-98.

69. See Thapar, *AISH*, pp. 242ff and Genealogical Table.
70. For details see *Vy.*, 91, 5-8 and 51; 92, 1-7; *Vṣn.*, IV, I, 16-17; *Br.*, Chs. 10-12; Pargiter, *op. cit.*, pp. 296-302; G.P. Singh, *op. cit.*, pp. 50 ff; Sankalia, "Prehistoric Colonization in India: Archaeological and Literary Evidences", in *AIHA*, pp. 308-10; J. Kennedy, "The Puranic Histories of the Early Aryas", *JRAS*, 1915.
71. Pradhan, *Chro. Anct. Ind.*, XI.
72. "Can we Reconstruct Pre-Bhārat War History" ?, *JBHU*, IV, pp. 183-223; also his presidential address, Section I: "Archaic and Early Cultural History", Indian History Congress, 3rd session, Calcutta, 15-17 Dec, 1939.

The traditional history of India from the earliest times to the accession of Parīkṣit II (thirty-six years after the war) is well recorded in the Purāṇas.

The kingdoms and dynasties of the post-Bhārata war period extending from the accession of Parīkṣit II or the beginning of *Kali yuga* down to the sixth or fifth century BC have also been covered in the Purāṇic records. Twenty-nine kings of Puru dynasty called the Pauravas of the Lunar family who ruled over Hastināpura, Indraprastha and Vatsa (Kauśāmbī),[73] thirty kings of Ikṣvāku dynasty of Kośala of the Solar family including the predecessors and successors of Prasenajit[74] and twenty-two kings of the Bārhadratha dynasty of Magadha (with regnal years) have all been incorporated in the dynastic list of the kings.[75] The genealogical lists containing the names of kings of the said dynasties have also been furnished. The information supplied by the Purāṇas about the shifting of capital from Hastināpura to Kauśāmbī during the reign of Nicakṣu (one of the successors of Parīkṣit), the rule of famous king Udayana over Kauśāmbī, the pedigree and progeny of Buddha of the Śākya clan and the kingdoms of Pañcāla, Śūrasena, Videha, Aṅga, Kāśī, etc., are of utmost importance. Ten dynasties of the *Kali* age ruled contemporaneously in northern, central and eastern India. The historical credibility of the information concerned is well established. The five kings of Pradyota dynasty who ruled over Avantī also find mention in the Purāṇas. They are said to have ruled for 138 years.[76]

The Purāṇic accounts of the major dynasties of early historical period are of exceptional value. Ten kings of Bimbisārian and Śaiśunāga dynasties, including Bimbisāra (*c.* 558-491 BC), Ajātaśatru (*c.* 491-459 BC), both contemporaries of the Buddha (*c.* 563-483 BC), Udāyin, Śiśunāga and others, are said to have ruled for 360 or 362 years.[77] They actually ruled for 200 years (*c.* 543-343 BC). The nine Nandas (Mahāpadmananda, the

73. *Vy.*, 99, 249-79; *Vṣṇ.*, IV, 21, 1-18; *Mts.*, 50, 57-89; *Bhāg.*, IX, 22, 33-44; Pargiter, *PDKA* (Oxford, 1913) pp. 4-5, 24, note 16.

74. *Vy.*, 99, 280-93; *Vṣṇ.*, IV, 22, 1-13; *Mts.*, 271, 4-18; *Bmd.*, 3, 74, 104-7; *PDKA*, pp. 10-11, 66-67.

75. *Vy.*, 99, 294-308; *Vṣṇ.*, IV, 23, 1-13; *Mts.*, 271, 18-30; *Bhāg.*, IX, 22, 46-49; *Bmd.*, 3, 74, 107-21; *HV.*, I, 32, 63-78; *PDKA*, pp. 13-22; see also Pargiter, *AIHT*, pp. 285-87; Pusalker, "Traditional History from the Acession of Parikshit to the End of the Bārhadratha Dynasty", in *The Vedic Age*, pp. 323-33; G.P. Singh, *op. cit.*, pp. 141-54.

76. *Vy.*, 99, 308-14; *Vṣṇ.*, IV, 24, 1-8; *Mts.*, 272, 1-5; *Bhāg.*, XII, I, 2-4; *Bmd.*, 3, 74, 121-25; *PDKA*, pp. 18-21, 68-69; H.H. Wilson, trans, *Viṣṇu Purāṇa*, p. 372.

77. *Vy.*, 99, 314-21; *Vṣṇ.*, IV, 24, 9-19; Wilson, *op. cit.*, pp. 372-75; *Mts.*, 272, 5-13; *Bhāg.*, XII, I, 5-7; *Bmd.*, 3, 74, 127-33; *PDKA*, pp. 21-66, 67-69; see also Max Müller, *HASL*, pp. 265-66.

founder of the dynasty, and his eight succcessors) are said to have ruled for 40 or 100 years.[78] In reality, only two of them, the first (Mahāpadmananda) and the last (Dhanānanda identical with Agrammes or Xandrammes of classical or Greek and Roman writers, and contemporary of Alexander), were the regining kings who altogether ruled for 22 years (*c.* 343-321 BC). We are also informed that a period of 1050 years had elapsed between the birth of Parīkṣit and the coronation of Mahāpadmananda.[79]It is also clearly stated in the Purāṇas that it was Cāṇakya (Kauṭilya) who uprooted the Nandas and installed Candragupta Maurya on the throne of Magadha (in 321 BC),[80] which is historically established fact. Ten kings of the Maurya dynasty, including Candragupta, Bindusāra, Aśoka and his seven successors, are said to have ruled for 137 years (*c.* 321-184 BC).[81] Ten rulers of the Śuṅga dynasty from Puṣyamitra to Devabhūti are said to have ruled for 112 years (*c.* 184-72 BC).[82] Four kings of the Kaṇva dynasty from Vasudeva to Suśarman ruled exactly for 45 years (*c.* 72-27 BC).[83] These six dynasties ruled successively over Magadha and other kingdoms from the sixth to the first centuries BC. Besides, thirty rulers of the Āndhra or Sātavāhana dynasty from its founder Simuka to Pulumayi IV are said to have ruled for 456 or 460 years.[84] The Purāṇas also supply the information that the period of 836 years intervened between Mahāpadmananda and the last Āndhra

---

78. *Vy.*, 99, 321-28; *Vṣṇ.*, IV, 24, 20-24; Wilson, *op. cit.*, p. 374; *Mts.*, 272, 14-21; *Bhāg.*, XII, I, 8-11; *Bmd.*, 3, 74, 139-44; *PDKA*, pp. 23-24, 69; *HASL*, p. 266.

79. *Vy.*, 99, 415; *Vṣṇ.*, IV, 24, 104; Wilson, *op. cit.*, p. 389; *Mts.*, 273, 36.

80. *Vy.*, 99, 329-31; *Vṣṇ.*, IV, 24, 25-28; *Mts.*, 272, 21-22.

81. *Vy.*, 99, 331-36; *Vṣṇ.*, IV, 24, 29-32; Wilson, *op. cit.*, pp. 374-76; *Mts.*, 272, 22-26; *Bhāg.*, XII, I, 12-15; *Bmd.*, 3. 74,145-49; *PDKA*, pp. 28-30; *HASL*, p. 266.

82. *Vy.*, 99, 336-42; *Vṣṇ.*, IV, 24, 33-37; Wilson, *op. cit.*, pp. 376-77; *Mts.*, 272, 26-33; *Bhāg.*, XII, I, 16-18; *Bmd.*, 3, 74, 150-55; *PDKA*, pp. 30-32, 70.

83. *Vy.*, 99, 343-47; *Vṣṇ.*, IV, 24, 38-42; Wilson, *op. cit.*, p. 377; *Mts.*, 272, 32-37; *Bhāg.*, XII, I, 19-21; *Bmd.*, 3, 74, 155-60; *PDKA*, pp. 33-38, 71.

84. *Vy.*, 99, 348-58; *Vṣṇ.*, IV, 24, 43-50; Wilson, *op. cit.*, pp. 378-80; *Mts.*, 273, 1-17; *Bhāg.*, XII, I, 22-28; *Bmd.*, 3, 74, 160-70; *PDKA*, pp. 38-43, 71; see also V.A. Smith, *EHI*, pp. 216-17, 220; R.G. Bhandarkar, *Early History of the Dekkan down to the Mahomedan Conquest*, pp. 15-23; *A Peep into the Early History of India*, pp. 36-37; S.P. Sen (ed.), *Historians and Historiography in Modern India*, pp. 32-34.

    For details of pre- and post-Maurya dynasties up to Sātavāhana, as recorded in the Purāṇas, see G.P. Singh, *op. cit.*, pp. 161-89; "A New Approach to the Study of Historical Data in the Epic and Purāṇic Literature Regarding Ancient India", *Proceedings of the UGC Sponsored National Seminar on History and Literature* (Sardar Patel University, Vallabh Vidyānagar, Gujarat, 9-11 February, 1991), p. 4; also *AIHT*, pp. 286-87.

king, Pulumayi.[85] According to this chronological data, the Āndhras' rule began 376 years after the Nanda and lasted for 460 years (376+460 = 836). In fact, they reigned in western India and the Deccan (Maharashra and Andhra) for not more than 252 years (*c.* 27 BC - AD 225). There are some epigraphic and numismatic evidence[86] to partly confirm the historicity of Purāṇic genealogy of this dynasty. The genealogical list of the dynasty contains the names of many actual rulers like Śrī Sātakarṇi I, Śātakarṇi II, Gautamīputra Śātakarṇi, Vāsiṣṭhīputra Śrī Pulumāvi or Pulumayi and Yajña Śrī Śātakarṇi. The political achievements of some kings of some of the aforesaid dynasties have also been highlighted in the Purāṇas. Some information supplied in this regard are very useful for our historical purposes.

It is worthy of remark that the above-mentioned seven dynasties that ruled over different kingdoms are historically authenticated. Their genealogies are chronologically arranged. Most of the kings mentioned in the genealogical lists are real. Only few of them are fictitious. The length of reign of each individual king as well as the total duration of the rule of each dynasty are given. Some figures are, of course, inflated and arbitrary, but some are accurate. There are some variations in the Purāṇas with regard to number of kings and their names, order of succession, regnal years and total duration of their rule. The chronological sequence of kings in case of some dynasties is also broken to some extent because of anachronism. However, the total duration of the rule of some dynastic given in some Purāṇas are absolutely correct which can be utilised for the purpose of chronlogical computation and interpretations to determine the period of the end of one dynasty and the beginning of the other. The Purāṇic data are no doubt extremely important for genealogical and chronological reconstruction of ancient Indian history of the periods concerned.

The historical value of the Purāṇic data from dynastic, genealogical and chronological points of view has been acknowledged by a number of scholars.[87]

---

85. *Vy.*, 99, 416-17; *Mts.*, 273, 37.

86. Bühler's Report, *Arch. Surv. of West India*, vol. IV, pp. 98, 110; vol. V, pp. 60-71; Luder's, 'A List of Brahmi Inscriptions from the Earliest times to about AD 400', published as an Appendix to *EP. Ind.*, vol. X, 1910, p. 160, nos. 1113, 1114, 1144; *JIH*, vol. LVI, pt. I, 1978, pp. 48-49, 52-53; D.C. Sircar (ed.), *SI*, vol. I, pp. 176-80, 197-201; *EP. Ind.*, vol. VIII, No. 5, pp. 36-49, 60-61 (1, 5, 7), 73-74; E.J. Rapson, *Catalogue of Coins in the British Museum, the Andhra dynasty, etc.*, 1908, p. XXX, K.P. Jayaswal, *JBORS*, vol. XVI, Pts 3 & 4, pp. 265-66; also *JNSI*, vol. III, pt. I, June 1941, pp. 43-45.

87. D.R. Mankad, "Studies in Puranic History, Genealogies and Chronology in Modern Times", *Purāṇa*, IV, I, 1962, pp. 3-22; *Purāṇic Chronology* (Vallabh Vidyānagar, 1951); A. Banerji Shashtri, →

The later Sātavāhanas and some contemporary minor dynasties of the kings of both indigenous and foreign origins that ruled over different parts of India sometime between the third century BC and the sixth century AD which include the dynasties of the post-Sātavāhana period also are vividly portrayed in the Purāṇas. The genealogies and chronology of some dynasties are also given therein.

The later Sātavāhanas or the successors of the Sātavāhanas of the Deccan have been referred to in the Purāṇas as Āndhravṛtyas. They belonged to the lineage of the servants or feudatories of the Āndhras. There were seven kings in this line. The Śrīparvatīya-Āndhras (of Teleṅgānā) have been assigned a reign-period of 52 years. One of the five minor dynasties that came into being after the dismemberment of the Sātavāhana empire was that of the Abhīras of western India (Maharashtra). The ten Abhīra kings are said to have ruled for 67 years. The kings of the Āndhra dynaśty (who established themselves in the Deccan and western India sometime after AD 236) are said to have ruled for over a period of 300 years. The eight Yavana kings (Greek princes of Bactria lying between the Hindukush and the Oxus who ruled from the third century BC to the middle of the first century BC) are said to have ruled for 80 to 87 years. The ten, sixteen or eighteen Śaka kings (Indo-Scythians, second century BC-second century AD) are said to have ruled (over Afghanistan, northern, central and western parts of India and in the upper Deccan) for 183 or 380 years. The fourteen Tuṣāras (the tribes settled on the banks of the river Cakṣu or Oxus in the north-western region) are said to have ruled for 500 years. The seven Gardabhinas or Gardabhillas (who established themselves

---

→ "On Ancient Indian Historical Tradition", *JBORS*, vol. XIII, pp. 62-79; V.R.R. Dikshitar, "The Purāṇa : A Study", *IHQ*, vol. VIII, pp. 747-67; R. Morton Smith, *DDEI*, ed. J.L. Shastri (Delhi, 1973), pp. 38ff; "The Early Chronology of India", *JAOS*, vol. 77, No. 2, April-June 1957 and No. 4, Dec. 1957; Pargiter, *PDKA*, pp. 4ff; "Ancient Indian Genealogies and Chronology", *JRAS*, 1910, pp. 26-56; "Earliest Indian Traditional History", *JRAS*, 1914, p. 267f; Max Müller, *HASL*, pp. 265-68; K. Venkatachalam, *The Plot in Indian Choronology*, pp. 23ff, 38ff, 80-100; *Chronology of Ancient Hindu History*, Pt. I, pp. 34ff; Thapar, "Origin Myths and the Early Indian Historical Tradition", in *AISH*, pp. 294-325; "Genealogy as a Source of Social History", in *ibid.*, pp. 326-60; see also William Jones, "On the Chronology of the Hindus", *As. Res.*, vol. II (1st Pub 1799, rept. Delhi, 1979), pp. 107-13 (all about Purāṇic dynasties); Lord Teignmouth (ed.), *The Works of Sir William Jones* (in 13 vols), vol. IV (London, 1807), pp. 36-46; F. Wilford, "Chronology of the Hindus", *As. Res.*, vol. V (Delhi, 1979), pp. 241-92; "An Essay on the sacred Isles in the West with other Essays...", Essay III, *A.Res.*, vol. IX (Delhi, 1979), pp. 116-210 (for kings and their chronology); J. Bentley, "On the Principal Eras and Dates of the Ancient Hindus", *As. Res.*, vol. V, pp. 315-43 (all about different dynasties of the post-war period as given in the Purāṇas); "On the Hindu System of Astronomy and their connection with History in Ancient and Modern times", *As. Res.*, vol. VIII (1st Pub. 1809, rept. Delhi, 1979), pp. 225ff.

in Avanti region with their seat of power at Ujjayini anterior to the Śakas) ruled for 72 years.' The thirteen Muruṇḍas (a branch or kinsmen of the Śakas) along with other kings of the śūdra class are said to have ruled for 200 to 450 years. The eighteen or nineteen Hūṇas (or Maunas) ruled for 300 years. The eleven kings of the contemporary *mleccha* dynasty are also said to have reigned for 300 years.[88] The kings of the said dynasties altogether are said to have ruled for 1090 to 1099 years.[89]

The historicity of the above-mentioned dynasties is well proven. Here it may further be added that the Muruṇḍas established their rule in some parts of central India sometime after AD 230. They continued to rule till the time of Samudragupta (AD 335-75) which can be substantiated by the epigraphic evidence and other relevant sources. The Allahabad Pillar inscription confirms that the "Śaka-Muruṇḍas" were one of those foreign powers who acknowleged Samudragupta as their overlord.[90] They were probably ruling as the Śaka lords or chieftains in the regions of Surāṣṭra and Ujjain at his time. The Gardabhinas were actually Garddabha princes who once ruled over Mālawā region of central India and some parts of western India.[91] This dynasty ruled over Avanti in western Mālawā with its capital at Ujjain before the Śaka kings established their supremacy there.

The details of Vikramāditya of Ujjain and his dynasty have been provided in the Pratisarga Parvan of the *Bhaviṣya Purāṇa*.[92]

Vikramāditya regained his ancestral kingdom of Ujjain by expelling the Śakas from there after nine years of their rule (which began in 66 BC). In order to commemorate his victory over them he introduced a new era called Vikram Saṁvat (or Mālawā Saṁvat) in 57 BC). He reigned for 60 years and his four successors altogether for 75 years which comes to total 135 years.

According to the same Purāṇa, Vikramāditya was succeeded by his son Devabhakta who ruled for 10 years only. He was either overthrown or killed by the Śakas.[93] His son,

---

88. *Vy.*, 99, 359-64; *Vṣṇ.*, IV, 24, 51-54 and 58; Wilson, *op. cit.*, pp. 380-82; *Mts.*, 273, 18-24; *Mts.*, *SBA*, pp. 339-41; *Bhāg.*, XII, I, 27-32; *Bmd.*, 3, 74, 170-77; *PDKA*, pp. 42-48, 540-51; also R.K. Arora, *Historical and Cultural Data from the Bhaviṣya Purāṇa*, p. 37f; Patil, *op. cit.*, p. 262.
89. *Vṣṇ.*, IV, 24, 53; *Bhāg.*, XII, I, 30-32.
90. Fleet, *CII*, vol. III, No. I, pp. 1-17; J. Allan, *Catalogue of the Coins of the Gupta Dynasty*, Introduction, pp. XXIX-XXX.
91. For details see *As. Res.*, VI, p. 35; IX, p. 147; *JASB*, December 1835, p. 688; *JRAS*, III, p. 385.
92. *Bhv.*, vol. I, pp. 337-40, vv. 8-26; vol. II, pp. 161-64, vv. 13-21.
93. *Bhv.*, II, pp. 163-64, v. 22.

Śālivāhana, of the same dynasty conquered the Śakas and celebrated his victory by commencing a new era called Śālivāhana Śaka era in AD 78.[94] He is believed to have established his rule over his kingdom with its capital at Ujjain in about AD 32. He was succeeded by ten rulers. The Śālivāhana dynasty and some other dynasties that ruled over Ujjain are briefly described in the same Purāṇa. The reign-period of individual ruler, the total duration of the rule of each dynasty and achievements of some of the rulers of some dynasties are also given therein.[95]

Some unanointed kings of Kilakila have also been depicted in the Purāṇas. They are stated to have belonged to either Yavana race or śūdra class.[96] They actually succeeded the Abhīras of Maharashtra after overthrowing them. The Kilakila princes were succeeded by the rulers of the dynasty founded by the Vindhyaśakti. After the extinction of this dynasty three Vāhlika kings for 30 years.[97] Sakyma, the famous king of Māhiṣmatī, seven kings who ruled over Mekala (situated on the bank of the Narmadā rivers), nine kings who governed Kośala, etc., also find mention in the Purāṇas.[98] They were all contemporary provincial rulers.

The Purāṇas also provide description of the rulers (called Mitras) who governed Mekala and Māhiṣmatī regions for about 30 years. Puṣyamitra was one of the famous rulers. The 'Puṣyamitras' are said to have ruled for 13 years.[99] The Bhītarī pillar inscription bears witness to the fact that towards the closing years of Kumāragupta's reign (AD 414-55) the Puṣyamitras invasion led to the eclipse of the Gupta power. It was Skandagupta (AD 455-67) who crushed them and restored the fallen fortunes of his family.[100]

We come across some inaccuracies and discrepancies in the Purāṇas with regard to the number of kings of the dynasties concerned and total duration of their rule. The trustworthiness of some reign-periods is doubtful. Sometimes one dynasty is merged or interwoven into another; sometimes dynasties are lengthened owing to various corrupt

---

94. *Ibid.*, pp. 163-64, v. 23; I, pp. 416-19., vv.17-19, 33.
95. *Ibid.*, pp. 164-67, vv. 24-42; I, pp. 419-20, vv. 1-4, 425, vv. 1-2.
96. *Vy.*, 99, 363-64; *Vṣṇ.*, IV, 24, 55; *Mts.*, 273, 23-24; *Bhāg.*, XII, I, 32-33.
97. *Vy.*, 99, 372-73; *Vṣṇ.*, IV, 24, 57.
98. *Ibid.*, 99, 374.
99. *Ibid.*, *Vṣṇ.*, IV, 24, 58; Wilson, *op. cit.*, p. 384; *Bmd.*, 3, 74, 187-88; *Bhāg.*, XII, I, 34; *PDKA*, p. 51, note 14; see also K.P. Jayaswal, *Hindu Polity*, pp. 156-57.
100. Fleet, *CII*, vol. III, pp. 53-55; H.R. Divekar, "Puṣyamitras in the Gupta Period", *ABORI*, 1919-20, pp. 99-103.

readings and sometimes their accounts appear to be conflicting and confusing because of fabrications, interpolations and distortions. History and myths have been jumbled up to an extent that sometimes it becomes difficult to extricate one from the other. However, they cannot be put aside as wholly unworthy of credence.

The Purāṇas do contain some useful information about the rule of the Nāga dynasties at Vidiśā (the capital of eastern Mālawā), Padmāvatī (modern Padam Pawaya near Narwar in the Gwalior State, Madhya Pradesh), Kāntipurī (modern Koṭwār, about 25 miles north of Gwalior) and Mathurā (Uttar Pradesh) between the second century BC and the fourth century AD.

The Nāga dynasty of Vidiśā has been divided into two parts in the Purāṇas. To the first part belonged those kings who flourished before the end of the Śuṅga and to the second belonged those who ruled in the post-Śuṅga period. The Purāṇas mention the names of Śeṣanāga, Bhogin, Rāmacandra, Sadācandra, Dharmavarman, Vaṅgara (who ruled during the Śuṅga and Kāṇva periods), Bhūtīnandī, Madhunandī, Śiśunandī, Yaśonandī and his descendants, Dauhitra, and Śiśuka, Śivanandī, etc. (who ruled in the post-Kāṇva period).[101] The historicity of most of the Nāga kings mentioned above has been proved, and they have been chronologically arranged by K.P. Jayawal.[102]

The Purāṇas refer to nine Nāga kings of Padmāvatī without mentioning their names Kāntipurī is said to have been one of the chief seats of their power.[103] The said nine kings known from coins and inscriptions were Bhavanāga, Ganapatināga, Nāgasena, Bhīmanāga, Skandanāga, Bṛhaspatināga, Devanāga, Vibhanāga and Vyāghranāga.[104] The archaeological excavation at Koṭwār has proved that Kāntipurī mentioned in the Purāṇas was once the seat of power of the Nāga kings.

The Purāṇas also refer to the seven Nāga kings who ruled at Mathurā[105] after the fall of the Kuṣāṇas. These seven kings from Mathurā continued to rule over doab for 383 years which can also be confirmed on the testimony of the Purāṇas.[106] The coins discovered

101. *Vy.*, 99, 366-70; *Vṣṇ.*, IV, 24, 56; Wilson, *op. cit.*, pp. 382-83.

102. *History of India* (AD 150-350), pp. 3-15.

103. *Vy.*, 99, 382-83; *Vṣṇ.*, IV, 24, 63; Wilson, *op. cit.*, p. 385; *Bmd.*, 3, 74, 194, 197; *PK*, p. 267.

104. E.J. Rapson, *Ind. Co.*, p. 28 and plate V; V.A. Smith, *CCIM*, vol. I, pp. 176-77 (Some Nāga coins of Padmāvatī belong to the second century AD); *JRAS*, 1897, p. 643 (coins of the fourth century AD); Cunningham, *CMI*, pp. 20-21; *JASB*, 1865, p. 115; Fleet, *CII*, vol. III, No. I, lines 20-21.

105. *Vy.*, 99, 382-83; Wilson, *op. cit.*, p. 385; *PK*, p. 393.

106. *Ibid.*, 99, 453; *Bmd.*, 3, 74, 194-95, 267; *PK*, p. 267.

from Mathurā bear the names of the said seven kings as Puruṣadatta, Uttamadatta, Rāmadatta, Kāmadatta, Śesadatta, Bhavadatta and Balabhūti.[107]

Pargiter on the authority of the Purāṇas has stated that the Nāga families ruled from more than one place, viz., Vidiśā, Padmāvatī and Mathurā.[108] K.P. Jayaswal while throwing light on the Hindu republics in the Nāga period (AD 150-284) has opined that the Nāgās of Mālawā and Padmāvatī were by and large republican communities.[109]

The archaeological evidence, including coins and inscriptions, about the Nāga kings and seats of their rule mentioned in the Purāṇas proves the historicity of the Purāṇic accounts of the Nāga dynasties. The Purāṇic style of presentation of subject-matter is completely different from what we find in other sources. There are, of course, some vacuums in the Purāṇic accounts of the subject. However, from the twilight of the Purāṇic history it appears that the Nāgas (mostly serpent-worshippers) had spread far and wide in central and northern India. Some Nāga rulers became powerful during the times of the later Kuṣāṇas in the second century AD and some of them reestablished themselves after the expulsion of the Kuṣāṇas from some parts of northern India in the early third century AD. Some Nāga chiefs ruling in the Yamunā valley and central India were exterminated by the Gupta ruler (Samudragupta) about the middle of the fourth century AD.

The information contained in the Purāṇas about the Vākāṭakas is very meagre but authentic.

The founder of the Vākāṭaka dynasty, Vindhyaśakti (who flourished about the middle of the third century AD), figures in the Purāṇas. He is said to have ruled for 96 years. His son and successor, Pravīra, is said to have ruled for 60 years. Kāñcanapurī was the capital of his kingdom. Being an ambitious ruler he carried his arms to the Narmadā and succeeded in annexing the kingdom of Purika, which was being ruled by a king named Śiśuka. He is said to have performed Vājapeya sacrifices after assuming the title 'Samrāṭ'. He had four sons but all of them did not become rulers.[110] Other details are conspicuous by their absence in the Purāṇas.

---

107. V.A. Smith, *CCIM*, *op. cit.*

108. *PDKA*, p. 49.

109. *History of India* (c. AD 150-350), pp. 53-54; *Hindu Polity*, pp. 154-55.

110. *Vy.*, 99, 365, 370-72; *Vṣṇ.*, IV, 24, 56; Wilson, *op. cit.*, pp. 382-83; *Bmd.*, 3, 74, 184-86; *PDKA*, p. 44.

There are some inscriptional and other reliable evidences to partly prove the historical authenticity of the information supplied by the Purāṇas about the Vākāṭakas, particularly about their genealogy and chronology. Vindhyaśakti and Pravīra have been identified on the basis of inscriptions with Vindhyaśakti I and Pravarasena I respectively. The former is said to have ruled from AD 250 to 270. It is said that he had his base in central India from where he occupied parts of Vidarbha or Berār in western India and the Deccan (Andhra Pradesh). The latter is said to have ruled from AD 270 to 330 (which is in full accord with the Purāṇic length of his reign, i.e., 60 years). It has also been established that out of his four sons only the second one, Sarvasena, had set-up a separate dynasty with his capital at Vatsagulma in the Akolā district of Vidarbha and ruled from about AD 330 to 335. This also confirms the authenticity of the Purāṇic testimony that he had four sons and all of them did not rule. The other rulers of the dynasty further continued to rule till AD 500. After the defeat of the Vākāṭakas at the hands of the Kalacūris (descendants of Kārttavīrya Arjuna of the Haihaya race mentioned in the epics and Purāṇas) of Māhiṣmatī in the second quarter of the sixth century AD the dynasty ultimately came to end or ceased to exist.[111]

The information available in some Purāṇas about the earliest phase of the Gupta rule is very valuable.

It is fairly stated in the Purāṇas that the "Guptas set-up their rule over Anugaṅga (the middle Gangetic basin), Prayāga (Allahabad), Sāketa (adjoining Ayodhyā) and Magadha (south Bihar)".[112] It is historically proven fact that the kingdom of the Guptas originally comprised only some parts of Uttar Pradesh and Bihar at the end of the third century AD. The earliest centre of their power was in Uttar Pradesh which can be confirmed by the discovery of early Gupta coins and inscriptions mainly from this part of India. They gradually expanded from Prayāga over the neighbouring regions and the whole of Magadha in south Bihar. The founder of the Gupta dynasty was Śrīgupta who ruled as a minor

111. For details see V.V. Mirashi, "Some Puranic passages Corroborated by Inscriptional and Numismatic Evidence", *Purāṇa*, I, I, pp. 31-38; "The Vākāṭaka Chronology", *IHQ*, XXIV, pp. 148-55; M. Govinda Pai, "Genealogy and Chronology of the Vākāṭakas", *JIH*, XIV, 1935, pp. 1-26, also 165-204; R.C. Majumdar, "Note on the Genealogy and Chronology of the Vākāṭakas", *JRASB* (L), XII, p. 150; S.K. Aiyangar, "The Vākāṭakas and their place in the History of India", *ABORI*, V, pp. 31-54; V.A. Smith, "The Vākāṭaka Dynasty of Berar in the 4th and 5th centuries", *JRAS*, 1914, pp. 317-18; K.P. Jayaswal's views cf *JBORS*, March-June 1933, p. 67.

112. *Vy*., 99, 383; *Vṣn*., IV, 24, 63; Wilson, *op. cit*., p. 385; see also D.R. Patil, "Gupta Inscriptions and Puranic Tradition", *BDCRI*, II, pp. 2-58; V.A. Smith's views, cf *Ind. Ant*., 1902, p. 258, note.

chief over a small territory in Magadha from *c.* AD 275 to 300. The Purāṇic passage shows the extent of the Gupta dominions of pre-Candragupta's period and not of Candragupta's time (AD 319-35) as held by Pargiter.[113] The *Bhaviṣya Purāṇa* informs us that the seven kings of the Gupta dynasty ruled for 245 years.[114] But we find that in the imperial Gupta line there were twelve or thirteen kings (from Śrīgupta to Bhānugupta) who ruled for 235 years (AD 275-510).

A.K. Warder opines that the Purāṇas provide a comprehensive view of ancient Indian history, a universal history from the origin of the state through the earliest recorded kings, and the ancient dynasties down to the early fourth century AD. They mention Guptas and history of early Vākāṭakas.[115] H.H. Wilson has also stated that the dynastic lists of kings of the post-war period (*Kali* age) have been preserved in the Purāṇic historical records with greater precision which offer political and chronological particulars. Their general accuracy has been incontrovertibly established. Some Āndhra and Gupta rulers mentioned in the Purāṇas find confirmation in the inscriptions on columns of stones or rocks and on coins deciphered by archaeologists and others.[116]

The Purāṇic history of the post-Harṣa period (AD 650-1200) is very reliable. It is only the *Bhaviṣya Purāṇa* (Pratisarga Parvan) which provides data about the Pratihāras (Parihāras), the Paramāras, the Cāhamānas (Cauhānas) and the Cālukyas or Solaṅkīs (Śuklas), the four Rājapūt-families of the Aganivaṁśa or Agnikula, and the Rājapūt rulers of other dynasties. They (except Cālukyas) actually dominated the politics of northern India after the death of Harṣa in AD 647. They established their rule in this part of India and founded several petty independent kingdoms which lasted for nearly five centuries and then one by one succumbed to the Muslim invaders.

The Pratihāras have been described in the said Purāṇa as the Parihāras. It is well-known fact that prior to the conquest of Kanauj (Kānyakubja), they established their rule in Avantī with its capital at Ujjain. A notable ruler of this dynasty named Vatsarāja (identified by all historians with the father of Nāgabhaṭa II AD 805-33) figures in the Purāṇa as a king of Avantī.[117] He ascended the throne in about AD 778. His empire

---

113. *PDKA*, Introduction, XII and p. 20.
114. See also Krishanamachariar, *HCSL*, Introduction, XLVIII-XLIX.
115. *Op. cit.*, p. 157
116. *Op. cit.*, preface, LXVIII-LXX.
117. *Bhv.*, II, p. 165, v. 32.

intially comprised Mālawā and eastern and central Rājapūtānā. Gradually he established his supremacy over a large part of northern India. Bhoja I (AD 836-85) and Bhoja II (AD 910-12) were also the Pratihāra rulers of Kanauj. We find the description of the Bhojas in the Purāṇa,[118] but neither their periods nor the details of their achievements are given therein. However, the Pratihāras continued to exercise their sway over Kanauj and Madhyadeśa. The last king of this dynasty, Rājyapāla (AD 991-1018), also figures in the Purāṇa.[119] His capital Kanauj was invaded by Mahmud of Ghazni in AD 1018, but he could not defend it and fled away out of fear.

The Candellās, who established their sway over the kingdom of Bundelkhaṇḍa (situated between the Yamunā and the Narmadā) in the tenth century AD, were the feudatories of the great Pratihāra emperors of Kanauj. The Purāṇic tradition confirms it that Kāliñjar (which was earlier one of the strongholds of the Pratihāras and later occupied by the Candellās) was founded by the king named Parihāra, who ruled for ten years.[120] The names of all his successors who ruled over Kāliñjar are given in the Purāṇa.[121] One of them called Karvarman can be identified with Kīrtivarman who ruled sometime between AD 1100 and 1129.

The Paramāras of Mālawā, according to the Purāṇa, were the descendants of king Pramāra of Avantī. He is said to have ruled over Avantīpura (Ujjain, which had an extent of 4 *yojana*) for six years.[122] Muñja or Muñjavarman (AD 974-98), who was the seventh king of this dynasty, also finds mention in the Purāṇa. He is said to have defeated the Śavaras and Bhīllas. The details about Sindhurāja are also given therein.[123] The most famous king of this dynasty was Bhoja (son of Sindhurāja) who ruled over Mālāwā with its capital at Dhāra (60 km from Indore). He was propularly known as Rājā Bhoja. He ruled for about 42 years from AD 1018 to 1060. The Purāṇa explicitly mentions his name as a king of this dynasty.[124] The later Paramāra kings of Mālawā are also mentioned in the Purāṇa.[125] But the historicity of only two of them, Naravarman and

118. *Ibid.*, I, pp. 419-20, 425; II, p. 165.
119. *Ibid.*, II, pp. 165-66, v. 35.
120. *Ibid.*, I, p. 366, vv. 1-2; II, pp. 184-85, vv. 1-4.
121. *Ibid.*, II, pp. 184-90, vv. 5-37.
122. *Ibid.*, I, pp. 335, v. 49, 337, v. 8; II, pp. 161-62, vv. 13-15.
123. *Ibid.*, II, pp. 175-77, vv. 25-30.
124. *PK*, p. 385; see also Wilford, *As. Res.*, IX, pp. 176-77.
125. *Bhv.*, II, pp. 176-77, vv. 31-35.

Udayāditya, has been established. The copper-plate of the former (nephew of Bhojarāja) preserved in Archaeologcal Museum of Indore proves that the latter (AD 1059-94) was brother of Bhoja. According to the Purāṇa, Udaya (Udayāditya) was the founder of Udayapura[126] which can be confirmed by 'Udepur' inscription,[127] which describes him as the successor of Bhoja.

The Purāṇic accounts of the Tomaras of Delhi and the Cauhānas of Ajmer and Delhi are of paramount historcial importance.

It is clearly mentioned in the Purāṇa that the Tomara dynasty founded by Anaṅgapāla I ruled in Indraprastha (Delhi).[128] It is further said that Tomara also ruled there. His descendants became known as Tomara kṣatriyas. Tomara's son Cauhānasubha became known as Sāmaladeva who ruled for seven years. One of his descendants was Ajaya (or Ajayapāla).[129]

Ajayapāla (Ajayarāja) was one of the Cauhāna rulers of Ajmer. He is credited with having founded that city. One of the famous rulers of this dynasty was Viśaladeva (or Vigraharāja IV, AD 1152-64) who captured Delhi about AD 1158 from the Tomaras. In the Purāṇic genealogy of the Cauhāna rulers, his name figures as Viśāla. One of the Tomara kings was Jayasiṁha who is said to have ruled for about fifty years. The two other noted rulers, Ānandadeva and Someśvara, have also been mentioned in the Purāṇa.[130] The most famous and illustrious king of the Cauhāna family, Pṛthvīrāja (AD 1179-92), inherited the kingdom of Delhi from his maternal grandfather, Anaṅgapāla II, the last king of the Tomara dynasty. It is clearly stated in the Purāṇa that the death of Anaṅgapāla he became the full-fledged ruler of Delhi. He made it a fortified city. It became an extensive and magnificent city during his time.[131]

The further historical narratives of the subject in the Purāṇa show that Pṛthvīrāja's overlordship of nothern India was disputed by Jayacandra of Kanauj, the most famous king of Gāhaḍavāla dynasty or Rāṭhor family, who ruled from AD 1170 to 1194. It is said that the former turned the latter into an enemy by forcibly carrying off his beautiful

126. *Ibid.*, p. 176, v. 34.

127. *Ep. Ind.*, I, pp. 232-38.

128. *Bhv.*, I, pp. 424, v. 5, 429-32, vv. 1-14.

129. *Op. cit.*, II, pp. 168-69, vv. 1-6.

130. *Ibid.*, pp. 170-71, vv. 15-22 (the pedigree and progeny of king Viśāladeva are given); also I, p. 430, v. 4.

131. *Ibid.*, p. 171, vv. 22-25; I, pp. 430-34, vv. 1-15, 22-28.

daughter, Saṁyogitā, from her *svayaṁvara*. The rivalry between the two ultimately resulted in the battle which was fought as Sūkar. In this battle the soldiers of both sides were killed. The hostility between the two potentates proved to be disastrous for the Agnivaṁśa[132] and blessing for Muhammad Ghori. The Purāṇa even records the 'death of Pṛthvīrāja at the hands of Saho-ddin (Sihabuddin Ghori)'[133] which is indicative of the fact that the latter after having defeated the former in the second battle of Tarāin (about 14 miles from Thāneśvar) fought in AD 1192 put him to death. And thereafter he occupied Delhi and Ajmer. It is also narrated in the same Purāṇa that after his death a large number of women of the Cauhāna family fell into the hands of the Muslims and their descendants were neither pure Āryans nor *mlecchas*. They were rather of mixed parentage. And the kṣatriyas sprang from the Cauhānas.[134]

The Purāṇa slightly touches upon the Cālukya (called Śukla) dynasty of Ānartta (Gujarat) in western India. The founder of the dyansty, Śukla, is said to have set-up his rule at Dvārakā and ruled for 10 years. He was succeeded by Viśvaksena who ruled for 20 years, Jayasena for 30 years and Visena for 50 years.[135] But it is very difficult to establish their identities and to confirm their reign-periods.

The Purāṇic accounts of some of the dynasties of Rājapūt princes shown above are neither systematic nor complete. There are some gaps in the dynastic accounts as well as in the genealogies. The overlapping of dynasties is also apparent. However, the historical validity of the information contained in the Purāṇa cannot be doubted. Some of the details are in full accord with the facts recorded in ancient and early medieval history of India.

While critically judging the value of the Purāṇas, E.J. Rapson observed: "The descriptions of ancient monarchs and of their realms (therein) are essentially historical. They may be compared to the Sagas and the medieval chronicles of Europe. They are the products of an imaginative and uncritical age in which men were not careful to distinguish fact from legend. It is the task of modern criticism to disentangle the two elements. . . ."[136]

---

132. *Bhv*., I, pp. 432-35, vv. 17-21, 29-38, 435-45, vv. 1-63, also 424-25, v. 4.
133. *Ibid*., II, p. 171, v. 25.
134. *Ibid*., pp. 171-72, vv. 26-28.
135. *Ibid*., I, p. 336, v. 4; II, pp. 172-76, vv. 1-28.
136. "The Purāṇas", in *CHI*, I, p. 267.

The historical material available in the Purāṇas about kingdoms and dynasties covers the period from primaeval king Manu Vaivasvata down to the times of Pṛthvīrāja Cauhān and not only up to the early fourth century AD as held by some scholars. It will not be correct to say that the Purāṇas provide dynastic history only up to the beginning of the Gupta rule.

There are some other aspects of ancient Indian history like towns and cities, *janapada*s (territories and peoples), kingdoms, state and government, polity and administration, society, religion and culture which are also recorded in the Purāṇas.

The Purāṇic data about the foundations, planning, naming, antiquity, growth and decay of towns and cities are very important for the study of history of urbanisation in ancient India. This is one of the aspects of judging the historical value of the Purāṇas. The Purāṇic records also throw light on the nature of urban settlements by showing the growth of towns as political, administrative, commercial, religious or educational centres. The town and cities described in the Purāṇas include Hastināpura and Indraprastha (the two capitals of Kuru kingdom), Ahicchatrā and Kāmpil or Kāmpilya (the northern and southern capitals of Pañcāla kingdom), Mathurā (the capital of Śūrasena kingdom), Ujjayinī or Ujjain (the capital of Avantī kingdom, western Mālawā), Virāṭa (the capital of Matsya kingdom), Ayodhyā (the earliest capital of Kośala kingdom), Vaiśālī (the capital of king Viśāla and later metropolis of eight confederate republican clans), Girivraja or Rājagṛha (the earliest capital of Megadha kingdom), Pāṭaliputra (the later capital of Magadha kingdom), Kauśāmbī (the capital of Vatsa kingdom), Vārāṇasī (the capital of Kāśī kingdom), Māhiṣmatī (the capital of southern part of Avantī), Tripurī (the early medieval capital of Cedi kingdom), Tāmralipti (modern Tāmluk), Takṣaśilā and Puṣkalāvatī (the eastern and western capitals of Gāndhāra kingdom), Śrāvastī (the capital of northern Kośala), Kuśāvatī (the capital of southern Kośala), Pratiṣṭhānapura (the capital of Purūrava and his descendants), Campā (the capital of Aṅga kingdom), Mithilā (the capital of Videha kingdom), Dvārakā, Bhārukaccha (modern Broach), Vidiśā (the capital of Daśārṇa, eastern Mālawā), Śūktimatipura (the early capital of Cedi kingdom), Kuṇḍinapura and Bhojakaṭapura (the earlier and later capitals of Vidarbha kingdom), Śūrpāraka (modern Sopārā), Śākalapura (the Madras' capital) and Kāñcī (modern Kanjeevaram, originally belonged to the Coḷas and later became the capital of the Pallavas). These towns or cities belong to different parts of India including those of the upper and middle Gaṅgā valley. The archaeological discoveries of the remains of most of the towns mentioned above not only confirm their existence but also prove the historicity of Purāṇic accounts of the subject. The archaeological evidences also throw light on the antiquity of the towns and settlement-patterns there. Of the towns mentioned above the first seven are archaeologically associated with PGW (Painted Grey Ware) and NBPW (Northern Black Polished Ware) phases of culture. The archaeologists on the basis of Carbon-14 dating place them in the first millennium BC. The urban growth of next twelve are ascribed to NBPW phase or second half of the first millennium BC. H.D. Sankalia, while placing his reliance on both tradition and archaeology, has reasonably concluded that the antiquity of towns and cities as occurring in the *Mahābhārata* and Purāṇas can also be proved by archaeological evidence.[137] The Purāṇas contain genuine historical tradition which also finds corroboration in archaeology. R. Morton Smith is perfectly correct in stating that. ". . . the Purāṇa makes a good historical sense consistent with the idea of archaelogy".[138]

The *janapadas* mentioned in the Purāṇas include Kuru, Pāñcāla, Kāśī, Kośala, Śūrasena and Matsya of Madhyadeśa, Bāhlika, Gāndhāra, Kamboja, Sindh, Sauvīra (northern part of Sindh), Madraka (northern part of the Punjab), Kashmir, the Śakas, Tuṣāras, Cīnas, Kirātas, Pahlavas (Persians) and Ambaṣṭhas of Uttarāpatha (north-western region), Aṅga, Baṅga, Prāgjyotiṣa or Kāmarūpa, Puṇḍra, Videha (Mithilā), Magadha and Tāmralipti of Prācyadeśa (eastern region), Sārasvata, Saurāṣṭra, Ānartta and Bhārukaccha of Aparānta (western region), the Pāṇḍyas, Keralas, Colas, Muṣikas, Śabaras, Pulindas, Māhisaka (Mysore), Kaliṅga (southern part of Orissa) and Aśmaka (southern part of Mahārāṣṭra) of Dakṣiṇāpatha (southern region), Avantī, Vidiśā, Tripurī, Daśārṇa and Bhojas of Vindhyan region, and the Kirātas, Khasas, Dārdas, Mālawas and Trigarttas of mountain region.[139]

The Purāṇas throw a good deal of light on the evolution of kingship, emergence of the state and its seven constituent elements (based on the *saptāṅga* theory), inter-state relations, administrative organisation (local, judicial, civil and military administration),

---

137. *AIHA*, pp. 277-78 and 280.

138. *DDEI*, preface, see also pp. 1-3.

139. *Vy.*, 45, 108-37; 47, 42-62; Patil, *op. cit.*, p. 270; *Vṣṇ.*, 2, 3, 15-17; *Mts.*, 114, 34-57; *Mkd.*, 54, 32-57; 55, 6-32, 49-52; *Br.*, 19, 15-18; 27, 41-64; *Vmn.*, 13, 35-57; *Km.*, I, 45, 39-42; *Padma Purāṇa* (Svargakhaṇḍa), ed by Ashoka Chatterjee Śāstrī (Vārāṇasī, 1972), 15, 41-59; *Garuḍa Purāṇa*, ch. LV, p. 146; see also S.M. Ali, *The Geography of the Purāṇas*, pp. 133-76; D.C. Sircar, *SGAMI*, pp. 26-74; B.C. Law, "Countries and Peoples of India" (Epic and Paurāṇic Sources), *ABORI*, vol. XVII, pt. III, 1936, pp. 225ff; *Geographical Essays*, pp. 119-71.

revenue system, etc.[140] The data concerned have their own value in the realm of study of ancient Indian polity and administration.

The Purāṇic descriptions of socio-religious life of the people with references to the *varṇāśrama dharma* (four-fold stages of life), caste system, Śaiva, Śakti and Vaiṣṇava cults of Hinduism, etc., have considerable historical value.

Several broken chains in the political and cultural history of ancient India can be restored back with the help of the historical data contained in the Purāṇas.

140. For details of all see *Mts.*, Chs 215-20, 225-27; *Agn.*, Chs 218-27; 233, 11-23; 234, 1-25; Chs 235-236; 239, 1-45; 240, 1-32; Chs 242-43, 251-52; B.B. Mishra, *Polity in the Agni Purāṇa*, pp. 27ff; *Padma Purāṇa*, Svargakhaṇḍa (*Supra*), Chs 36-37; 38, 1-40, 59-65; *Vṣṇ. Dh.*, II, 65, 2-70; II, Chs 6, 18, 68, 150, 177-181; Patil, *op. cit.*, pp. 47-54; J.L. Shastri, *Political Thought in the Purāṇas*; Om Prakash, *Political Ideas in the Purāṇas*.

5

Buddhist and Jain Traditions

THE Buddhist and Jain traditions of historiography also deserve our notice. Both the Buddhist and Jain scholars made substantial contributions to the evolution of historiographical tradition in ancient India. They also like the Hindus felt the need to record the past as well as contemporary events of historical nature in their respective works. They did not ignore the incorporation of historical subjects in their writings and their preservation. They like the scholars of the Brāhmaṇical historical schools presented history in literary form. They have both historical and semi-historical works to their credit. The historical narratives, dynastic genealogies and chronology, biographies and chronicles from very important parts of their historical writings. There were different schools of historical writing in the Buddhist and Jain communities. The historical records were compiled and preserved by the Jains and Buddhists of various schools. Like the Sanskrit literature, the Buddhist and Jain literatures too contain a good number of works of historical value. The Jain historical literature, which is marked by its variety, vastness and richness, is of special importance. The Buddhist and Jain historical traditions are preserved in different classes of works of different periods. Both the traditions have their own authenticity and value.

Buddhist Historiography

Of all the Buddhist works of some historical importance, mention may first be made of the three Piṭakas, *Vinaya*, *Sutta* and *Abhidhamma,* which from parts of canonical Pāli literature ascribed to the period extending from the fifth century BC to the first century BC. Their historicity can be proved by the historical facts they contain.

The *Vinaya Piṭaka* contains valuable historical information about two powerful Magadhan rulers, Bimbisāra and his son Ajātasattu (Ajātaśatru), the events that took place during their times, socio-eonomic and political life of the people, towns and cities and kingdoms and republics in the time of the Buddha, Buddhism, etc. Bimbisāra is said to have ruled over the kingdom of Magadha with its capital at Rājagaha (Rājagṛha). The economic prosperity of this capital city is also highlighted. We are further told that Ajātasattu employed his two ministers, Sunidha and Vassakāra, to build a fort at Pāṭaligāma (which later developed as a city of Pāṭaliputta or Pāṭaliputra) to repel the invasion of the Vajjians. Brahmadatta, king of Kāśī, entered into a war with king of Kośala in which the latter suffered most, but friendship was soon restored. The republican states of Pāvā and Kuśinārā of the Mallas were in a flourishing condition at the time of the Buddha. The towns and cities of Majjhimadesa (Madhyadeśa) which were intimately associated with the Buddha and Buddhism include Rājagaha, Vesāli (Vaiśālī), Sāketa, Sāvatthi (Śrāvastī), Campā, Kośambī, Pāṭaliputta, Kapilavatthu and Vārāṇasī. A brief account of the first two Buddhist Councils held at Rājagaha in *c.* 483 BC (three months after the death of the Buddha) under the patronage of Ajātasattu, and at Vesāli in about *c.* 383 BC during the reign of Kālāsoka respectively has also been provided in this Piṭaka. Interesting sidelights are also thrown on the political history, and social and economic conditions of the people of the Buddha's time.[1] The *Mahāvagga* provides us with information about Gautama's attainment of enlightenment and the first sermon he delivered at Sāranāth near Vārāṇasī. The entire history of the foundation of the Buddhist community (Saṁgha) is recorded therein. It records in chronological order the subsequent events of a century in that community. It presents a systematic history of the development of the Buddhist order. It also records a few important episodes in the life of the Buddha. It deals with his life history. In fact, it starts history just from the Buddhahood of Gautama.[2] The *Cullavagga* provides historical anecdotes connected with the life of the Buddha and history of constiution of the order.[3] These two important sections of the said Piṭaka constitute very important sources of the history of Buddhism.

We find wealth of historical material in the *Sutta Piṭaka*. It consists of the five Nikāyas, *Dīgha*, *Majjhima*, *Saṁyutta*, *Aṅguttara* and *Khuddaka*.

The *Dīgha Nikāya* contains a number of historical Suttas. The *Sāmaññaphala Sutta* furnishes us with valuable information about the crafts and occupations of the time. The weavers, potters and basket-makers have been mentioned as important occupational groups. Another important historical allusion in this Sutta is to the murder of Bimbisāra at the hands of his son Ajātasattu. The *Ambaṭṭha Sutta* refers to king Pasenadi of Kośala who was the contemporary of the Buddha. This Sutta also throws light on the

1. B.C. Law, *HPL*, II, Appendix A, pp. 648-51.
2. *Ibid.*, I, pp. 61ff, 65.
3. *Ibid.*, p. 65 f.

social position of the four *vaṇṇa*, khattiya, brāhmaṇa, vessā and suddā. The *Sonadaṇḍa Sutta* refers to Campā visited by the Buddha with 500 monks, to king Bimbisāra of Magadha and king Pasenadi of Kosala. This Sutta also tell us how the Aṅga kingdom with its capital Campā was absorbed in the Magadhan empire. The *Mahāli Sutta* makes an incidental reference to the Buddha's dwelling at Vesāli. The *Lohicca Sutta* states that king Pasenadi used to collect taxes from the inhabitants of Kāśī-Kośala. He enjoyed the income not alone but with his subordinates. The *Mahāparinibbāna Sutta* contains the details of how the Magadhan monarch, Ajātasattu, hatched a plot to annihilate his Vajjian rivals. It relates that when the Buddha heard of this plot, he remarked that so long as the Vajjians remain united and fulfil the seven conditions of their welfare, there would be no danger to them. But soon Ajātasattu succeeded in annihilating them with the help of his tow ministers. Sunidha and Vassakāra. These ministers are stated to have created dissensions among them which resulted in their fall and annexation of their metropolis Vesāli to Magadha kingdom. This Sutta further relates that Buddha on his way to Vesāli visited Pāṭaligāma where the said two ministers built a fort to crush the Vajjians. The same Sutta speaks of the Mallas of Kuśinārā. It further mentions Sāvatthi, Campā, Rājagaha, Sāketa, Kosāmbī and Vārāṇasī as great cities. The *Janavasabha Sutta* refers to Bimbisāra of Magadha as a righteous king. This Sutta also refers to Kāśī, Kośala, Vajji, Cedi, Vaṁsa (Vatsa), Kuru, Pañcāla, Maccha (Matsya) and Śūrasena kingdoms. The *Sangiti Sutta* informs us that Mahāvīra, the founder of Jainism, died at Pāvā. It also mentions the Mallas of Pāvā who were republican communities. The *Mahānidāna Sutta* and the *Mahāsatipaṭṭhana Sutta* refer to the land of the Kurus where the Buddha dwelt for sometime. The *Mahāsudassana Sutta* mentions Campā, Rājgaha, Sāketa, Sāvatthi, Kośāmbī, Vārāṇasī and Kuśinārā (also named as Kuśāvatī) as rich and prosperous cities. The *Mahāgovinda Sutta* refers to a number of great cities built by Govinda. They are Dantapura of the Kaliṅgas, Poṭana of the Assakas. Māhissati of the Avantīs, Roruka of the Sovira, Mithilāof the Videhas. Campā of the Aṅgas and Vārāṇasī of the Kāśīs. The *Dīgha Nikāya* is also an important record of the dialogues and discourses in which the Buddha expounded his doctrine.[4]

The historical information contained in the *Majjhima Nikāya* are mainly concerned with the life and itinerary of the Buddha. In this respect the *Ariyapariyesana Sutta* is very important. It deals with different phases of his life and activities. We are told that he in the course of his wanderings stayed at Rājagaha, Campā, Nālandā, Mithilā, Kuśinārā,

4. *DN*, I, pp. 47-126, 150-58; II, pp. 72-168, 220-52, 290-358; Eng. trans. by T.W. and C.A.F. Rhys Davids, *The Dialogues of the Buddha*, 3 vols. PTS (London, 1899-1921).

Kośāmbī, Vesāli, Sāvatthi and other places. There are historical references in this Nikāya to the Vajjis and Mallas, the Śākyas of Kapilavatthu, the Kāśīs of Vārāṇasī, the Aṅgas and the Magadhas, etc. It tells us of the Vajjis and the Mallas as forming Saṁghas and *gaṇas*, that is, clans governed by organised corporations. We are also informed that the political relation between the Licchavis of Vesāli and king Pasenadi of Kośala was friendly.[5]

The *Saṁyutta Nikāya* refers to king Pasenadi of Kośala the capital of which was Sāvatthi. The whole of the *Kosala-Saṁyutta* is devoted to him. It contains historical narratives of a war that broke out between Ajātasattu, king of Magadha, and Pasenadi. Each claimed the possession of the twonship of Kāśī. At first the former was victorious but later on he was defeated and taken prisoner by the latter. Pasenadi, however married his daughter, Vajirā, to Ajātasattu and granted to him the township of Kāśī.[6]

The *Aṅguttara Nikāya* contains a list of sixteen *mahājanapadas* (large territorial states) that existed in the age of the Buddha. These were Aṅga, Magadha, Kāśī, Kośala, Vajji, Malla, Ceti, Vaṁsa, Kuru, Pañcāla, Maccha, Śūrasena, Assaka, Avantī, Gāndhāra, and Kāmboja.[7] The list includes the names of the people as well as states.

The *Khuddaka Nikāya* is of inestimable value from the point of view of the study of history of Indian civilisation in the pre- and post-Buddha period. The *Jātaka* records (assigned to the second century BC) contain a lot of valuable historical data about political and socio-economic history of ancient India. It is clearly stated therein that Aṅga was once a powerful kingdom. Magadha was once under the sway of Aṅgarāja (*Jāt.,* Fausboll, VI, p. 272). It is said that king Manoja of Brahmavardhana (another name of Vārāṇasī) conquered Aṅga and Magadha (*Jāt.*,V, pp. 312-16). It appears from the same records that before the Buddha's time Kāśī was the most powerful kingdom in the whole of northern India (*Jāt.* III, pp. 115ff; I, pp. 262 ff). Mahākośala, father of king Pasenadi of Kośala, is said to have given his daughter in marriage to king Bimbisāra of Magadha. The pin-money was the village of Kāśī yielding a revenue of a hundred throusand for bath and perfume. We are also told that there took place many a fierce fight between the sons of Mahākośala and Bimbisāra, Pasenadi, and Ajātasattu respectively (*Jāt.* II, p. 237; IV, pp. 342 ff). In one of the *Jātakas* (IV, pp. 144 ff) it is narrated that Viḍūḍabha, in order to crush the Śākyas who deceived his father Pasenadi by giving him a daughter of a slave

5. *MN*, I, pp. 160-75, 231; II, pp. 100-1.
6. *SN*, I, pp. 68-102.
7. *AN*, I, p. 213; IV, pp. 252, 256, 260.

girl to marry, deposed his father and became king. He marched out with a large army and succeeded in annihilating the Śākyas. But he with his armymet also with destruction. The river Rohiṇī was the boundary between the territories of the Śākyas and Koliyas, the two republican communities. A quarrel flared up between the two over the possession of the river. But the Buddha succeeded in restoring peace among his kinsfolk (*Jāt.*, I, pp. 327 ff; IV pp. 207 ff). A king of Vārāṇasī attacked the kingdom of Kośala and took the king prisoner. The king of Kośala had a son named Chatta who fled while his father was taken prisoner. Afterwards Chatta recovered his kingdom (*Jāt.*, III, pp. 115 ff). The kingdom of Kāśī was seized by a king of Sāvatthi named Vaṅka. But it was soon restored to the king of Kāśī (*Jāt.*, III, pp. 168-69). It is said that Campā, the capital of the kingdom of Aṅga, was at a distance of 60 *yojana* from Mithilā (*Jāt.*, VI, p. 32). In the *Assaka Jātaka* (II, p. 155) we are told of the Assaka territory, the capital city of which was Poṭali. In the *Bhimasena Jātaka* (I, pp. 356 ff) Takkasilā is mentioned as a great certre of learning. from the *Sivi Jātaka* (IV, p. 401) we know that Ariṭṭhapura was the capital of the Śivi kingdom. The kingdom of Bāveru is referred to in the *Bāveru Jātaka* (III, p. 126), Bharukaccha, a seaport town, is referred to in the *Sussondi Jātaka* (III, pp. 187ff). In the *Cetiya Jātaka* (III, p. 454) it is said that Sotthivatinagara was the capital of the kingdom of Ceti. In the *Gandhārra Jātaka* (III, pp. 363-69) the Kāśmīr-Gāndhāra kingdom and the Videha kingdom are also mentioned. The kingdom of Kāśī with its capital Vārāṇasī also finds mention in the *Jātaka*s. The extent of the city is mentioned as 12 *yojana* (IV, p. 160). There are also references to the Kośala kingdom (*Jāt.*, III, pp. 211-13, 237). The Kāmboja kingdom is also referred to in the *Jātaka*s (IV, p. 208). There are innumerable references to the Magadha kingdom (*Jāt.*,IV, pp. 454-55; V, p. 316., VI, p. 272). The city of Mithilā, the capital of the Videhas, was 7 leagues and the kingdom of Videha 300 leagues in extent (Cowell's *Jāt.*, III, p. 222). In the *Kumbhakāra Jātaka* (*Ibid.*, III, p. 230) Kampilla has been mentioned as the capital of Uttara-Pañcāla. The river Campā formed the boundary between Aṅga and Magadha (*Campeyya Jātaka* — *Jāt.*, IV, p. 454). There are some *Jātaka*s which throw light on different categories of the brāhmaṇas, their position in the society and different professions and occupations they chose, the position of the khattiyas who were warrior *par-excellence*, agriculture and industry and trade and commerce both internal and external.

Apart from the *Jātaka*s the *Khuddaka Nikāya* contains some other books which are historically very important. The *Udāna* (p.11) makes mention of king Bimbisāra of Magadha and king Pasenadi of Kośala. The *Sutta Nipāta* deals with social and economic conditions of the people of the time. The social position of the brāhmaṇas and various pursuits they followed as means of their livelihood are sufficiently highlighted in it (p. 122). It also speaks of internal trade system (vv. 1012-13). It contains historical references to Rājagaha and Kapilavatthu visited by the Buddha (pp. 86, 192), Patiṭṭhāna, Māhissati, Ujjeni, Vedisā, Kośāmbī, Kuśinārā, Magadha, etc. (p. 194). The *Mahāniddesa* speaks of India's commerce by sea with Yona and Paramayona. Towards the east, it mentions Kālamukha, Suvaṇṇabhūmi, Vesuṅga, Verāpatha, Takkola, Tamali, Tambapaṇṇi and Java as countries visited by the Indian sea-going merchants and speaks also of the manner in which they followed the difficult land-route after reaching the harbour (pp. 154-55, 415). The *Cullaniddesa* (pp. 4-5) makes mention of a trade route from Patiṭṭhāna to Magadha. There are references to Mulaka, Patiṭṭhāna, Māhissati, Ujjeni, Vedisā, Kośāmbī, Sāketa, Sāvatthi, Kapilavatthu, Kuśinārā Pāvā, Bhoganagara, Vesāli and Megadha. The *Buddhavaṁsa* contains in verse the life history of Gautama Buddha. It also refers to the cities of Amarāvatī, Kuśinārā, Vesāli, Kapilavatthu, Allakappa, Rāmagāma, Pāṭaliputta, Avantīpura and Mithilā.[8] The *Cariyāpiṭaka* (a post-Aśokan work) mentions the city of Indapatta ruled by Dhañanjaya who met some brāhmaṇas from Kaliṅga, Kuśāvatī, Pañcāla where there was a king named Jayadissa in the city of Kappila or Kampil, etc. (pp. 74-75, 90 f). The *Apadāna* contains a list of occupational groups like basket-makers (*nalakāra*), weavers (*pesakāra*), leather-workers (*cammakāra*), carpenters (*tacchakā*), metal-workers (*kammāra*), blacksmiths, goldsmiths, tinsmiths, jewellers (*manikāra*), potters (*kumbhakāra*), cloth merchants (*dussikā*) and dyers (*rajakāra*) (II, p. 357 f). The hereditary craftsmen or those who followed different occupations and professions organised themselves into various guilds (called *seṇis*, *pūgas*) agreeing to be governed by their laws and customs. This work also speaks of India's external trade relations with outside world. It bears witness to be fact that traders and merchants from various countries including Malaya (Malay Peninsula), Soṇṇabhūmi (Suvaṇṇabhūmi) and Cīna (China) visited India (I, p. 2 and II, p. 357).

The *Kathāvatthu*, the thrid book of the *Abhidhamma Piṭaka* also deserves mention here. It is work of the Aśokan age. It was composed by Thera Moggaliputta Tissa, president of the Third Buddhist Council held at Pāṭaliputra under the patronage of king Aśoka. It is important from the point of view of history of Buddhism and development of Buddhist doctrine of the ages after Buddha. It is evident from it that at the time of Aśoka there existed different schools of Buddhism.

The *Tripiṭaka* throw a good deal of light on social, economic, political and religious

8. *Buddhavaṁsa*, Eng. trans. by Law, PTS (London, 1938).

history of ancient India from the time of the Buddha or rise of the Magadhan empire to the third or second century BC. They also provide the narratives of historical events that took place during the lifetime of the Buddha (sixth and fifth centuries BC). It cannot, however, be denied that in the canonical Pāli texts the history is mixed up with legends.

The post-cononical Pāli literature of the period extending from the beginning of the Christian era to the end of the fifth century AD also contains some works including the commentaries and chronicles which are very important for historical purposes.

The *Milindapañho* (a non-canonical or an extra canonical work) perserves the history of rule of the Bactrian Greek king, Menander (*c.* 165-145 BC), over the Punjab with its capital at Sāgala (Śākala = modern Siālkoṭ). He became popularly known as Milinda after being converted to Buddhism by Nāgasena, the learned Buddhist monk. It appears from this work that the capital city was adorned with splendid and magnificent buildings, parks, gardens, tanks, well-laid out streets, strong defences and market-places. It was one of the important centres of trade and commerce. It had shops for the sale of Banāras muslin, jewels and other costly articles indicating the wealth and prosperity of the kingdom. It had also trade relation with Pāṭaliputra.[9] The full details of conversations between king Milinda and Nāgasena have been provided in all the seven books of this work. It contains valuable information about the Buddhist monks who were persecuted by the brāhmaṇa ruler, Puṣyamitra Śuṅga (*c.* 184-148 BC), and protected by Menander, a zealous Buddhist. The Śuṅga king was no doubt a persecutor of Buddhism and zealous champion of Brāhmaṇism. He after having usurped the throne of Magadha in 184 BC actually extended his sway over Śākala in the Punjab. In one of the Buddhist Sanskrit texts, *Divyāvadāna*, also it is recorded that Puṣyamitra made the notorious declaration at Śākala setting a price of one hundred gold *dīnāra*s on the head of every Buddhist monk.[10] There is hardly any reason to doubt the historicity of such information.

One of the important historical facts recorded in the *Milindapañho* is about Dhana-nanda, the last reigning Nanda king, who was uprooted by Cāṇakya in a war in which Bhadrasāla was the commander-in-chief of the Nanda army and the carnage was terrible.[11] There are some other facts and contents of historical interest in this work. It contains a list of kingdoms, towns and cities, etc. It refers to the province of Yavana (Bactria in

9. Eng. trans. From Pāli by T.W. Rhys Davids, *The Questions of king Milinda SBE*, XXXV, I (Oxford, 1890, rept. Delhi, 1969) pp. 1-27.

10. *Divyāvadāna*, ed. E.B. Cowell and R.A. Neil (Cambridge, 1886, rept. 1976), pp. 433-34.

11. *SBE*, XXXVI, II, (Oxford, 1894, rept. Delhi, 1969), pp. 147-48.

north Afghanistan watered by the Oxus) where the Bactrian Greeks established their rule. Alsanda (the town of Alexandria on the Indus founded by Alexander which was famous for coral trade), Bharukaccha (an seaport town equivalent to modern Broach), country of Cīna (China), the kingdoms of Gāndhāra (that had its capital at Puruṣapura), Kaliṅga (that had its capital at Dantapura ages before Bhddha's time), Kaśmīr, Kośala, and Magadha with its capital at Pāṭaliputra, the cities like Sāgala, Sāketa, Ujjeni, Madhurā (Mathurā) and Vārāṇasī, and places like Sovīra (Sauvīra adjacent to Sindh), Suvaṇṇabhūmi (identical probably with Lowel Burma and Malay Peninsula) and Takkola which were visited by Indian merchants.[12] It also throws some light on the socio-economic life of the people. It is explicitly stated in it that in a well-laid city or town, rooms had to be made for the residence of the various classes of khattiyas, brāhmaṇas, vessas, suddas, goldsmiths, silversmiths, workers in lead, tin, iron and brass, blacksmith, jewellers, weavers, potters, leather-workers, wagon-makers, ivory-workers, basket-makers, dyers, money-exchangers, cloth merchants, traders and merchants from various countries and places and other professional groups.[13]

The authorship of *Milindapañho* and date of its composition are controversial aspects of the subject. According to Mrs. Rhys Davids, the recorded conversations of Milinda and Nāgasena were edited in the new book from after the former's death by special commission by a brāhmaṇa of Buddhist collegiate training named Mānava. But it is disputable. The generally accepted view is that it had originally been written in northern India at or little after the beginning of the Chirstian era in Sanskrit or in some north Indian Prākṛt by an anonymous author. It appeared again in an enlarged and modified form in the second century AD. It saw its Pāli recension before the fifth century AD.

The Buddhist historical writing in the commentatorial tradition is also worthy of our notice. Buddhaghoṣa, a native of Bodha-Gayā, flourished in the first half of the fifth century AD. He went to Ceylon and wrote fourteen commentaries on the Pāli texts there during that period or between AD 410 and 435. Of all the commentaries written by him, the *Sāmaṇtapāsādikā* (on the *Vinaya Piṭaka*) is the most important from a historical point of view. It provides dynastic history of Magadha from the sixth century BC to the time of Aśoka. It provides dyunastic genealogies and chronology of the kings of Bimbisāra, Śisunāga, Nanda and Maurya dynasties who ruled over Magadha with its capital at Pāṭaliputra. Bimbisāra is stated to have ruled over the kingdom of Magadha maintaining

12. *Milindapañho*, ed. by V. Treckner (London, 1880), pp. 327, 331, 359.

13. *Ibid.*, p. 331.

a powerful army. He had many sons. He was succeeded by his eldest son Ajātasattu, who is said to have ruled for 24 years. He bore the cost of repairing at Rājagaha 18 *mahāvihāras* which were deserted by the Buddhist monks after the *parinibbāna* of the Buddha. The Buddha passed away in the eighth year of Ajātasattu's reign. Udāyi Bhadda, the successor of Ajātasattu, reigned for 16 years. The other two kings of Magadha are mentioned Anuruddha and Muṇḍa. They altogether ruled for 18 years. Then came Nāgadāsaka who reigned for 24 years. He was banished by the citizens who anointed the minister named Susunāga (Śiśunāga) as king. He ruled for 18 years. Kālāsoka ruled for 28 years. He had ten sons (the most prominent among whom was Nandivardhana). They altogether ruled for 22 years. Then came the Nandas who also ruled over Magadha for the same period. The Nanda dynasty was overthrown by Candagutta (Candragupta) Maurya who ruled the kingdom for 24 years (*c*. 321-297 BC). He was succeeded by Bindusāra who ruled for 28 years (*c*. 297-269 BC).[14] He was succeeded by Aśoka (Dhammāsoka) who is said to have enjoyed undivided sovereignty over the kingdom after slaying all his brothers except Tissa. It is clearly stated in this work that he reigned without coronation for four years[15] which means that he ascended the throne four years before he was formally crowned as a king. While furnishing an account of Aśoka this work also records that he followed his father for sometime in making donations to non-Buddhist ascetics and institutions, and gave charities to the Buddhist *bhikkhus*. His income from the four gates of the city of Pāṭaliputta was 400000 *kahāpanas* daily. He is said to have built 84000 *vihāras* all over India. The missionaries who were sent to various places to preach the *dhamma* of Aśoka were all natives of Magadha.[16] These are positive evidences of historical writing in the said tradition. The other historical contents in this work are about Kuśinārā, the town of the Mallas, where Buddha passed away, the cities of Vārāṇasī, Vesāli, Campā, Sāvatthi and Kapilvatthu, the sea-port of Bharukaccha, Suvaṇṇabhūmi, visited by Indian traders, the kings of the Licchavigaṇa, the places visited by the Buddha in the course of his wanderings, etc.[17] The historicity of the work is established by the facts stated above.

There are some other historically important commentaries of Buddhaghoṣa. The *Sumaṅgalavilāsinī* (on the *Dīgha Nikāya*) describes Ajātasattu as a partricide monarch.

---

14. *Sāmantapāsādikā*, ed. by J. Takakusu and M. Nagai, vol. I, PTS (London, 1924), pp. 72-73, also 8-9, 41.

15. *Ibid*., p. 41.

16. *Ibid*., pp. 44, 52, 63f, 115.

17. *Sāmantapāsādika*, pp. 175, 210, 212, 241.

It further relates that he had hostile relationship with his father, Bimbisāra, whom he imprisoned and kept confined in a room and starved to death.[18] Ajātasattu's two ministers, Sunidha and Vassakāra, built fortress at Pāṭaligāma to repel the attacks of Licchavis of Vesāli.[19] The Śākyas, Koliyas and other republican tribes, the Aṅga kingdom with its capital Campā, the other tow kingdoms of Kośala and Gāndhāra, the towns of Rājagaha and Kośāmbī of the Buddha's time, the economic importance of Varāṇasī as a trading centre and the weavers who produced soft and beautiful garments there, etc., are also recorded in it.[20] It also contains information about Nālandā which grew as a town and a Buddhist University in the fifth century AD.[21]

The *Dhammapada-aṭṭhakathā* abounds in references to some of the important kings like Bimbisāra and Ajātasattu of Magadha and Pasenadi of Kośala, some principal cities like Takkasilā, Kapilavatthu, Kośāmbī, Vārāṇasī, Rājagaha, Sāvatthi and Vesālī and the republican tribes like Licchavis, Mallas, etc.

The *Sutta Nipāta* commentary is a mine of various sorts of valuable historical information. It deals with two important kingdoms of Magadha and Kośala. It states that Bimbisāra was a lord of Magadha, and being possessor of big army was called Seniya. Kośalarāja Pasenadi is also described as a powerful ruler. It mentions Vārāṇasī, Sāvatthi, Kapilavatthu, Rājagaha and other famous cities of the Buddha's time. It also throws light of the socio-economic life of the people and trade and commerce of the time.

The *Aṭṭhasālini* (commentary on the *Abhidhamma Piṭaka*) contains references to some historical personages including Udāyi Bhadda of Magadha. It supplies us with information about the kingdom of Kośala, the urban life of the people, the cities, Kāśīpura, Pāṭalputta, Bharukaccha, Rājagaha, Sāvatthi, etc.

The *Khuddakapātha* commentary furnishes us with many important historical materials concerning political and religious history of ancient India. The details of the Licchavis of Vesāli, the kingdom of Magadha, king Bimbisāra, growth of Buddhism, eighteen great monasteries in Rājagaha, the importance of Kapilavatthu in the time of Buddha, etc., have been provided in it.

---

18. *Sumaṅgalavilāsinī*, ed. by Rhys Davids and J.E. Carpernter, 3 vols, PTS (London, 1886-1932), I, pp. 133-40.
19. *Ibid.*, II, pp. 516-17.
20. *Ibid.*, I, pp. 132, 239, 258f, 279, 317-19, 389.
21. *Ibid.*, I, p. 35, III, p. 873.

The above commentaries afford an ample testimony of Buddhaghoṣa's knowledge of history.

The two Ceylonese chronicles, the *Dīpavaṁsa* and the *Mahāvaṁsa*, are important historical records. Their association with Indian Buddhist historical tradition justifies their inclusion here. Both the chronicles deal with some aspects of ancient Indian history.

The *Dīpavaṁsa* was written at the end of the fourth century AD or the beginning of the fifth century AD by an anonymous Buddhist writer. Some of the kings of Magadha with the length of their reigns and the events of their times are mentioned in it. Bimbisāra is said to have ruled for 52 years, Udāyi Bhadda for 16 years and the ten sons of Kālāsoka for 22 years. Candagutta Maurya ascended the throne 162 years after the death of Buddha (i.e., 483 - 162 = in *c.* 321 BC) and ruled for 24 years (i.e., till 297 BC).[22] It further deals with the reign of the great Maurya king Aśoka (the grandson of Candagutta and son of Bindusāra) and the notable events that took place in his time. It was during his reign or in *c.* 246 BC that Mahinda (Mahendra, his son) went to Ceylon and spread Buddhism there.

The *Mahāvaṁsa* (Great History) compiled by Mahānāma in AD 431 is an authoritative work. A dynastic list of the kings of Magadha to Asoka with regnal years of most of them is preserved in it. It is recorded therein that Bimbisāra was fifteen years old when he was anointed king by his own father and then reigned for full 52 years. (Thus he was born in 558 BC, ascended the throne in 543 BC and regined till 491 BC). His son Ajātasattu reigned for 32 years (*c.* 491-459 BC). It was the eighth year of his reign when the great Gautama Buddha died (i.e., in 483 BC) Ajātasattu's successor Udāyi Bhadda reigned for 16 years. His lineal descendants, Anuruddha and his son Muṇḍa, conjointly ruled for 8 years and Nāgadāsaka for 24 years. The throne of Magadha was then offered by the citizens, ministers and officials of Pāṭaliputta to Susunāga (Śiśunāga) who ruled for 18 years. His son Kālāsoka ruled for 28 years. At the end of the tenth year of his reign a century had passed after the *nirvāṇa* of the Buddha. Kālāsoka's ten sons (including Nandīvardhana and Mahānandin) together ruled for 22 years. All the above-mentioned rulers altogether ruled for 200 years (*c.* 543-343 BC). It is further stated in this chronicle that during the reign of Kālāsoka's sons the Nanda dynasty became powerful and usurped the sovereignty of Magadha. The nine Nandas have been assigned 22 years as the length of their reigns (*c.* 343-321 BC). It was Cāṇakya who uprooted this dynasty by putting

---

22. *Dip.*, ed. and trans. by H. Oldenberg (London, 1879, rept. Delhi, 1982) III, 50-60; V, 97.

Dhanananda, the last reigning Nanda king, to death.[23] All the three traditions, Purāṇic, Buddhist and Jain, are unanimous about this historic event. The genealogies and chronology of the kings mentioned above are very reliable. The genealogical lists of kings of the dynasties of pre-Maurya period do not agree with those of the Purāṇas in respects of their names, order and regnal years and total duration of their rule. However, the Purāṇic and Buddhists lists are supplementary to each other so far as their names are concerned and they have relative value but about the rest the latter stands as corrective to the former.

The Nanda dynasty came to an end in 321 BC. It was supplanted by the Maurya dynasty. The *Mahāvaṁsa* also supplies us with information about the origin or parentage of its founder, Candagutta. He was the son of the chief queen of the king of kṣatriya or Moriya clan (a branch of the Śākyas then ruling over Pippalivana).[24] He is said to have ruled for 24 years which exactly agrees with the Purāṇic chronology. (Thus he ruled from *c*. 321 to 297 BC.) And his son Bindusāra ruled for 28 years (*c*. 297-269 BC). But according to the Purāṇas, the length of his reign is 25 years (*c*. 297-272 BC) which appears to be more correct than the former.

The *Mahāvaṁsa* as well as the *Dīpavaṁsa* state that Aśoka was formally crowned as a king 218 years after the death of the Buddha.[25] Thus it was (483 - 218=) 265 BC. Since he was crowned four years after his accession, the actual beginning of his reign, according to the Buddhist historical tradition, will go back to 269 BC. However, there is another evidence to show that his coronation did not take place until 269 BC[26] which means that he ascended the throne in 273 BC which is in near approximation to the truth. According to Purāṇic historical tradition, he ruled for total 40 years (4 years before + 36 years after his coronation), i.e., from 272 to 232 BC. This is generally accepted reign period of this Maurya king. Both the chronicles deal with the propagation of Buddhism in Ceylon by Aśoka's son Mahinda and Buddhist establishments there. The historical statements are, of course, not always infallible. They also provide trustworthy accounts of three Buddhist Councils (already mentioned), eighteen different sects in the Buddhist order with their respective schools and systems that arose after the Second Council, and the Buddhist

23. For all *Mhv*., ed. by by W. Geiger, PTS (London, 1908, rept. 1958), II, 28-32; IV, 1-8; V, 14-15; trans. by W. Geiger and M.H. Bode, PTS (London, 1912, rept. 1950), introd. pp. XL-XLVI, 12, 15, 21, 163f, 168f.

24. *Dip*., trans, Geiger, p. 27; comm. ed. by Turnour, introduction, pp. XXXVIII-XLII.

25. *Dip*., VI, I; *Mhv*., V, 21; also Eng. trans. of both by E.M. Coomaraswamy (Colombo. 1908).

26. *Mhv*., trans. Geiger, p. 28.

missionaries sent to far-off lands for spreading Buddhism after the Third Council. They furnish a good deal of information regarding towns and cities of the Buddha's time. The chronicles refer in common to all those places in India and Ceylon which are especially important in the history of Buddhism. The *Mahāvaṁsa* in particular throws some light on the relations between Coḷa-rattha and Ceylon. We are told that about the middle of the second century AD a Coḷa prince named Elāra conquered the Island and ruled there for a fairly long period. These two chronicles have great value as sources of authentic historical tradition and information.

A.K. Warder, while dealing with historical writing in ancient India, has correctly stated that some of the Pāli canon and commentaries, and the two chronicles are historical records.[27]

The Buddhists presented history also in the form of an *avadāna*. We have, of course, some *avadānas* in Sanskrit in which we find some evidences of historical writing.

The *Aśokāvadāna* was composed in the first century AD by an anonymous Buddhist writer of the Sārvāstivāda school. Some scholars suggest a later date of its composition, i.e., second or early third century AD.[28] It is basically a biographical work. It speaks of Aśoka and his times. Besides, it contains some other historical indormation too. It is primarily based upon the *Aśokasūtra* composed in Mathurā sometime after the middle of the second century BC or between 150 and 50 BC which is no longer extant in original. It contains some stories of historical character about the great king Aśoka himself. The *Aśokāvadāna* consists of four chapters or sections titled *Pamsupradanāvadāna, Vitasokāvadāna*, *Kunālāvadāna* and *Aśokāvadāna.* The text throws light on the Aṅga kingdom with its capital at Campāpurī of the time of Bindusāra of Magadha. It refers to the Magadhan capital Pāṭaliputra as having been attacked by his son Susīma when his younger brother Aśoka was reigning there, but the former was overpowered by the latter. It mentions the *vihāras* built during the time of Aśoka. It is also stated therein that Upagupta, the teacher at Aśoka, was the son of Gupta, a rich merchant of Mathurā. The information supplied in it about Aśoka and his successors particularly Kuṇāla are of great value.[29] There are, of course, some discrepancies in the stories narrated in it about

27. C.H. Philips (ed.), *Historians of India, Pakistan and Ceylon*, vol. I of *Historical writing on the peoples of Asia*, pp. 46-56.
28. S.K. Mukhopadhyay (ed.), *The Aśokāvadāna*, p. IX.
29. *SBLN*, pp. 8-11.

them. It also contains some information about Prasenajit, king of Kośala, and Buddha's visit to Vaiśālī and other areas in its vicinity.[30]

The *Divyāvadāna* in its present from is datable to the fourth century AD. It is one of the important historical compositions. It throws light on the prosperity of the Magadha kingdom.[31] Its capital Rājagṛha is described as a rich, prosperous and populous city at the time of Bimbisāra and Ajātaśatru.[32] It was an important centre of inland trade where merchants flocked from different quarters to buy and sell their merchandise.[33] From Rājagṛha to Śrāvastī there was a trade route for the merchants.[34] In and around the city of Rājagṛha there were a number of important localities hallowed by the history of their associations with the Buddha and Buddhism.[35] The Magadhan capital Pāṭaliputra at the time of the Buddha was a great city.[36] The Gaṅgā formed the boundary between the kingdom of Magadha and the territory of the Licchavis, who were followers of the republican system of government. The Licchavis and the Vaiśālakas have been mentioned as two different confederate clans. Vaiśālī was the metropolis of the entire confederacy of eight confederate clans including the Vṛjikas and the Licchavis.[37] The wonderful city of Vaiśālī was visited by the Buddha more than once.[38] The Videha kingdom with its capital Mithilā (which had originally monarchical constitution) also finds mention in it.[39] The Mallas, who were republican community, had their headquarter at Kuśinārā which become famous because of the Buddha's *parinirvāṇa* there.[40] Vārāṇasī, the capital of Kāśī kingdom, is described as a prosperous, extensive and populous city. It was a famous trading centre in king Brahmadatta's time. The traders in his time used to come from Uttarāpatha.[41] Hastināpura, capital of the Kuru kingdom, is described as a rich,

30. *SBLN*, pp. 12-13.
31. *Divyāvadāna* (supra), p. 425.
32. *Ibid.*, p. 545.
33. *Ibid.*, p. 397.
34. *Ibid.*, pp. 94-95.
35. *Ibid.*, pp. 143, 554.
36. *Ibid.*, p. 544.
37. *Ibid.*, pp. 55-56, 136.
38. *Ibid.*, p. 208.
39. *Ibid.*, p. 424.
40. *Ibid.*, pp. 208-9.
41. *Ibid.*, pp. 73 and 510ff.

prosperous and populous city which was visited by the Buddha.[42] The *Mākandika-avadāna* has preserved the tradition about king Udayana of the Vatsa kingdom.[43]

The existence of king Muṇḍa, one of the descendants of Udāyi Bhadra, and king Kālāśoka called Kākavarnin, son of Śiśunāga, of Magadha is attested by the *Divyāvadāna*.[44] This work also contains a genealogy of the rulers of Maurya dynasty from Candragupta down to Puṣyadharman (Śatadhanvan) who preceded the last ruler; Bṛhadratha.[45] Chapter XXVI to XXIX contain many legends about some pre-Maurya and Maurya rulers with some Kernel of historical truth. The *Aśokāvadāna*, which forms very important part of this work, mainly deals with Aśoka and his successors. It is also recorded in this work that the citizens of Takṣaśilā revolted against the oppression of the Maurya officials during the reign of Bindusāra. Prince Susīma, his eldest son and viceroy there, could not quell the disturbance. Then Aśoka was deputed by his father to put down the revolt. He succeeded in restoring order.[46] The *Aśokāvadāna* states that Aśoka was immediately succeeded by his grandson, Samprati, and not by his son, Kuṇāla.[47] The historical tradition recorded in the Purāṇas is also conflicting about the immediate successor of Aśoka. It contains some anecdotes about his son and grandson. It further offer a glimpse into the conditions prevailing during the last phase of the reign of the great monarch Bṛhadratha which led to the disintegration of the Maurya empire. The last king of the Maurya dynasty was murdered by his own commander-in-chief, Puṣyamitra, whose name also figures in this work.

The *Mahāvastu-avadāna* is one of the earliest extant works in Sanskrit composed before the beginning of the Christian era by an anonymous writer of the Lokottaravāda school. Its Rājavaṁśa section is of exceptional value from a historical point of view. It deals mostly with the history of the life of the Buddha. It appears that the Buddhist historians were not ignorant of biographical tradition. It also contains a traditional record of the sixteen *mahājanapadas* or big states of his time.[48] It describes in detail the Licchavis of Vaiśālī and their close association with him. It also states that there were twice

---

42. *Divyāvadāna*, p. 435.
43. *Ibid.*, pp. 515-44.
44. *Ibid*, Ch. XXVI, p. 369.
45. *Ibid.*, pp. 370-71, 409, 433-34.
46. *Ibid.*, pp. 234, 262, 371, 407-8.
47. *Ibid.*, Ch. XXIX.
48. Mahāvastu, ed. E. Senart, 3 vols (Paris, 1882-97), vol. I, p. 34; II, p. 2, line 15.

84,000 Licchavirājās residing within the city of Vaiśālī.[49] It speaks of all important kingdoms and towns and cities which flourished before and after the rise of Buddhism. It refers to the Kuru kingdom with its capital Hastināpura, the Pañcāla kingdom with its capital Kāmpilya, the Aśmaka kingdom with its capital Poṭana, the kingdom of Magadha with its capital Rājagṛha of Bimbisāra's time and Puṣpāvatī (identical with Pāṭaliputra) of later time, the Vatsa kingdom with its capital Kauśāmbī ruled by king Udayana in the Buddha's time, the Kośala kingdom with its capital Sāketa, the Aṅga kingdom with its capital Campā, the kingdom of Kāśī with its capital Vārāṇasī, the Videha kingdom with its capital Mithilā, etc.[50] It also highlights the political relation between the kings of Kāśī and Kośala kingdoms. We are informed that Kāśī came in conflict with Kośala several times and each time the king of Kāśī was defeated. At last when he was going to make desperate final attack the king of Kośala refused to fight and abdicted his throne.[51] Vārāṇasī's commercial importance is also highlighted in this work. The place is described as a great trading centre of Buddhist India. Rich merchants of the city used to travel to far-off countries with ships laden with merchandise. It is also stated therein that a wealthy merchant came to Vārāṇasī from Takṣaśilā with the object of carrying on trade.[52] The history of the foundation of Kapilavastu and the settlement of the Śākyas (republican clan) there is also related in this work.[53]

In the *Avadānaśataka,* it is fairly recorded that the ancient Kośala kingdom was divided into two great parts the river Sarayū serving as the wedge between the two, and that there was a war between the kings of North and South Kośala.[54] The kingdom of Magadha with its capital Rājagṛha, the localities in and around this city important in the history of Buddhism, the city of Vaiśālī and the adjoining area and the Buddha's travels to all these places, the importance of Śrāvastī, the famous capital of the Kośala kingdom in the time of the Buddha, as a trading centre, etc., also find mention in it.[55]

The *Bodhisattvāvadāna-Kalpalatā* of Kṣemendra (*c.* AD 1028-63 or 1028-89), a

---

49. Mahāvastu, ed. E. Senart, I, pp. 253ff.
50. *Ibid.*, I, pp. 34f, 120, 283, 289, 348; II, pp. 2, 94-95, 419, III, pp. 47, 57, 90f, 172, 208-9, 231, 361-63, 402.
51. *Ibid.*, III, p. 349.
52. *Ibid.*, II, pp. 166-67; III, p. 286.
53. *Ibid.*, I, pp. 350ff.
54. *SBLN*, p. 20.
55. *Ibid.*, pp. 17-25; *Avadānaśataka*, ed. by J.S. Speyer, 2 vols (St. Petersburg, 1906).

historian of Kashmir school, is an extremely important work. It refers to Hastināpura, the capital of the Kuru kings (3rd *pallava*, p. 116; 64th, pp. 9 and 62), the kingdom of Pañcāla with its capital Kāmpilya (66th, p. 4; 68th, p. 9) the kingdom of Videha with its capital Mithilā ruled by a king named Puṣpadeva (83rd, p. 9), the Kāśī kingdom with its capital Vārāṇasī (6th, pp. 31-32), Kośala which was an important kingdom during the days of early Buddhism and its king Prasenajit (100th, p. 2) and one of its capitals, Sāketa, which was adorned with domes (3rd, p. 2) and the visit of merchants of Śrāvastī to Ceylon (7th, p. 50). It is stated therein that Kauśāmbī, the capital of Vatsa kingdom, was ruled by the king Udayana, the contemporary of the Buddha (35th p. 3). It throws some light on the Licchavi republic. The Vaiśālikas or the inhabitants of Vaiśālī called *gaṇas* are said to have followed the republican constitution (20th, p. 38). It mentions Buddha's visit to Vaiśālī and neighbouring places (90th, p. 73). It furnishes us with fragments of historical information about the rule of king Aśoka over Magadha with its capital at Pāṭaliputra and his different activities and *stūpas* and *caityas* built by him (69th, pp. 6-7). This work also contains many stories about the Buddha of both legendary and historical character.

The *avadānas* contitute an important part of Buddhist historiography.

The *Lalitavistara*, an important Sanskrit Buddhist text of the early first century AD is memoirs of the early life of the Buddha. The stories narrated about him therein are partly mythical and partly historical. Besides, it contains some other valuable information about kingdoms and republics, towns and cities, etc., of his time. Kapilavastu, famous in the history of Buddhist India and the home of the republican kṣatriya tribe Śākyas, is described copiously therein as *mahānagara* or great city with four gates, tower, market places, etc. It gives 500 as the number of member of the Śākya council.[56] It also refers to the sixteen kingdoms of the Buddha's time including those of Magadha, Kośala, Vatsa, Cedi, Avantī, Kāśī, Matsya, Śūrasena with its capital Mathurā which was a rich, flourishing and populous city, and Kuru.[57] It is further stated therein that Rājagṛha, the capital of Magadha kingdom, was a *mahānagara* or great city. It was much frequented by the Buddha.[58] It also provides a description of the people of Magadha. Vārāṇasī, the capital of Kāśī kingdom, was very famous for manufacturing cloth called *kāśika-vastra*.[59] This city

56. *Lalitavistara*, ed. R.L. Mitra, BIS, ASB (Calcutta, 1877), pp. 28, 58, 77, 98, 101-2, 113, 123, 136-37, 243.
57. *Ibid.*, pp. 20-22, 27, 109, 405-6, 412-13.
58. *Ibid.*, pp. 239, 243, 246, 318, 398.
59. *Ibid.*, p. 215.

was also visited by the Buddha. Śrāvastī, the most important capital city of Kośala kingdom in the Buddha's time, was full of kings, princes, ministers, councillors, brāhmaṇas, kṣatriyas, householders, etc.[60] The Videha dynasty is described as wealthy and prosperous. The Licchavis of Vaiśālī and the system of the government they followed are also recorded in it.[61]

The Sanskrit Buddhist texts unlike some of the Pāli texts contain hardly any contemporary evidence of a historical character. They deal mostly with past events.

The *Buddhacarita* of Aśvaghoṣa, who flourished in the first century AD and adorned the court of Kaniṣka, is a biographical work (semi-historical) in Sanskrit. It deals with main events of the life of the Buddha from his birth to his death or *mahāparinirvāṇa*, but the extant portion of this work covers only up to his attainment of enlightenment. It in the original form throws some light also on his teachings and Buddhist doctrine. Since the celebrated author does not treat of the Buddha as a historical personality, this work cannot be considered a historical biography. It was originally composed in twenty-eight cantos as is proved by its Chinese translation of the fifth century AD. But the Sanskrit text is available only in seventeen cantos.[62] It is significant to note that despite the absence of an established tradition of biographical writing in those days the Buddhist scholars made some contributions in this field as appears from this work as well as the *Aśokāvadāna* which deals with the life history of Aśoka and some of the other Sanskrit texts which deal with the life of the Buddha, mentioned before.

The *Mahābodhivaṁsa* composed by a monk Upatissa in the eleventh century AD has also some considerable historical value. A credible list of the names of king Kālāśoka's ten sons including the most prominent Nandīvardhana of pre-Nanda period and that of nine Nandas including the last king Dhanananda who ruled over Magadha is provided therein (p. 98). It also provides us with an account of attainment of enlightenment of the Buddha. There is a general historical reminiscence underlying of the stories of the three Buddhist Councils recorded in it. The different Buddhist schools that arose after the Second Council also find mention in it (pp. 96-97). It deals partly with the history of

60. *Lalitavistara*, ed. S. Lefmann and A.S. Halle (London, 1902 & 1908), rept. by P.L. Vaidya, Buddhist Sanskrit Texts Series (Darbhanga, 1958), Ch.I.

61. *Ibid*, Ch. III, p. 21.

62. *Buddhacarita* of Aśvaghosa, ed. and trans. by E.H. Johnton, 2 vols, 2nd edn. (Delhi, 1972); Eng. trans. (cantos I-XVII) by E.B. Cowell in SBE, vol. XLIX, pt I (Oxford, 1894, rept. Delhi 1972), pp. 1-200.

bodhi-tree in Ceylon which has its own importance in the realm of spread of Buddhism there.

Each Vaṁśa work is part of history. The tradition of composing and preserving such work was handed down from age to age. This tradition of the Buddhists continued till the nineteenth century. It may casually be mentioned here that the *Śāsanavaṁśa* which belongs to this period deals with the history of the growth of Buddhism from the time of the *parinirvāṇa* of the Buddha to the period concerned.

The early Buddhist literature is important for the history of ancient India from the time of the Buddha down to Aśoka. While estimating the historical value of this literature, B.C. Law observes: "From a time when Indian history emerges from confusion and uncertainties of semi-historical legends and traditions to a more definite historical plane, that is from about the time of the Buddha to about the time of Aśoka the Great, the literature of the early Buddhists is certainly the main, if not the only, source of the historical . . . information of ancient India, supplemented however, by Jain and Brahmanical sources here and there."[63]

The *Mañjuśrīmūlakalpa*[64] composed in the ninth century AD in Sanskrit is one of the ancient historical records of the Indian Buddhists. It carries the political history of ancient India down to the eighth century AD dealing with the Nandas, Mauryas, Guptas, Maitrakas (of Valabhī), Maukharis, Puṣyabhūtis and the Pāla ruler of Bengal, Gopāla, though in a sketchy manner. The author of the work states that Cāṇakya survived his master (Candragupta) and further served Bindusāra as minister for a few years. The information contained in this week about the succession of the Gupta emperors is very important. This Tibetan Buddhist work also throws light on the early history of Nepal from the fifth to the eighth century AD.

Jain Historiography

The historical writings of the Jains are found in different categories of literature. Some of their canonical and non-canonical works also contain such writings. Their other works which form part of historical literature include (besides some of the non-canonical texts) the *paṭṭāvalī*s (political succession lists or dynastic lists), the *guruvāvalī*s (pontifical

63. *Geographical Essays*, p. 2.
64. Ed. by T. Ganapati Śāstri, 3 vols (70, 76 and 84), Trivandrum Sanskrit Series.

succession lists or the lists of Jain *gurus*, religious prechers and teachers), the *rājāvalīs* (chronicles of kings), biographies (the life stories of ancient Jain persons of note, mostly historical), Purāṇas, *praśastis* (or colophons) at the beginning or end of Jain works, or at the end of some or all chapters of a work, which supply reliable historical information about the authors, donors, kings, etc., and *prabandhas* (collections of historical narratives akin to chronicles and biographies, or narrative histories). The *paṭṭāvalīs* and *rājāvalīs*, the two important historical records, were compiled and preserved by them with great care. All these works are very important from the point of view of historiography as they throw light on different aspects of ancient Indian history and culture. Besides the above- mentioned works, there are some other semi-historical and historical works of the period preceding and succeeding *circa* AD 900. The bulk of Jain historical literature was produced after AD 900. The Jain literature is as extensive as Buddhist one. The historical works of the leter period have been preserved in a better way then those of the earlier period by the Jain historians unlike their Buddhist counterparts. The period of rule of the Cālukyas of Gujarat and the Rāṣṭrakūṭas of Dekkan was a blooming one in the history of Jain historiography. Some very important historical works were composed under the patronage of some Cālukya and Rāṣṭrakūṭa kings. The Jain writers, who made contributions to Indian historiography, belonged to both Śvetāmbara and Digambara school.

The Jain tradition of historical writing began in the fourth century BC with the biographical one preserved in the canon. Bhadrahāhu I, who was a contemporary of the last Nanda king Dhanananda of Magadha and Candragupta Maurya, wrote the biography of Vardhamāna Mahāvīra sometime before *c.* 300 BC which is contained in his *Kalpasūtra*. The work consists of three different sections. The first section contains the biographies of the twenty three Jain *tīrthaṅkaras* (prophets of Jainism) who preceded Mahāvīra, the last and twenty-fourth *tīrthaṅkara* and a historical personality like Buddha. The main part of this section contains the detailed biography of Mahāvīra. The twenty-third *tīrthaṅkara* named Pārśvanātha who lived 250 years before Mahāvīra was a real historical figure. He was the son of king Aśvasena of Vārāṇasī. He is said to have founded the Jain doctrine which Mahāvīra later followed. In the said work we find the history of Jainism from its inceptions to the close of the fourth century BC. A short biography of Mahāvīra has also been preserved in the first book of the *Ācārāṅga Sūtra* and in the *Bhagavatī Sūtra.* According to these three sources, Mahāvīra was born in Kuṇḍagrāma, a suburb of Vaiśālī (in north Bihar), in *c* 599 BC in a rich kṣatriya family. His father Siddhārtha was the head of a kṣatriya clan called the *jñātrikas*, and his mother, Triśalā was the sister of Cetaka, the most famous among the Licchavi Princes and rulers of Vaiśālī. As king Bimbisāra called *śreṇika* of Magadha had married Cellana, the daughter of Cetaka, Mahāvīra was related to the ruling family of Magadha. Mahāvīra was married to Yaśodharā. In *c.* 570 BC or in his thirteenth year, on the demise of his parents he renounced the world, left his home and became an ascetic in the quest of truth. He wandered for thirteen years. In *c.* 557 BC, when he was forty-two he attained spiritual knowledge of enlightenment near the Pārśvanātha hills and thereafter became popularly known as Mahāvīra. For the next thirty years he moved from place to place and preached his doctrine. He paid frequent visits to Magadha during the first sixteen years of Bimbisāra's rule. He died at Pāvā near Rājagṛha at the age of seventy-two in *c.* 527 BC.

The biographical writings embodied in the above three works form part of the Jain canonical literature which was redacted thrice between the fourth century BC and the fifth century AD. The Jain canon of the Śvetāmbara set was finally compiled in the present from in the latter half of the fifth century AD at Vallabhī in Gujarat. The Digambara section of the Jains redacted their traditional canon by the beginning of the Christian era.

The anonymous *Kālakācārya-Kathānaka* related in the *Kalpasūtra* (*circa* fifth century AD) and further repeated in a number of later works throws light on the role the Jain saint Kālaka played in the overthrow of king Gardabhilla (Gandharvasena Mahendrāditya *c.* 74-61 BC) of Ujjayinī (Ujjain capital of the kingdom of Avantī or western Malawā) who was none other than the father of famous king Vikramāditya. The story tells us that Kālaka in his bid to depose Gardabhilla because of his hostility with him and opposition to his unjust and tyrannical rule proceeded to 'Sagakula' (the Prākṛt version of the Sanskrit Śakakula, i.e., Śakasthān or the lands of the Śakas or Scythians in Sindh which they had conquered after entering India) whose king was styled as '*Sāhānusāhī*' (Prākṛt version), i.e., 'King of Kings', stayed therefor sometime and persuaded the Śaka chiefs or Sāhīs to accompany him to the kingdom of Mālawā and to invade it and overthrow the dynasty of the ruler of Ujjayinī and occupy the rich kingdom. The Śaka *satrapas* 96 in number marched with their forces towards Mālawā. They crossed the Indus and first came to Surāṣṭra and encamped near Dhakkagiri.[65] We are further told that they entered Lāṭadeśa (Gujarat) and therefrom reached Mālawā and invaded it. They first entered Ujjayinī (in *c.* 66 BC) and besieged the city. After having finally defeated Gardabhilla and expelled him from his homeland (in *c.* 61 BC)they occupied Ujjiayinī and settled there

65. See *Ind. Ant.*, XLIII, 1914, p. 125.

and continued to rule till they themselves were expelled from there. It was only after 4 years of their rule that the Mālawā people led by their valiant leader Vikramāditya, the son of Gardabhilla, rose in open revolt and ousted the Śakas from Ujjayinī. Thereafter the glorious king Vikramāditya reestablished himself on the throne of his ancestors (*Kālak Kathā*, p. 43). This national victory was celebrated, and to commemorate this events a new Mālawā or Vikrama era (or Saṁvat) was introduced in *c* 57 BC. The Śaka chief or Sāhī who occupied Ujjayinī at the instance of Kālaka was probably the first Kṣaharāṭa, a predecessor of Nahapāna, and the Śaka overlord Sāhānusāhī probably the predeccessor of Maues. The work provides a glimpse of the Scythian rule in western India during the first century BC. The *Prabhāvakacarita* of Prabhācandra Sūri (AD 1276) also contains the details of some important episodes in the life of Kālaka. The story narrated in the ancient work *Kālakācārya-Kathānaka* has, undeniably, some historical basis. K.P. Jayaswal has also admitted that it records a genuine historical tradition.[66]

Of all those Jain non-canonical works which are of historical importance, mention may first be made of the *Tiloyapaṇṇatti* of Yativr̥ṣabha (*c.* AD 150-80)[67] of Digambara School. This Prākr̥t text was originally composed by him in *c.* AD 176. Its later recension may be ascribed to either *circa* AD 478[68] or 483.[69] The work in the present form in any case cannot be placed later than the sixth century AD. It is divided into nine major chapters and contains 8,000 verses. It is the most important of the early texts from a strictly historical point of view. It contains a biographical description of all twenty-four *tīrthaṅkara*s and records Purāṇic traditions about them. There are also some incidental references to Jain doctrine in it. Besides, it supplies pontifical genealogy of Mahāvīra's successors or a list of succession of Jain *guru*s after Mahāvīra up to ME 683, i.e., AD 156 (IV, 1474-95). It also throws some light on the dynastic history of ancient India from the first century BC to the fifth century AD. It provides information about the Śakas occupation of Ujjayinī and the beginning and end of their rule (IV, 1496, 1501-03), some rulers of Pradyota and Śuṅga dynasties, minor dynasties of the post-Sātavāhana period like the Muruṇḍas and the Gaddava, and the Guptas with period of their respective rule, etc. The full dynastic list with chronological details is contained in the text (IV, 86-99; also IV, 1501-14). On the whole, the work is important for the study of social, political and religious history of ancient India to a considerable exent.

66. *JBORS*, XVI, p. 233.

67. Ed. by A.N. Upadhye and H.L. Jain.

68. N.R. Premi, *Jaina Sāhitya aur Itihāsa*, rev. edn., p. 64.

69. J.K. Mukhtar, *Varni Volume*, p. 331.

The *Vasudevahiṇḍī*, a prākṛt work of the fifth century AD by Saṁhadāsa (also called Dharmadāsa)[70] and later completed by other writers probably in the latter half of the sixth century AD contains some historical information about the Yadu dynasty that ruled the kingdom of Śūrasena with its capital at Mathurā, the Magadhan kingdom of Bimbisāra's time, trade and commerce during the period from the first century BC to the third century AD, etc. It is a work of quasi-historical nature having half legends and half history.

The *Kuvalayāmalā*, a Prākṛt work composed by Udyotanasūri[71] of Jābālipur (Jālor) in *circa* AD 778, is very valuable as it supplies the long colophon (27 verses) at its end much useful historical information. The colophone has both historical and chronological importance. Vatsarāja of the colophon is none else but the Gurjara-Pratihāra king of Avantī. We are further informed that his great grandfather Nāgabhaṭa I had founded the kingdom of Bhinnamāla and had extended it up to Broach. He was a great conqueror. The epigraphic records also speak of his glory.[72] The work provides good source material for the history of Gurjaradeśa around Bhinnamāla where Jainism had a big following. It furnishes a very reliable account of internal and external trade and commerce of India.[73] It is also stated in the said Jain work that the Hūṇa chief, Tormāṇa, who had established his sway over a large part of north-western India in the late fifth and early sixth centuries AD, was converted to the Jain faith.

Somadeva Sūri of Digambara School flourished in the reign of Rāṣṭrakūṭa king Kṛṣṇa III (*c.* AD 940-48). His *Nitivākyāmṛta* (composed in *c.* AD 959)[74] is an excellent treatise on the science and art of politics covering the period from *circa* 100 BC to AD 900. It deals with evolution of kingship, state, government, etc. His another work, *Yaśastilaka-Campu*,[75] was composed in the same year (*c.* AD 959) at the capital of Baddiga, the eldest son of Cālukya prince Arikeśarī. He was probably patronised by the later Cālukyas of Bādāmī. The author himself tells us that "he finished that work in Caitra Śaka year 881 (AD 959) during the rule of the Cālukya prince Kṛṣṇarāja Deva" which shows both his

---

70. Bhavnagar, 1930.
71. Ed. by A.N. Upadhye, Pts I & II, rev. edn.
72. *Ep. Ind.*, XII, pp. 202-03.
73. See also J.C. Jain. "Trade and commerce in Ancient India from Less known Jain sources", *QRHS*, XVII, I, 1977-78, p. 47.
74. *MDJG*, Bombay, 1887-88.
75. Ed. by Sivadutt and K.P. Parab (Bombay, 1901-03); trans. by G.C. Jain, *Yaśastilaka kā Sāṁskṛtika Adhyayana*; K.K. Hindiqui, *Yaśastilaka Champu and Indian Culture*.

historical sense and chronological consciousness. The work portrays a vivid picture of contemporary life and society. It also throws light on the economic life of the people with special reference to trade and commerce.

Jaṭila or Jaṭāsiṁhanandī in his *Varāṅgacarita* (*c.* AD 700), Vīranandī (*c.* AD 978) in his *Candraprabha-carita* (*sarga* 5) and Hariścandra (*c.* AD 900) in his *Dharma-Śarmābhyudaya* (*sarga* 18) have provided though meagre but very important information about state and government, practical politics, etc. These are useful works on political theories and institutions in ancient India. They are to some extent useful for historical purposes.

The *Jambūdvīpaprajñapti-Saṁgraha,* a Prākṛt text in 13 chapters by Padmanandī (*c.* AD 700),[76] is almost a semi-historical work. It contains useful information about historical geography of ancient India in Jain tradition.[77] It is also important for religious history. It contains a record of pontifical succession for about seven centuries after Mahāvīra's *nirvāṇa.* It is also speaks of 18 settlements of Bhojas of the Yādava group of pre-Bhārata war period (1.12).

Haribhadra Sūri, a Śvetāmbara scholar, who belonged to the latter half of the eighth century AD, in his *Āvaśyakavṛtti* (*c.* AD 775) in Sanskrit provides reliable information about Mahāvīra's last phase of life.

Dhanapāla, Śvetāmbara poet, wrote *Tilakamañjarī,*[78] in about AD 970 during the reign of Siyaka-Harṣa (AD 949-72), the father of Vākpati *alia*s Muñja (AD 974-94), the two early Paramāra rulers of Mālawā. The work provides a trustworthy account of the social, economic, cultural and artistic life of the people during the early medieval period. It is said that it "ranks among the few first-rate works written after Bāṇabhaṭṭa".[79]

The *Trilokasāra* (AD 973), a Digambara work by Nemicandra, preserves a dynastic list containing the names of Śaka kings, and rulers of the Pradyota and Śuṅga dynasties with their reign periods. It also contains the information about the period of the rule of the Guptas and that of the post-Sātavāhana dynasties, etc.

The *Titthogāli-Painna*, an old Prākṛt text by an anonymous Śvetāmbara scholar,

76. *Jambūdvīpaprajñapti* with the commentary of Śānticandra.

77. *IHQ*, XIV, pp. 188 ff; XIV, 2, pp. 388-91.

78. *Ed.* by Bhavadatta Śāstrī, 2nd edn. (Bombay, 1938); also Virendra Kumar, *Tilakamañjarī kā Ālocanātmaka Adhyayana*.

79. G.P. Yādava "Position of women as depicted in Dhanapāla's *Tilakamañjarī*", *QRHS*, XXI, 1, 1981-82, p. 28.

and *Tīrthoddhāra-Prakaraṇa* contain lists of some important dynasties like Pradyota that ruled over Avantī in central India, Nanda, Maurya and Śuṅga that ruled over a big empire Magadha in eastern India, the Śaka of western India and Gaddabhilla of Ujjayinī. The important kings of some dynasties are also mentioned, and the total regin periods of the kings and the dynasties are also given. The dynastic lists are incomplete and the total reign periods as given by the Jain scholars are not fully reliable.

Hemacandra (AD 1125-72), a celebrated poet, grammarian, and historian of Śvetāmbara School, made significant contribution to the evolution of historiography in ancient India. He adorned the court of Jayasiṁha Siddharāja (AD 1093-1143), and also enjoyed the patronage of his successor Kumārapāla (AD 1143-72), the Cālukya kings of Gujarat. His *Pariśiṣṭaparvan* (in Sanskrit)[80] is a work of immense historical value. It deals with the history of Magadha from Bimbisāra down to the time of Candragupta Maurya. It furnishes a dynastic list containing the names of some of the prominent kings of different dynasties that ruled over this kingdom with their genealogies, chronology and other relevant details. We are told that Bimbisāra (called Śreṇika) was the real founder of the Magadhan imperial power. He governed Aṅga as a sparate province with Campā as its capital. During his lifetime his son Ajātaśatru (called Kuṇika) acted as a viceroy at Campā. His son and successor, Udāyin before ascending the throne of Magadha also acted as his father's viceroy at Campā. But being overpowered with sorrow at the death of his father he transferred his capital from Campā to Pāṭaliputra (*pariśiṣṭa*, VI, 22-188, pp. 42-43) which accords with the Buddhist tradition but is at variance with the Purāṇic tradition, according to which, he shifted his capital from Rājagṛha to Kuśumapura (Pāṭaliputra). We are further informed that Udāyin was a powerful king. He defeated and killed the king of a certain country in a battle whose son went to Ujjain (*ibid*, VI, 189-91). He had political relation with king of Avantī (VI, 208). Nandīvardhana (one of the sons of Kālāśoka, successor of Śiśunāga) was offered the throne of Magadha 5 years before 415 BC (i.e., in 420 BC). Nanda (Mahāpadma, the founder of Nanda dynasty), the son of a courtesan by a barber, became king of Magadha 60 years after the death of Mahavīrā (i.e., in 417 BC). He and his descendants continued to rule Magadha for 95 years or till the last Nanda king was deposed by Viṣṇugupta (Cāṇakya) 155 years after the death of Mahāvīra (VI, 231-43). Thus, according to Jain Śvetāmbara tradition recorded in the said work, the Nanda dynasty ruled from 417 to 322 BC. This dynasty is said to have been supplanted by the Maurya dynasty. The work further throws some light on the origin of the Mauryas. According to the said tradition. Candragupta was the son of a

80. *Pariśiṣṭaparvan* (*Sthavirāvalī-Carita*), ed. by H. Jacobi, 2nd edn. BIS.

daughter of the chief of a village of peacock-tamers (*mayura-poṣaka*) which belonged to the Nandas (VIII, 229, p. 56f) which does not agree with Purāṇic tradition, according to which, he was the son of last Nanda monarch by his śūdra wife named Mura after whom Candragupta and his descendants were styled as Mauryas. The author of the work further tells us that Candragupta asccended the throne of Magadha 155 years after Mahāvīra's *nirvāṇa* (VIII, p. 339) which may be probably 322 BC. His son Bindusāra (whose mother's name was Durdharā) succeeded him on the throne (VIII, pp. 439-43). In the absence of corroborative evidence it is difficult to prove the historicity of the said queen mother. However, the succession of the king is well prove. Apart from dynastic history, the work also deals with the history of Jainism of ancient period.

The Jain *paṭṭāvalīs*, which are very important historical documents of both the Digambaras and the Śvetāmbaras, were maintained from the early times. The Prākṛt *paṭṭāvalī* of the Nandi *saṁgha*, which is one of the oldest Digambara *paṭṭāvalīs*, and the equally old Śvetāmbara *Tapāgaccha-paṭṭāvalī*[81] belong to AD 500-900 and are sufficiently reliable. Most of the *paṭṭāvalīs* in their present form belong to later medieval times (i.e., fifteenth-seventeenth century AD). They are full of discrepancies and are not very reliable about early times. Some of the old *paṭṭāvalīs* supply useful historical, cultural and geographical information. Some of the Śvetāmbara *paṭṭāvalīs* refer to Magadhan dynasties of the pre-Maurya period (from Bimbisāra to the end of the Nanda dynasty). Śreṇika (Bimbisāra), Kuṇika (Ajātaśatru) and Udāyin have been mentioned as powerful kings of Magadha. Pālaka mentioned in the lists was the son of king Caṇḍa Pradyota of Ujjayinī and in the period of 60 years allotted to him Kuṇika and Udāyin were ruling at Pāṭaliputra (*cf. Paṭṭāvalī-Samuccaya*, p. 17). The dynastic lists include Pālaka, the Nandas, the Mauryas, some of the Śuṅga rulers, the Śakas and the Gaddabhas or Gaddabhilla, and the period of their rule are also clearly stated (*ibid*, p. 197; *Tapāgaccha-paṭṭāvalī*, vv. 1-3). Apart from dynastic succession lists, pontifical genealogy of Mahāvīra's successors in both Digambara and Śvetāmbara tradition are contained in some of the *paṭṭāvalīs*. The Prakṛt *paṭṭāvalī* of the Nandī *saṁgha* gives the years of individual *gurus* who succeeded Mahāvīra during that period of 683 years. On the basis of a close and comparative examination of the *paṭṭāvalīs* the history with a detailed and exact chronology of the

---

81. Eng. trans. of the Digambara *Paṭṭāvalīs* by Hoernle, *Ind. Ant.*, XIX, pp. 233-42; XX, pp. 341-61; XXI, pp. 57-84; also in *Jaina Antiquity*, *Arrah*, XV, 2, pp. 1-7; *Jaina Siddhānta Bhāskara*, *Arrah*, I, I, p. 37; 1, 2-3, p. 32; I, 4, pp. 43. 51, 71, 78, 81, 103; *Paṭṭāvalī-Samuccaya* (A collection of Śvetāmbara *Paṭṭāvalīs*, ed. by Muni Darśanavijaya, 2 vols (Viramgam, 1933); see also *Ind. Ant.*, XI, p. 245.

Jain *saṁgha* through the ages may be reconstructed, and an interesting detail about the political history of the country during those centuries may be furnished. The *paṭṭāvalīs* and *guruvālīs* of the different Jain *saṁghas*, *gaṇas*., etc., that developed in both the sects, besides the respective genealogies, contain the faithful accounts of the achievements of important *gurus*, often give the names of the royal patrons and devotees of such *gurus* and also shed some light on religio-cultural history of the period. Dr. Walthur Schubring observes: "It was based upon some misunderstandings which naturally arose when India was measured with the scale found in China, Bablyonia and Egypt. Her sources of history often flow not so plainly by far as those empires of the past, but there are some where no historian would have the right to deny the existence of historical exactness. It is specially Jaina authors who develop this praiseworthy quality. History cannot be told more exacly than has been done, for instance, in the Jaina *Guruvāvalis* and *paṭṭāvalis*, The care with which the history of the primitive Jaina community is written by Hemacandra and other later authors is highly meritorious. Of course, the *Pariśiṣṭaparvan* (and such other Jaina works) contains much legendary by-work, but is it not the some thing in the west where nobody would think of not taking notice of our own mediaeval chronicles where history and legend so often intermingle? . . . ."[82]

Equally important like the *paṭṭāvalīs* are the *rājāvalīs* — brief chronicles of kings with details of some important events that took place in their times. The *Rājāvalī Kathā* (an anonymous work of unknown period) about Candragupta Maurya deals with his life and achievements. Some important *rājāvalīs*, particularly about the rulers of Delhi, have come down to us. They generally begin in the seventh or eighth century AD and end at the time of their respective compositions. The *rājāvalī* of Delhi in Hindi verse composed by poet Kisanadāsa starts with Anaṅgpāla Tomara of Delhi in AD 852. The exact date of its composition is not known. A number of important *rājāvalīs* were produced by the Jain scholars during the medieval period which do not fall within the scope of this work.

There are a number of biographical works or the *carita-kāvyas* in both Prākṛt and Apabhraṁśa which deal with the life-stories of some historical Jain heroes, religious leaders and great teachers of early time. The tradition of writing *caritras* in Purāṇic style dealing with the lives of individual heroes had already begun by the sixth century

82. Quoted in J.P. Jain's *The Jaina sources of the History of Ancient India* (100 BC-AD 900), pp. 216-17.

AD, but only few of them were written perior to AD 800. In fact, such works in historical style began to appear from the ninth century onwards. Some of the important works in Prākṛt are the *Mahāvīracarita* of Asaga (AD 853),[83] of Guṇacandra (AD 1082),[84] of Guṇabhadra Sūri (AD 1139) and of Nemicandra (AD 1170)[85] which relates the life and teachings of Mahāvīra, the *Pārśvanāthacarita*,[86] which deals with the life of Pārśvanātha, the real founder of Jainism, the *Ādināthacarita* of Vardhamāna (1103), etc. They supply us with such salient facts about the lives of these heroes as may be taken to be credible. The contemporary royal personalities also find incidental mention in some of these works. The facts and fictions have jumbled up in the stories narrated about them. However, the works to a certain extent bear the character of historical biographies. The other works include the *Mallināthacarita*, the *Neminātha-cariu* and the *Sanakumara-cariu* of Haribhadra (AD 750-75), the *Karakandu-cariu* (in Apabhraṁśa) of Kanakamāra (tenth century), the *Sudarśanacarita* of Nayanandī (AD 1042), the *Jambu-carita* (in Prākṛt) of Guṇapāla (the post-eighth century AD), of Vīra (AD 1019) and of Sāgaradatta (AD 1020) the *Śāntināthacarita* of Devacandra (1108), the *Sumatināthacarita* of Somaprabha, the *Nemināthacarita* of Māladhārī Hemacandra, the *Supasanahacarita* of Lakṣmanāgani (1142) and the *Sanatkumāracarita* of Śrīcandra (1157). They chiefly deal with the spiritual life and religious deeds of the Jain saints concerned. These works are more of a legendary than historical character. Their values lie only in those facts which are related to the Jain doctrine. The most important among the Jain biographical works in Apabhraṁśa is Puṣpadanta's *Mahāpurāṇa*[87] which was composed sometime between AD 940 and 968 under the patronage of the Jain ministers of the Rāṣṭrakūṭa king Kṛṣṇa III. This work consists of biographies of nearly 63 *śalākāpuruṣas* (persons of great note). The work besides containing bipgraphical accounts deals with socio-economic life in the early period. The two other notable works by the same author are the *Jasahara-cariu*[88] and the *Nayakumara-cariu.*[89] The *Triṣaṣṭiśalākapuruṣacarita* of Hemacandra[90] also contains

83. *Vardhamāna-carita* of Asaga (Sholapur, 1931).
84. *Mahāvīracarita* of Guṇacandra (Bombay, 1929).
85. Premi, *op. cit.* pp. 74-91, 111-14, 199 (for all important Jain biographical works).
86. See *Pārśvanāthacaritam, The Life and stories of the Jain Saviour Pārśvanātha*, trans. M. Bloomfield (Baltimore, 1919).
87. Ed. by D.K. Jain, 4 vols *MDJG* (Delhi, 1979-83); P.L. Vaidya, 3 vols (Bombay, 1937-41).
88. Ed. by P.L. Vaidya (Karanja, 1931).
89. Ed. by H.L. Jain (Karanja 1933).
90. Trans. by H.M. Johnson, I-VI (Baroda, 1931-62).

biographies of some important historical personages including Kumārapāla, the Cālukya king of Gujarat who was one of his patrons. The tradition of biographical writing was further carried on by the Jain scholars in the medieval period.

The period falling in between the accession of Dantidurga in AD 733 and the end of the rule of Amoghavarṣa I in AD 877 or 878 (the two famous Rāṣṭrakūṭa kings) produced a marvellous gallaxy of Jain authors who produced a large number of valuable works in different languages on different subjects many of which are important for political and cultural history of early India. The authors were acturally patronised by the Rāṣṭrakūṭas. One of the authors was Swāmī Vīrasena (AD 710-90) of Digambara school who wrote the *Dhavala*, the *Jayadhavala* and *Mahādhavala* in Prākr̥t and Sanskrit (mixed). He completed his famous work, *Dhavala* in AD 780 but his other works remained incomplete. His *Jayadhavala*[91] was completed by his disciple Jinasena III in AD 837. The *Dhavala* transmits information about some contemporary kings with their dates. The *Dhavala* of Vīrasena and the *Jayadhavala* of Jinasena contain almost the identical dynastic lists with the names of the rulers of Pradyota and Śuṅga dynasty. The Śaka king, the post-Sātavāhana kings and the dynasties, the Guptas, etc., also figure in the lists. The reign periods of all are also mentioned. The historical and chronological data contained in the works are of equal importance. The genealogy of the 28 immediate successors of Mahāvīra divided into 5 groups together with the periods taken by each group has been preserved in both these works. This historic record of pontifical succession for about seven centuries after Mahāvīra's *nirvāṇa* is of unique value.

Some of the Purāṇic records of the Jains are also rich in historical contents. The *Padma Purāṇa* (*c.* AD 676-77) in Sanskrit (with 18,000 verses divided into 123 Parvas) of Ravisena,[92] the *Harivaṁśa Purāṇa* (AD 783) in Sanskrit (with 10,000 verses divided into 66 *sargas*) of Jinasena II[93] (Jinasena I of the third century AD being the author of the *Vardhamāna Purāṇa* about Mahāvīra), who flourised in the Rāṣṭrakūṭa age, the *Ādi Purāṇa* (AD 840) with 47 *sargas* of Jinasena III[94] (the religious preceptor of the Rāṣṭrakūṭa emperor Amoghavarṣa I, AD 815-77) and the *Uttara Purāṇa* (AD 898) with *sargas* 48-73 of Guṇabhadra[95] (who was patronised by the Rāṣṭrakūṭa king, Kr̥ṣṇa II, AD 877-914), forming

91. *BGP*, Kāśī, 1947.
92. Ed. Pannālal Jain, 3 vols, 1st edn. *BGP* (Kāśī, 1958-59).
93. Ed. Pannālal Jain, *BGP* (Kāśī, 1962).
94. Ed. Pannālal Jain, 1st edn. *BGP* (Kāśī, 1951); see also Nemicandra Śāstrī, *Ādi Purāṇa mein Pratipādita Bhārat* (Vārāṇasī, 1968).
95. Ed. Pannālal Jain, *BGP* (Kāśī, 1954).

two different part of the *Mahā Purāṇa,* are valuable from a historical point of view. These Purāṇas contain some historical portions. The abundant wealth of historical material are embodied in them. They in common throw a good deal of light on different aspects of history and culture of India of ancient and early medieval period. They deal with society, economy, trade and commerce, polity and administration, state and government, king and kingdoms, towns and cities, religion and culture, art and architecture, Āryan and non-Āryan peoples, etc. The authors of the works furnish useful information about the life and society of their respective contemporary age.

Jinasena III defines history "as an account of past happenings, which must be authoritative, truthful and righteous" (*Ādi Purāṇa*, I, 24-25). This Purāṇa deal with the history of 63 famous men including kings, emperors and the Jain heroes. Jinasena II, the author of the *Harivaṁśa Purāṇa,* in particular was more or less a *itihāsakāra*. He gives history of Jainism down to his own time. He mentions Indrāyudha (AD 783-84), the ruler of Kānyakubja (Kanauj) in the north, Vatsarāja, the Gurjara-Pratihāra king of Avantī in central India, whose identity as the father of Nāgabhaṭa II (AD 805-33) is well established, and Dhruva Nirupama also called Śrī-Vallabha (AD 779-94) the Rāṣṭrakūṭa king of Dekkan, who were all his contemporaries. The dynastic list furnished by him contains the names of some rulers of the Pradyota and Śuṅga dynasties. The Gaddava kings of Ujjayinī, the Śakas, the Hūṇas, etc., also figure in the said list with length of their respective reign. He also supplies the dynastic chronology for the first one thousand year beginning with Mahāvīra's *nirvāṇa* and ending with the termination of the age of the Hūṇas (*Harivaṁśa*, *sarga* 60, vv 487-92, 551-52). The dynastic list given in this Purāṇa is almost identical with the corresponding list of the *Uttara Purāṇa.*

The Jain *purāṇakāras* were endowed with a remakable historical sense. They have, in fact, preserved ancient Indian history in their respective works. They have maintained to a great extent the objectivity in their presentation of the subject-matter. They have debunked brāhmaṇical history and myth in the sense of making the narratives or stories more rational.

The *praśastis* of Jain authors also constitute a valuable literary source of ancient Indian history. These *praśastis* occur in the works which were produced after the seventh century AD. They are generally found at the beginning or end of the works, or at the end of some or all chapters of a work. They are of various types. The *praśasti* of the author gives details about himself, his religious genealogy, when and for whom he wrote the work, etc. It sometimes mentions the name of the place and that of the ruler of the territory as well. The *praśasti* of the donor provides facts about his family and about the *guru* to whom the manuscript was given as a gift. We come across such information more in manuscripts from Gujarat and Central India than in those from Karnataka and Tamiladeśa. The works produced prior to the tenth or eleventh century AD contain mostly the first type of *praśasti*. The *praśasti*s of a number of later works contain useful historical information pertaining to older times the most notable example of which is *Vadnagar Praśasti*s of Kumārapāla (AD 1143-72), the Cālukya ruler of Gujarat, found in AD 1152, according to which, Vanraj Chavda founded the capital of Paṭan in AD 746 and his dynasty ruled in Gujrat for about two centuries.

The Jain works of the ancient period mentioned above as a whole deal with different aspects of history and culture of India. They provide a systematic history of India from the time of Mahāvīra to the rise of the Maurya empire. The history of Jainism recorded in them is of exceptional value. They provide only little information about the post-Maurya dynasties, Gurjara-Pratihāras, Cālukyas, Rāṣṭrakūṭas, etc. We do not find continuity in the presentation of Jain authors about them. They are selective in picking out the regions and historical personalities and usually do not give continuous history. Some historical works deal in part with the events of the post-Mahāvīra period. However, the details of contemporary life and society, general economy, polity, religion, art and culture, etc., provided in some of the works are of great historical value. The works of the period under discussion, in fact, provide the general history of ancient India as they cover various regions and touch on various dynasties.

The *prabandha*s were written by the Śvetāmbara scholars of Gujarat from the thirteenth to the fifteenth century. These works are purely of historical character and very valuable for a reconstruction of the history of Gujarat. But, since they belong to the medieval period, we cannot include them here because of limitation of period. The *prabandha*s of Rajasthan too belong to the same period.

6

Historical Writing of Kālidāsa and Viśākhadatta

Historical Writing of Kālidāsa

The historical sense of Kālidāsa, who may undoubtedly be ascribed to the first century BC, is eloquently reflected in his *Mālavikāgnimitra,* a drama in five Acts. The political events narrated by the poet in his work bear to a great extent historical character. From this it appears that Puṣyamitra Śuṅga, who after having assassinated Bṛhadratha, the last Maurya ruler of Magadha, in 184 BC usurped the throne and ruled till 148 BC with his capital at Pāṭaliputra, was having hostile relationship with Yajñasena, the king of Vidarbha. The first event which the author records is conflict between two sovereigns because of their long hostility. Yajñasena's brother-in-law, who was the counsellor or minister of king Bṛhadratha, was imprisoned by Puṣyamitra before he himself established on the throne and founded the Śuṅga dynasty. The latter refused the request of the former to release his brother and eventually also murdered him which created bitterness in their relations. The former had declared himself independent in Vidarbha taking advantage of the confusion following Bṛhadratha's murder, and as soon as Puṣyamitra felt his position secure on the throne he demanded the allegiance of Yajñasena but could not secure it. The hostility further erupted between the two and continued for sometime. Agnimitra, Puṣyamitra's son and viceroy (during his father's time for eight years, 156-148 BC) at Vidiśā (once the prosperous capital of the western dominions of the Śuṅgas situated in the fork of the Betwā and Beās rivers, 10 km from Sāñcī) carried on hostility with great vigour and consummate skill and diplomacy. He succeeded in winning over to his side Yajñasena's cousin, Mādhavasena and launched an expedition against the former under the command of his brother-in-law Vīrasena and inflicted crushing defeat on him. After the struggle ended, the kingdom of Vidarbha was divided between the two cousins each ruling over each side of the river Varada. In order to establish his claim as a paramount sovereign Puṣyamitra performed the famous horse-sacrifice (*aśvamedha*). Vasumitra (*c.* 141-131 BC), Agnimitra's son, valliantly guarded the sacrificial horse of his grandfather when a young prince. He is also said to have defeated certain Yavana troops.[1] Kālidāsa has given to events and characters a substantially correct historical setting. Puṣyamitra, Agnimitra (hero of the drama) and Vasumitra, the three illustrious Śuṅga kings, are real historical personages and some incidents (e.g., the sacrifice performed by Puṣyamitra) are parts of authentic history, which do not need any corroboration or confirmation. In addition to these, many other historical information may be gathered from the play. The poet also mentions Vāhataka, the minister of Agnimitra, Vīrasena, Agnimitra's brother-in-law, Yajñasena, the Vidarbha king, Mādhavasena, the cousin of Yajñasena, and Sumati, the minister of Mādhavasena. A "Maurya-Saciva" mentioned in the work (1.7) was none other than the minister of king Bṛhadratha Maurya, slain by Puṣyamitra. The *Mālavikāgnimitra* is, no doubt, a historical drama, though not denying some mythical and imaginary elements in it. Kṣemendra, a Kaśmīrī chronicler of the eleventh century AD, has rightly called Kālidāsa *itihāsadarśī* in his famous work, *Kaṇṭhāvaraṇa*.

Historical Writing of Viśākhadatta

The two important historical dramas, *Mudrārākṣasa* and *Devī-Candraguptam*, were written by Viśākhadatta during the reign of his patron, Avantīvarman (AD 579-600) of Kanauj.

The *Mudrārākṣasa* basically deals with the end of the Nanda dynasty and the establishment of the Maurya dynasty. The *itivṛtta* or narrative of the events concerned are fully historical in character. The main story of the drama revolves around the overthrow of the Nandas who were ruling over Magadha with its capital at Kuśumapura (Pāṭaliputra) and installation of Candragupta Maurya on the throne. The author highlights the role of Candragupta and Cāṇakya in dethronement of the Nandas in a dramatised form. His drama is one of the valuable works on the fall of the Nandas and rise of Candragupta Maurya. We are told that Candragupta and Cāṇakya entered into an alliance with the Pauravas and the Himālayan chief, Parvataka, against the Nandas. This alliance strengthened the position of the former two and made their task easier. In fact, Parvataka was a close associate of Cāṇakya. We are further informed that Cāṇakya through his diplomacy and politics took the Śakas, Yavanas, Kirātas, Kambojas, Vāhlikas, Pārśikas and other tribes to his side. They joined the combined forces of Candragupta and Parvataka. Candragupta virtually raised the banner of revolt against the Nandas with

1. For details see *Mālavikāgnimitram* of Kāidāsa with Eng. trans. by M.R. Kale, rev. by J.L. Dave and A.S. Upādhyāya (Delhi, 1985), Acts I-V.

the help of Cāṇakya. The said combined forces besieged the city of Kuśumapura, and the battle that ensued resulted in the defeat of the Nandas and victory of Candragupta Maurya. Thereafter the latter ascended the throne of Magadha as its ruler with his capital at Kuśumpura. After the defeat of the Nandas, the Paurava prince was also killed. The enemies of Candragupta were overcome one by one by Cāṇakya. Rākṣasa, who has been depicted in the drama as a supporter of the Nandas and an enemy of the Maurya emperor, was also brought under control. He was actually for resurrection and resurgence of the Nandas so as to restore their fallen fortunes, but Cāṇakya applying his political wisdom and sagacity made him surrender at his feet.[2] Pravartaka mentioned in the drama and also some Buddhist and Jain works in all probability was a Trigartta chief with his headquater at Jālandhara. And some of the tribes were recruited from Punjab (Vāhika) and adjoining hill region for joining the army of Candragupta and fighting on his behalf against the Nandas. The Kirātas and Khasas, who also joined his army, are said to have been from the Himachal Hills. At the time of recruitment both Candragupta and Cāṇakya were in Punjab after returning from Takṣaśilā. After the departure of Alexander from Punjab both of them evidently took full advantage of the situation.[3] They were fully aware of the political situation prevailing in north-west India. Cāṇakya imbued with patriotic feelings or as a nationalist of high order was on the lookout for a man who could prove himself a powerful king, dispel the dark cloud of misfourtune hovering on the political horizon of north-west India, wrest back the territories captured by the Greeks in the course of Alexander's invasion, save India from passing under foreign rule and defend the territorial integrity of the country, politically unify it and keep it bound together. He found all these qualities in Candragupta. He was bent upon divesting the Nandas of their royal authority and dignity and destroying them, deposing the last Nanda ruler, Dhanananda, who was weak, inefficient and incompetent, and replacing in his place Candragupta who could come up to his expectation. He succeeded by all means in accomplishing his mission and his dream eventually turned into reality.

The *Mudrārākṣasa* also provides us with the information regarding the social, economic and religious condition of the people. It throws sidelights on the religious condition of the people in the Gupta period. We are informed that the worship of Viṣṇu was prevalent. It appears that there was religious toleration which is proved by the position occupied by the Jain Jīvasiddhi. It also supplies a list of the various tribal groups

2. For details see *Mudrārākṣasa* of Viśākhadatta, ed. with the Śaśikalā Sanskrit and Hindi commentaries by S.V. Singh, Acts I-VII.
3. See also M.G. Singh, *History of Himachal Pradesh*, pp. 50-51.

that existed in the time of Candragupta Maurya and later and focuses on their activities. The author in "Bharat-Vākya" of his drama has also highlighted the exploits of Avantīvarman, a Maukhari prince of Kanauj. And while doing so he has extolled his virtues.

In the *Devī-Candraguptam*, Rāmagupta, the son and successor of Samudragupta, has been described as a worthless and cowardly ruler. He was having the hostile relationship with the Śaka king. In the war between the two, Rāmagupta was defeated and in response to the Śaka king's demand he agreed to hand over even his queen Dhruvadevī to him. It is stated in this work that he accepted the humiliating terms on the advice of his ministers and not of his people. However, her honour was saved owing to the intervention of Rāmagupta's younger brother Candragupta II, the famous Gupta monarch, who in the guise of a woman killed the Śaka ruler in the latter's camp. Candragupta then killed Rāmagupta too, and himself ascended the throne of Pāṭaliputra (sometime between AD 375 and 380) with Dhruvadevī as his queen amidst the applause of the people. This historical event finds mention also in Bāṇa's *Harṣacarita*, Rājaśekhera's *Kāvyamīmāṁsā* and other Sanskrit texts, and in some epigraphic records. The facts in the said drama are mixed up indissolubly with myths and legends. The existence of Rāmagupta, the hero of the said drama, can no longer be doubted by the historians in view of the fact that the three image-inscriptions referring to Mahārājādhirāja Rāmagupta discovered at Vidiśā (Madhya Pradesh) have already proved his historicity.

7

The Writing of Historical Biographies

Introductory Remarks

A historical biography in the true sense of the words deals with the life, character and deeds of a historical personality, royal personage, eminent king, great ruler or emperor, who occupies an important place in the history of a particular nation or region. It is based more on facts than fictions. It can easily be distinguished from a biography of literay figure, religious saint or particular individual and a biography of semi-historical nature.

The history of historical biography in India is not as old as in China, Greece and Rome. The Chinese historian, Ssu-ma Chien (*c.* 145-85 BC), produced *Shih-chi* in *c.* 100 BC which apart from other details contains biographies of important personalities who were his contemporaries. The art of writing historical biography further developed in Greece and Rome in the first and second centuries of the Christian era. The *Lives of the Noble Grecians and Romans* by the Greek Plutarch (*c.* AD 50-125), who is considered the "father of biography" and the *Life of Agricola* by the Roman Tacitus (*c.* AD 55-120) are the two notable specimens of historical biography produced in the ancient world. In India, it was the seventh century AD which marked the beginning of the tradition of writing historical biography. The ancient Indians had their own conception of a biographical history which needs no comparison with that of ancient Greeks and Romans. Their historical tradition including the biographical one was different from each other. And so is the case with the themes and qualities of their biographical works.

Historical biographies in ancient and early medieval India were generally composed in royal courts under the patronage of kings or princes concerned. The court historiographers not only enjoyed the royal patronage but also received the encouragement to record the history of their respective times which gradually led to the development of historical writing in ancient India.

The authors of historical biographies while dealing with the lives and achievements of their patrons have also touched on side by side their pedigree or genealogies, political relations with other kings and the historical events which took place before and during their times, and also the culture and civilization of the contemporary age. Some authors have focused mainly on the contemporary history and culture. The writing of historical biographies in ancient India marked the significant stage in the development of the *itihāsa* tradition. Carlyle pointing to the place of biography in history observed: ". . . history is the biography of great men". Again, "History is no more than the sum total of innumerable biographies".

Historical biographies of ancient period as a whole are in Sanskrit, Prākr̥t and Apabhraṁśa. These works are faithful records of the lives of kings who left indelible imprints of their personalities on the history of the said period. The remark of a great orientalist, Maurice Winternitz, that "History and biography have in India never been treated other than by the poets and as a branch of epic poetry"[1] is not an absolute truth. Historical works including biographical ones have been written also by other than the poets and most of them are in prose.

Historical Biographies

Of all the extant historical biographies of ancient times, mention may first be made of the *Harṣacarita* of Bāṇa (Bāṇabhaṭṭa),[2] the court poet-cum-historian of Harṣa (AD 606-48) of Sthāṇviśvara (modern Thāneśvar in Haryana) and Kānyakubja (Kanauj). Bāṇa himself calls his work an *ākhyāyikā* as it has a historical basis. It consists of eight *ucchavāsas* (chapters). In the first chapter, the author speaks of his own ancestry and lineage. According to the information supplied by him, he was the son of Citrabhānu in the Vātsyāyana line of the Bhārgava brāhmaṇas. His ancestral home was at Pritikūṭa, a village situated on the western bank of the river Sona within the limits of the kingdom of Kānyakubja. The first three chapters are devoted, of course, partly to the life and family of the author himself. He belonged to the family which was famous for scholarly tradition. His inclination towards or interest in history was quite consistent with his family tradition.

Harṣa's ancestors find mention in the third chapter of the *Harṣacarita*. The author

1. *HIL*, I, intorduction, p. 3.
2. Ed. P.V. Kane (Bombay 1918, rept. Delhi, 1965); K.P. Parab, 3rd edn. (Bombay 1912); Eng. trans. E.B. Cowell and F.W. Thomas (London, 1897, 2nd edn. 1929); Hindi trans. V.S. Agrawala, *Harṣacarita : Ek Sāṁskr̥tika Adhyayana* (Patna, 1964).

of the work informs us that it was Puṣyabhūti who founded the kingdom of Śrīkaṇṭha with its capital at Sthāṇviśvara (in the late fifth or early sixth century AD). He has been described also as the founder of the royal Vardhana dynasty. His successors, Naravardhana, Rāyavardhana and Ādityavardhana (mentioned in Madhuvana copper-plate inscription of Harṣa) do not find place in the genealogy perserved in the work. These kings who floursihed probably between AD 500 and 580 were the feudatory chiefs. They might have acknowledged the supremacy of the Guptas and the Maukharis. The next king in the line of Puṣpabhūti, as mentioned in the work was Prabhākaravardhana who was blessed with two sons, Rājyavardhana and Harṣavardhana, and a daughter, Rājyaśrī.

Prabhākarvardhana (AD 580-605) was an eminent and powerful king. After having expanded the frontiers of his paternal kingdom by annexing to it the territories of the conquered kings he assumed the titles, *mahārājādhirāja* and *paramabhaṭṭāraka*. His wars and conquests have been described in the fourth and fifth chapters. The information Bāṇa provides about him in the former, of course, in the metaphorical style is useful to a historian. He says that he was "A lion to the Hūṇa deer, a burning fever to the king of Sindhudeśa, a troubler of the sleep of Gurjara king, a billious pleague to that scent-elephant, the lord of Gandhara, a destroyer of the pride of the Lāṭas, and an axe to the goddess of fortune and glory of Mālavā". He appears to have extended his political sway to the Hūṇa territories in the Punjab which marked the limit of the north-western frontier of his kingdom. In the east it was conterminous with the Maukhari state of Kanauj and on the west and south it just covered portions of the Punjab and Rājapūtānā desert. He achieved partial success in subduing the king of Sindhudeśa. However, the latter accepted the political hegemony of the former. Gāndhāra, which was then under the rule of Kuṣāṇas (a branch of those who had established themselves in the Kabul valley), could not be brought within the limits of the kingdom of Prabhākaravardhana. The Gurjaras of Bhinnamāla and the king of Lāṭadeśa simply tendered their submission. Mālawā was, of course, annexed to his kingdom which can be substanitated by the fact that the two sons of the defeated Mālava king, Kumāragupta and Mādhavagupta, were sent to his court to confirm their acceptance of his overlordship, as stated in the text. In the fourth chapter itself it is stated that Rājyaśrī was married to Grahavarman, the son of the Maukhari Prince Avantīvarman of Kanauj.

The fifth chapter is devoted to Prabhākaravardhana's and his eldest son Rājyavardhana's conflicts with the Hūṇas. The former has been called 'Hūṇahariṇakeśarī' because of his resounding victory over the Hūṇas. The Hūṇas, who were defeated by him with the help of his relative, Avantīvarman of Kanauj (in AD 575 or 582), were none other than the petty Hūṇa chief of the northern Punjab with their metropolis at Śākala where they continued to rule after the dismemberment of the Hūṇa kingdom in about AD 563 or 567. In order to strike another blow to the Hūṇas Prabhākaravardhana sent Rājyavardhana on a military expedition against them in the Uttarāpatha. But before they could be finally subdued Rājyavardhana returned back to the capital on account of the illness of his father. His father had already expired and his mother had burnt herself to death on the bank of the Sarasvatī river. We are further told in the sixth chapter that Rājyavardhana because of being shocked and terribly upset offered the throne to his yonger borhter, Harṣa. The latter too was not willing to accept the throne and ultimately the former had to ascend the throne of Thāneśvar (in AD 605). No sooner had Rājyavardhana ascended the throne he received the sad news that the king of Mālawā or Avantīdeśa (who is identical with Devagupta of the Madhuvana and Bānskherā charter) had attacked and killed Grahavarmana and imprisoned his wife Rājyaśrī and put her into the dungeon cell in Kānyakubja. He chalked out a plan to attack also Thāneśvar. However, Rājyavardhana in order to avenge the death of his brother-in-law and the humiliation of his sister at once marched with his troops for Mālawā leaving his younger brother Harṣa in capital. He had successfully routed the Mālawā army and defeated king Devagupta but he was himself treacherously assassinated by the king of Gauḍa called Śaśāṅka (contemporary of Harṣa) who had come all the way from his distant kingdom to assist his ally, king Devagupta of Mālawā. This is the coalition of common enemies of Rājyavardhana which has been perhaps called by Bāṇa 'Śaśāṅkamaṇḍala'. He says that "Śaśāṅka threw Rājyavardhana off his guard by offering to marry his daughter to him as a token of submission and friendship and when he was weaponless, confiding and alone, the Gauḍa king despatched him to his own quarters and killed there". Having thus avenged the defeat of Devagupta of Mālawā the Gauḍa monarch Śaśāṅka occupied Kanauj and released the widowed Maukhari queen, Rājyaśrī, from captivity in her own capital. Bāṇa has, maintained sequence and coherence to a considerable extent in the narration of events.

Harṣa was only sixteen years of age at a time when he heard the news of the tragic end of Rājyavardhana. He was bit reluctant to occupy the throne. But after being persuaded by the councillors of the state he agreed to take the reign in his hand, and ultimately ascended the throne of Thāneśvar (in AD 606). The immediate task before him was to rescue his sister, who after having escaped from the prison had entered the Vindhya forest, and to relieve Kanauj from the control of Śaśāṅka. When he was about to set out on his *digvijaya* (conquest) with a strong force, Haṁsavega, a messenger of king Bhāskaravarman of Prāgjyotiṣa (Assam), entered his court with gifts and message of friendship. A perpetual treaty of friendship between these two contemporary kings was concluded as stated by Bāṇa in the seventh chapter of his work. The said messanger in the course of narrating the early history of Assam told Harṣa the names of some of the prominent rulers of different dynasties including those of the predecessors of Bhāskaravarman of Varman dynasty who ruled over the kingdom concerned, as we find in the same chapter.

After the departure of Haṁsavega from Thāneśvar, Harṣa entered the Vindhya forest and made a vigorous search for her sister, Rājyaśrī, and at last with the help of forest chiefs like Vyāghraketu, Bhūkampa and Nirghāta and a Buddhist monk, Divākaramitra, rescued her at the moment when she was about to immolate herself. He along with his sister returned to his camp on the bank of the Gaṅgā, as described in the seventh and eighth chapters of the work. In these two very chapters Bāṇa has described in detail the life and culture of the tribal people of the Vindhya region with special reference to the Śabaras.

We are informed by Bāṇa that Harṣa made an elaborate preparation to wage war against the Gauḍa king Śaśāṅka, who is described as 'the vilest of Gauḍas' and the 'vile Gauḍa serpent'. But he does not provide us with any detail of the war between the two. It seems that the friendly alliance between Harṣa of Thāneśvar and Bhāṣkarvarman of Kāmarūpa (one of the ancient names of Assam) struck fear in mind or Śaśāṅka, and instead of facing an impending danger he withdraw from Kanauj which paved the way for Harṣa to establish his rule there. He probably in the last phase of his life transferred his capital from Thāneśvar to Kanauj and made it the seat of his power. Thus, he not only inherited the paternal kingdom but also got the Maukhari throne of Kanauj. The amalgamation of these two kingdoms helped him in consolidating his position and extending his authority and influence in all directions.

Bāṇa, while describing Harṣa as a warrior and conqueror, informs us (in third chapter) that he conquered Sindhudeśa and annexed it to his kingdom and thereby completed the unfinished task of his father. The river Indus formed the western boundary of his empire. In the same chapter we are further informed that kings of the states in the Himālayan region were also subjugated by him. They after acknowledging his political supremacy started paying taxes to him. His conquest of Mālawā and its annexation to his kingdom finds mention in the seventh chapter of the author's work.These initial success he achieved as a king of Thāneśvar. We do not get a clear picture of the extent of Harṣa's empire.

However, it is true that he earned name and fame as the last great Hindu emperor of north India.

The information furnished by Bāṇa in the second chapter of his work regarding the administrative system and military organisation of Harṣa is of considerable historical value. He has higlighted the feudal structure of his administration. It may be stated here that the increase in the number of *sāmanta*, *mahāsāmanta* and feudatory chiefs after the disintegration of the Gupta empire had great bearing on the administrative system of Harṣa. Bāṇa has presented an enlarged picture of the feudal system that had already existed in ancient India prior to Harṣa's time. The same system continued in the time of Harṣa. According to Bāṇa, there were different categories of *sāmanta*, viz., *sāmanta*, *mahāsāmanta*, *āptasāmanta*, *pradhānasāmanta*, *satrumahāsāmanta* and *pratisāmanta* who offered their services to Harṣa and his predecessors. The *sāmanta*s ruling over the territories assigned to them used to pay taxes annually to the said kings. They used to render all kinds of services to the kings. Those who occupied high posistion among the *sāmanta*s were designated *pradhānasāmanta*. *Satrumahāsamanta*s were conqured chiefs who had to obey the orders of the king. They were treated with some respect. All other *sāmanta*s had to offer their services in the kingly court and royal palace whenever needed. The loyal and faithful *mahāsāmanta*s used to accompany the kings while going on military expedition. Some of the feudatory kings in the time of Harṣa also find mention in the work. Bāṇa has also focused on the inter-state relations in the time of Harṣa. The policies he followed towards kings are in perfect harmony with what we find in the *Prayāga-praśasti* of Samudragupta. In the same chapter Bāṇa has provided the details of military strength of Harṣa with special description of elephant force and cavalry.

With regard to religious beliefs and faiths of the people, Bāṇa informs us that altogether twenty-one religious sects existed in India. He has referred to three popular cults of Hinduism, the Śaiva, Śakti and Vaiṣṇava, the Lokāyatika sect, Buddhism, Jainism, etc., that had already flourished before the dawn of the seventh cetnury AD. On the combined testimony of the data available in the third, fifth and eighth chapters of his work it can plausibly be concluded here that Hinduism, Buddhism and Jainism were three popular forms of religion. Their co-existence is a proven fact. In the times of Harṣa and his predecessors, Brāhmaṇism and Buddhism flourished side by side. After having reigned for about four decades Harṣa passed away in AD 647 or 648.

A long list of twenty-seven kings of different dynasties that ruled over different kingdoms in ancient India furnished by Bāṇa in the sixth chapter of his work on the basis of his knowledge of the past history also deserves our notice. The list includes Somaka of Paurava dynasty, Nāgasena of Nāga dynasty of Padmāvatī (Pavāyā), Vatsarāja Udayana (or Kauśāmbī), rulers of Ayodhyā, Śrāvastī, Videha, Kāśī, Kaliṅga, Mathurā, Aśmaka, Sovīra and of Pradyota dynasty, and Kākavarṇa of Śiśunāga dynasty, Bṛhadratha of Maurya dynasty, Agnimitra, Sumitra and Devabhūti of Śuṅga dynasty and rulers of Gupta dynasty that ruled over Magadha, and Kṣatravarman of Maukhari dynasty. Even the killing of a Śaka king at the hands of Candragupta II attracted the attention of Bāṇa. Actually, his elder brother, Rāmagupta, after being defeated by the Śaka king agreed to surrender even his wife. Dhruvadevī, to him incompliance with his desire, but Candragupta in the guise of a woman killed that Śaka king in his camp itself, which Viśākhadatta in his *Mudrārākṣasa* has highlighted, already mentioned before. These are some of the additional historical information which Bāṇa has supplied in his work.

Bāṇa has not only provided the life history of Harṣa but also a true picture of social, economic, political, religious and cultural life of the people of India in his time. Some other historical information of great value have also been incorporated in his work. His historical knowledge was superb. He has nowehre in his work lavished extravagant praise on his patron. Nor do we come across any exaggeration in his presentation of the subject-matter. He has dealt with main theme of the work without much bias and prejudice. He has plainly stated the truth. Most of the facts stated by him are historically authenticated. However, it is undeniable that his work suffers from rhetorical descriptions and literary embellishment. The work after all belongs to a branch of literature called *kāvya* (epic).

> "Indeed, it is possible to prove by a diligent and critical examination of our sources that the Indians in the ancient and the early mediaeval periods possessed a sense of history, which at present appears to be imperfect and rudimentary, and that they developed a tradition of writing historical biography through its concrete evidence comparable to the lives of plutarch is not available. Were the sense of history or the tradition of biography-writing completely absent in ancient India, the emergence of Banabhatta and Kalhana would not have been possible. The works of Bana and Kalhana among others, represent the mature expression of historiography and historical biography and thus presuppose the continuity of literary and historical efforts and experiences of several generations."[3]

3. K.K. Dasgupta, "Historical Biography in Sanskrit Literature", in S.P. Sen (ed.), *Historical Biography in Indian Literature*, p. 5.

Cowell and Thomas have spoken very highly of Bāṇa and his work. They have observed that he in his Sanskrit work "has woven the story out of actual events". His work, in fact, is "based on real events". It contains "a living and contemporary picture wherein we can see something of the India of that time, just as we see in Arrian and Plutarch something of the India of Alexander's time". The work "has another interest from the vivid picture which it offers of the condition of Indian society and the manners and customs of the period". Bāṇa's "descriptions of the court and village life abound with masterly touches which hold up the mirror to the time. . . . The court, the camp, the quiet village and the still more quiet monasteries and retreats, whether of Brahmans or Buddhists, are all painted with singular power and his narrative illustrates and supplements the Chinese travellers's travel at every turn".

Devabhūti has also admitted that despite some defects typical of the courtly literature of the time, one can find a realistic picture of contemporary life and many valuable facts about Harṣa's character and achievements in Bāṇa's *Harṣacarita.*[4]

Vākpatirāja in his Prākr̥t work, the *Gauḍavaho*,[5] which consists of 1209 *gāthās*, describes the exploits of his patron, Yaśovarman (*circa* AD 725-52) of Kanauj, whose court he adorned as a poet. In fact, this work was composed by the said poet in AD 736 to celebrate with sense of honour and praise the victory of his patron over king of Gauḍa. We are told that "the king of Magadha fled when Yaśovarman advanced, afterwards some of his vassals stood and fought in a great battle but were annihilated after which Yaśovarman pursued, defeated and killed the king of Magadha" who was most probably identical with Jīvitagupta II. He further continued his victorious march and conquered the king of Vaṅga (Bengal). The inclusion of Magadha in his great empire in north India and the extension of his political sway to the eastern sea in Bengal may be confirmed by Nālandā stone insciption and other reliable sources. The poet credits his patron with extensive conquests as far as the south. He is said to have defeated the king of the Dekkan, crossed the Malaya mountain and reached the southern sea. The poet, while extolling Yaśovarman's success as a conqueror, further informs us that he conquered the Arabas who had occupied Sindh and expelled them from there, and also vanquished the Parasikas (Persians) in the west. He received tribute from the regions of Western Ghāṭs, come to the banks of the Narmadā, entered into Marudeśa or Rajasthan and therefrom advanced towards Śrīkaṇṭha or Thāneśvar, passed through Kurukṣetra,

4. *Harsha : A Political Study*, pp. 9-12.

5. Ed. S.P. Pandit, Bombay Sanskrit & Prakr̥t Series, No. 34 (Bombay, 1887).

proceeded to Ayodhyā and finally conquered the northern Himālayan region. But afterwards, in about AD 740, he was himself vanquished by king Lalitāditya (AD 724-60) of Kashmir but was allowed to rule as a feudatory. The poem of Vākpati contains, no doubt, little history in *kāvya* manner. Another work of the eighth century AD, the *Yaśoharacarita* (*Yaśodharacarita*) of Kanakasena Vādirāja,[6] is also important from a historical point of view. It is supplementary to Vākpati's work.

The *Navasāhasāṅkacarita* (in Sanskrit) of Padmagupta (also called Parimalgupta)[7] written about AD 1005 in 18 cantos deals with the hisotry of the Paramāra king Sindhurāja Navasāhasāṅka of Mālawā. He was the younger brother and immediate successor of Vākpati-Muñja (AD 974-94). The author of the work first graced the court of the latter as a poet and later enjoyed the patronage of his two successors. In the twelfth canto of his work he has provided the description of all the rulers of the Paramāra dynasty preceding Sindhurāja in a chronological order whose historical authencity is proved by the contemporary stone inscriptions. He has immortalised the achievements of Sindhurāja testifying to the success of his arms against a Hūṇa prince, Dakṣiṇa-Kośala (i.e., the Kalacūris of Tummāna), the Cālukyas of Lāṭa (Gujarat) and other neighbouring powers. After a short reign (AD 995-1005) Sindhurāja was followed by his son, Bhoja, the most striking and versatile Paramāra ruler. He ruled over Mālawā from 1005 to 1054 with Dhārā as its capital.

The *Rāmacarita* (in Sanskrit consisting of four cantos) of Sandhyākaranandī[8] may be regarded as one of the best specimens of historical biography produced in ancient India. It provides in detail the history of the life and achievements of Rāmapāla, one of the greatest Pāla kings of Bengal. He was the patron of the author who graced his court as a poet. The events which took place during the times of his two predecessors and successors are also recorded in the said work. The author begins with the origins of the Pāla dynasty, and just touches on his patron's ancestry. He throws little light on the parentage of Gopāla's son and successor, Dharmapāla (*c.* AD 780-815). Thereafter he relates the history from the time of Vigrahapāla III (*c.* AD 1055-70) onwards. He mentions his wars with the Kalacūri king, Karṇa of Tripurī. His death was followed by troublous times owing to the rivalry of his three sons (Mahipāla II, Sūrapāla II and Rāmapāla) over the succession issue. However, Mahipāla II being the eldest son of his father succeeded

6. Ed. T.A. Gopinatha Rao (Tanjore, 1912).
7. Ed. V.S. Islampurkar (Bombay, 1895).
8. Ed. R.C. Majumdar, R.G. Basak and N.G. Banerjee (Rajsahi, 1939).

him in about AD 1070 and ruled till about 1075. We are told that he imprisoned his two brothers relying on the mischievous rumours that they were plotting against him. 'While they were fighting among themselves, the Varmans rose to power in eastern Bengal and the Pāla territories, which were already reduced to portions of Bihar and Northern Bengal diminished still further.' In Vārendra, a chief of the aboriginal Kaivarta tribe named Divvoka took advatage of the internal dissension in the imperial family and raised the banner of revolt. Mahipāla attempted to put it down but failed. We are informed that against the advice of his minister he marched to fight the rebels but was defeated and killed. Despite his ill-judged actions, he has been referred to by the author in a poetic style and laudatory term as a good king. After his death the rebel leader successfully established an independent kingdom in northern Bengal. The rebels, in fact, ruled over part of the empire confining the Pālas to the part south of the Gaṅgā. Taking advantage of the prevailing situation and the misfortune that assailed the Pālas, some of the feudatories also started raising their heads. Mahipāla was succeeded by his younger brother, Sūrapāla II, who ruled only for about a couple of years (*c.* AD 1075-77). His reign was not eventful at all.

When Rāmapāla ascended the throne (in *circa* AD 1077) after the brief reign of his elder brother. Sūrapāla II, he found himself confronted with several problems. He appeared on the scene at a very critical moment. It appears from the most *Rāmacarita* that the period immediately preceding his ascendency was the most turbulent in the history of the Pāla rule in Bengal. The immediate task before him was to restore the fallen fortunes of his family by overcoming the political adversaries. In order to achieve his goal he adopted skillful policy. The author of the said work tells us that by his judicious presents and grants of land to the feudatories who were militarily very powerful he won them over and with their help raised a strong army. He sent his most able and loyal general Śivarāja ahead across the Gaṅgā to carry out military operation against the Kaivartas, and after his initial success he himself led the main army and had a pitched battle with the Kaivarta chief, Bhīma (the successor of his father Divvoka), who was defeated and captured. Hari, Bhīma's nephew, continued the war for sometime but was ultimately forced to capitulate. The captive (Bhīma) was eventually put to death, and Hari was given a high position as a feudatory in recognition of his honourable capitulation. Thus after being crowned with glorious victory, Rāmapāla was able to recover his paternal dominions in northern Bengal. He also overran the neighbouring kingdoms (Kaliṅga and Kāmarūpa). 'His protection was even sought by the Yādava Varman rulers of eastern Bengal. The revival of Pāla supremacy was, however, only temporary.' Towards the end of his rule he devoted his attention to the reorganisation of administration of the empire and promotion of learning. He entrusted the government to one of his sons, Rājyapāla, Rāmapāla died after a reign of about forty-five years. The author further informs us that in the time of Rāmapāla's son Kumārapāla, a revolt broke out in Kāmarupa, but it was quelled by the minister, Vaidyadeva, who virtually became independent there. Kumārapāla's successor, Gopāla III, was weak and died trying to destroy his enemies. The narrative ends with the reign of Madanapāla (AD 1140-58). The author completed his work with an autobiography at its end only in the reign of this Pāla king. He has been praised for his successful, victorious and generous rule. But the fact remains that the feudatories reasserted themselves, and the rise of Vijayasena even resulted in his expulsion from northern Bengal. The spell of disaster befell the weak successors of Rāmapāla one after another, and they could not arrest the decline of the family.

> "Sandhyakaranandin's object in this work seems primarily to be to contrast kings of good and bad judgment as demonstrated in their policies, with strong hints that they should submit to the guidance of the ministers, civil servants and of course writers like himself, scholars and poets, who generally belonged to the same bureaucratic class from which the administration was recruited."[9]

Sandhyākaranandī has unhesitatingly bestowed praise on the rebel Kaivarta chief, Bhīma, "who had shaken the fortunes of the family of his patron, Rāmapāla" which is a fairly good specimen of objective treatment of history. The corroboration of some of the facts highlighted by him by inscriptions enhances the value of his work. "For instance, the defeat of the ruler of Pithi in Magadha, Devarakshita, by Mahana, the uncle of Ramapala mentioned in the *Rāmacarita* (II.8) gets confirmed by verse 7 of the Sarnath inscription of Kumāradevi, Rāmapāla's daughter's daughter."

Sandhyākaranandī's *Rāmacarita* possesses great value as a contemporary historical record on the Pālas' rule in Bengal from AD 1070 to 1155, though it is a poetical composition.

The *Rāmacarita* composed in the eleventh century AD by Abhinanda (also called Gauḍābhinanda) contains short biopgraphies of two Pāla monarchs of Bengal, Dharmapāla and his son Devapāla (*c.* AD 815-55).

The *Kumārpālacarita* of Hemacandra (the celebrated Jain scholar and historian of the twelfth century AD)[10] is another important historical biography.

---

9. Warder, *An Introduction to Indian Historiography*, p. 54.
10. Ed. S.P. Pandit (Bombay, 1900); P.L. Vaidya (Poona, 1936).

In *c*. AD 1160, Hemacandra composed a historical epic in two parts one in Sanskrit and other in Prākṛt, called the *Dvyāśrayakāvya*. It being a comtemporary work is of immense historical value. The first part of it consisting of twenty cantos in Sanskrit constitutes a history of the Cālukya dynasty of Anhilwāḍa (identified with modern Paṭan in Gujarat) from its founder Mūlarāja (*c*. AD 941-94) down to Jayasiṁha Siddharāja (*c*. AD 1093-1143), who accorded a place of honour at his court to the author of the said work. The second part consisting of eight cantos in Prākṛt deals with the life and achievements of Kumārapāla (*c*. AD 1143-72), the successor of Jayasiṁha Siddharāja. Hemacandra, in fact, enjoyed the royal patronage of both. He tells us that Kumārapāla after having come under his influence embraced Jainism and proclaimed it as a state religion. The author provides an extensive description of his discourage with the said Cālukya prince on the doctrine of Jainism. He has presented an authentic history of the Cālukyas of Gujarat in his work.

We further learn from the *Kumārapāla-Pratibodha* (composed at Paṭan in Prākṛt by Somaprabhācārya towards the end of the twelfth century AD or in about AD 1195) that Kumārapāla was converted to the tenets of Jainism. And it was due to Jain influences that he issued stringent orders prohibiting the slaughter of animals throughout his vast dominions.

Jayasimha Sūri II, who is believed to have flourished in the middle of the thirteenth century AD, also wrote a historical epic called the *Kumārapālacarita*[11] in which he has given an authentic account of the achievements of Kumārpāla aṣ a conqueror. We are told that "after having overcome all opposition to his accession he pursued a policy of active militarism. He attacked Arnorāja, the Cāhamāna ruler of Sākambhari, and completely overpowered his forces. He also quelled the revolt of the Paramara prince of Abu, and reasserted the Cālukya authority in Mālavā, which had raised his head during his initial difficulties. He next turned his arms successfully against a chieftain of Saurāṣṭra, but his most remarkable exploit was the defeat of Mallikārjuna of Konkan".

The work contains some of those incidents or episodes connected with the life of Kumārapāla which are not found in earlier works available to us, such as his murder by his nephew. As a biography this is far more useful than the two other works mentioned above. However, these biographical works as a whole enable us to trace the history of Gujarat under the Cālukyas.

---

11. Ed. Kṣāntivijaya Gani (Bombay, 1926).

The school of historical writing in Gujarat developed under the influence of the Jains.

Bilhaṇa in his *Vikramāṅkadevacarita*[12] recounts the exploits of his patron Vikramāditya VI Tribhuvanamalla (*c.* AD 1076-1126), the famous Cālukya ruler of Kalyāṇī (in the Kanarese district of Karṇāṭaka). The said work in Sanskrit consists of eighteen contos. The author originally belonged to Kashmir as it distinctly appears from his biography in the last eighteenth canto of the work. He belonged to a branch (Sārasvasta) of the Bhārgava clan of brāhmaṇas. He travelled all the way from his native place to the court of Vikramāditya VI in search of a good patron which he fortunately found in him. He flourished at his court under his royal patronage. He was known for his historical scholarship and poetic talent. He composed his work in about AD 1088. He has related in detail the history of the Cālukyas of Kalyāṇī up to AD 1088 in seventeen cantos of his work which covers their origin, wars and conquests of Vikramāditya and of his father, Someśvara I Ahavamalla (*c.* AD 1043-68), and other historical themes.

Bilhaṇa, while dealing with exploits of Someśvara I, informs us that he first inflicted crushing defeats on Coḷa princes and occupied their capital, Kāñcī. In his wars he was assisted by his son, Vikramāditya VI, then a valiant yourth. Further, he invaded Mālawā, defeated its Paramāra king Bhoja, and expelled him from his capital Dhāra. He also defeated the Kalacūri ruler, Lakṣmī-Karṇa. These glorious victories enabled him to consolidate his imperial position. He founded a new capital at Kalyāṇī probably in AD 1053. He was succeeded by his eldest son, Someśvara II Bhuvanaikamalla. He did not attain any noteworthy distinction during a rule of about eight years (AD 1068-76). Vikramāditya VI, the most striking personality among the Cālukyas of Kalyāṇī and a valiant worrior, emerged victorious in some of the wars which he fought during the reign of his father. After having overrun Mithilā, Magadha, Aṅga and Vaṅga meeting with little or no opposition he vanquished the kings of Gauḍa and Kāmarūpa in the course of his northern incursions (sometime between AD 1050 and 1053). The king of Gauḍa may be identified with Nāyapāla. Vikramāditya VI met with feeble opposition from the decadent Pāla monarchy. But he along with his army was pushed back by king of Kāmarūpa who may be identified with Ratnapāla (*c.* AD 1030-53). The invasion of Kāmarūpa eventually ended in fiasco. We are further told by Bilhaṇa that after having subdued the ruler of Koṅkaṇ, Jayakeśin by name, the Coḷa monarch, Vīra-Rājendra of Kāñcī, and Kulottuṅga I (Rājiga) of Veṅgī, and deposed his elder brother, Someśvara II,

12. Ed. G. Buhler, Bombay Sanskrit Series, No. 14 (Bombay, 1875); trans S.C. Banerji and A.K. Gupta (Calcutta, 1965).

who was tyrannical and distrustful, Vikramāditya VI assumed the reigns of government at Kalyāṇī in AD 1076. After becoming king he directed his energies more towards peace than military adventures. After the cessation of hostility and restoration of friendly relations with the Paramāras of Mālawā he soon got entangled into hostilities with the Cālukyas of Anhilwāḍa. Another storm he had to face was the revolt of his younger Jayasiṁha, whom he had appointed vicerory of the Banvāsī province (north Kanārā). But this uprising was suppressed with firm hand. Further, he curbed the inroads of the Coḷa king and of the Hoysala Viṣṇuvardhana, who challenged the might of the Cālukya monarch towards the close of his career. The contemporary social life has also been depicted in Bilhaṇa's work.

G. Buhler's remarks on the themes of the *Vikramāṅkadevacarita* deserves to be placed here: "The main theme of this laudatory poem is royal wars and royal marriages. The poet begins wigh a short account of the Chalukya race and the kings of the restored dynasty which begins with Tailapa (AD 973-997); he dwells at some length upon the exploits of Vikramaditya's father and describes with all customary amplifications the conquests of Vikramaditya before his accession to the throne, his dethronement of his elder brother, Someswara II, his defeat and capture of his younger and his numerous wars with the faithless Cholas."[13]

Most of the facts stated by Bilhaṇa in his work with regard to Vikramāditya's conquests have been corroborated by contemporary epigraphical records. However, he is not free from bias M.A. stein has also opined that "The narrative of Bana and Bilhana, too treats of historical facts yet their heroes are painted all white and their enemies all black".[14]

The *Vikramāṅkābhyudaya carita* of Someśvara III Bhūlokamalla (AD 1126-38) one of the later Cālukya rulers of Kalyāṇī, is an incomplete biography of his father, Vikramāditya VI. The author is a solitary example of historian of royal family in ancient India. His work consists of three chapters which are fragmentary in nature. It is the third chapter which traces the history of the Cālukyas of Kalyāṇī from the time of Tailapa down to Vikramāditya VI. This chapter throws some light on the lives and activities of Vikramāditya including his anointment as an heir-apparent and his military campaigns, and of other kings who preceded him. The first chapter provides a graphic description of the people of Karṇāṭaka, and the second deals with the splendour of the Cālukya capital Kalyāṇī.

13. *Op. cit.*, Introduction.
14. *Rājataraṅgiṇī*, Eng. trans. (Westminster, 1900), introduction, pp. 32-33.

Estimating the historical value of the *Vikramāṅkābhyudaya* V.S. Pathak writes: "Save the *Harshacharita* of Bana, this *Vikramāṅkabhyudaya* is the only historical prose-narrative of ancient India available to us, and hence its discovery is of more than usual interest to the study of the historical literary writings inasmuch as by comparison with the earlier *ākhyāyikā*, it affords an opportunity of discovering patterns, motifs and devices — the way through which the objective facts of history are moulded into a literary story. In the case of *Vikramāṅkabhyudaya*, there is an additional advantage as the authentic information on the life of Vikramāditya VI, the hero of the prose-narrative, is available from inscriptions containing much historical detail, which in the case of few inscription which mention Harsha, celebrated in the Harshacharita is sadly lacking."[15]

The *Somapālavijaya* of Jalhaṇa, the celebrated Kaśmīrī brāhmaṇa scholar of the twelfth century AD, is a short biography of king Somapāla (the son of Saṁgrāmapāla), who was his patron. The author was a minister at the court of Rājapurī, the capital of his patron. His work deals with the life and achievements of his patron. His delineation of the conquests of king Somapāla bears the impact of the writings of historians of Kashmir school.

Jayānaka in his *Pṛthvīrājavijaya* (in Sanskrit consisting of twelve contos)[16] provides the life-history of his patron, Pṛthvirāja III (AD 1179-92), the illustrious Cāhamāna (Cauhān) king of Ajmer. Jayānaka, a Kaśmīrī brāhmaṇa, came to Ajmer, graced the court of Pṛthvirāja and flouished under his royal patronage as it appears from the twelfth canto of his work. The author begins with the origin of the Cāhamānas. He has traced their connection with the Solar dynasty. They are said to have descended from an eponymous Cāhamāna, born of the sun. He has narrated their earlier history in several cantos of his work. Of the several branches of the clan, the most important was that of Śākambharī or Sāmbhar. He has traced their genealogy to Vāsudeva, who established a branch of the family in the Sapādalakṣadeśa (northern Rajasthan). He may be ascribed to the seventh century AD, and the family then served for three centuries as vassals of the emperors of Kānyakubja. From this period the account becomes more historical. The author seems to have used the records preserved in the Cāhamāna archives. He tells us that Ajayarāja (in the early twelfth century AD) founded the city of Ajayameru (modern Ajmer) made it his capital and issued new coins to mark the occasion. A

15. *Ancient Historians of India*, p. 88.

16. Ed. with commentary of Jonarāja, G.H. Ojha and C.S. Guleri (Ajmer, 1941); Hindi trans. in *Nāgarī Pracāriṇī Patrikā*, (*Kāśī*), 5, 1981, pp. 133-83; Eng. abstract in *JRAS*, 1913, pp. 259-81.

resounding victory of his successor Arṇorāja over the Turks in the desert is celebrated with more poetic effect than factual detail. There is also reference to his marriage with the daughter of Siddharāja, the Cālukya prince of Gujarat.

In conformity with the prevailing literary conventions Jayānaka relates that Pṛthvīrāja III had to get rid of the *mlecchas* (i.e., the Muslim Turks) who had attacked and desecrated the sacred places and destroyed temples. In the concluding part of his work (which seems to have been lost) the author gives a picturesque description of the glorious victory (*vijaya*) of his patron king (Pṛthvīrāja Cauhān, the lord of the territories of Ajmer and Delhi) over Sahāvadina (Shihabuddin Muhammad Ghori) in the first battle of Tarāin or Taroari (situated near Thāneśvar or Bhaṭiṇḍā) in AD 1191. Pṛthvīrāja thus freed Rajasthan and the Punjab from the Muslim invaders. In order to celebrate the victory of his patron be composed his work in about AD 1192. It also appears from his work that Pṛthvīrāja married Tilottamā (Saṁyogitā of *Pṛthvīrāja Rāso*), a princess of perfect beauty. It appears that after the defeat and death of Pṛthvīrāja at the hands of his enemy, Jayānaka returned to Kashmir leaving his work incomplete on which the Kaśmīrī historian Jonarāja (fifteenth century) wrote a commentary.

Jayānaka has presented an authentic biographical history of the Cāhamānas of Śākambharī in his *Pṛthvīrājavijaya*. It being a contemporary work is of inestimable historical value. It constitutes a valuable source of information about Pṛthvīrāja the last independent Hindu sovereign of northern India, and some other Cauhān rulers who preceded him. Many incidents narrated in it have found corroboration from inscriptions and other records. It is a near approach to genuine historical biography in its modern sense.

Another important biography of Pṛthvīrāja III is the *Pṛthvīrāja Rāso*[17] by his court-poet Cand Bardāī, who belonged to a class of bard. The said work consists of 1400 verses, mostly in Apabhraṁśa, then the spoken language in the greater part of northern India. It forms part of bardic literature. It has not been preserved in its original form. It saw several recensions with additions. A vast amount of additional material seems to have been incorporated in it over the centuries. Its considerable parts are believed to be much later than the fourteenth century.

Cand, while dealing with the origin of the Cāhamāna family in his *Rāso,* explicitly states that like the Pratihāras, the Paramāras and the Cālukyas (Solaṅkīs) the Cāhamānas

17. Ed. S.S. Das (Banāras, 1904); Pandia and Das (Banāras, 1913).

belonged to 'Agnikula'. It is also traditionally believed that the descendants of those four persons who took the vow before the fire-altar in the presense of brāhmaṇas to repel the foreign invaders to defend the country were believed to be of the Agni Dynasty. It has, of course, some historical significance. However, the bardic tradition regarding the origins of the four Rājpūt families is not much relied upon in view of the evidence recorded in the extant inscriptions and other contemoporary records of the Cāhamānas, the Pratihāras and the Cālukyas that the former two belonged to the Solar dynasty and the latter to the Lunar dynasty. We are told by Cand that Paramāra was assigned the region from Arbuda to Avantī, Cālukya Anhilwāḍa (modern Paṭan in Gujarat), Pratihāra Marusthalī (the mostly desert country to the west of which the old capital was Māṇḍavyapura) and Cāhamāna Mahiṣadeśa (the middle Narmadā Valley with Māhiṣmatī as capital) from where the Cāhamānas eventually came to Sapādalakṣadeśa (northern Rajasthan) and settled there. The historical authenticity of the information concerned may be proved by the available evidences. His *Rāso* contains the genealogy of the Cāhamānas, the detailed information about the family of Pr̥thvīrāja, etc.

Cand, while highlighting the heroic deeds (*vira-gāthā*s) of Pr̥thvīrāja Cauthān in his poems, informs us that he attacked and defeated the Candella king, Paramardi, in AD 1182 and occupied Mahobā, Kālañjara and other fortresses in Jejākabhukti (Bundelkhaṇḍ). We are further informed that Pr̥thvīrāja was not on friendly terms with Jayacanda (AD 1170-94) of Kānyakubja (Kanauj). The latter's daughter, Saṁyogitā, had heard much of the former's valour and wished to marry him, but her father did not approve of it. She could not keep her cherished desire secret for a long time. She conveyed her desire to Pr̥thvīrāja through correspondence and invited him to come to Kānyakubja and take her away. When Jayacanda held a *svayaṁvara* (selection of bridegroom) for her daughter, Pr̥thvīrāja appeared just in the mist of the ceremonies and carried her away fighting off the persuing or chasing army of the enemy. This resulted in the hostility between the two which ultimately proved to be fatal for both. The said incident is supposed to have taken place immediately after Pr̥thvīrāja's victory over Muhammad Ghori in AD 1191. It has without any doubt historical basis.

The poet, Cand, has furnished an eye-witness account of the second battle of Tarāin which was fought in AD 1192 between Pr̥thvīrāja Cauhān and Muhammad Ghori. According to him, the former fell wounded from his horse in the course of the battle but at his instance killed the latter by an arrow and himself died which is not taken as worthy of acceptance. The information supplied in some of the later recensions of his *Rāso* that Ghori after having defeated Pr̥thvīrāja made him captive, took him along with Cand to

Ghazni and tortured them to death is taken equally incredible. What generally historians accept is that Pṛthvīrāja fled from the battlefield to save his life, but was captured near Sarasuti and taken to Ajmer where he was later put to death. And then Muhammad Ghori occupied Ajmer and Delhi. However, it is still a riddle or mystery of history as to how and where Pṛthvīrāja met his tragic end.

Cand's *Rāso* also records that the Tomara king Anaṅgapāla I (a feudatory of the Pratihāra king of Kanauj) founded a new city (on the ruins of Indraprastha which was devastated by the Śakas and Hūṇas) in VE 848 = AD 791 and named it Lāl Koṭ (a Rājpūt citadel) which was one of the seven names of modern Delhi. There are many other information in the said work which have kernel of historical turth. The *Pṛthvīrāja Rāso* has, no doubt, some historical value. The tradition of composing *Rāso*s in Rajasthan was further carried on in the medieval period.

The school of historical writing in Rajasthan flourished under the patronage of the Cāhamānas. The historical tradition of Rajasthan is different from that of other parts of India in terms of dynastic records or family histories.

The writers of the bardic tradition made some contributions to the development of historical writing in India. Bards may be regarded as the "Primitive historians of mankind". They *(bhāṭas)* got recognition in the royal courts as a class of poetic writer not before the seventh century AD. The professional bards were conspicuous by their absence in the time of Purāṇic *sūta*s. The bards of Rajasthan played an important part in preserving its local history in oral tradition. They preserved it also by recording real events and commemorating real personages. The records and oral tradition of such bards were repositories of many valuable data and facts, incidents, past and contemporary events and other historical material. It was their profession to memorise events and put them in writing. This tradition among them was handed down from generation to generation. Traditionally the bard followed his father's profession. He learnt from him his techniques of writing and reciting poetry, to chronicle historical facts and to glorify his Rājpūt patrons. The bards very carefully compiled the genealogies of the Rājpūt families. They earned their livelihood by this profession. They used to preserve with all meticulous care the genealogical records and the family histories of their Rājpūt patrons. At the death of a bard the records in his possession were passed to his son. Thus the bards became the permanent custodians of the family histories and genealogists of the most of the ruling clans of Rajasthan. Histories of some princes or royal personages of Rajasthan were recorded by their respective family bards both in ancient and medieval period. The heroic poems of the bards including that of Cand Bardāī constitute a valuable source of history. The bardic poems (*Rāsos*) are historical records of Rajasthan. It is significant to note that when written historical records were being destroyed by the Muslim invaders in the course of their invasions of India, the bards thought it proper to memorise the contemporary historical events and to preserve them in their memories instead of recording them. History of Rajasthan (*Annals and Antiqutities of Rajasthan*) of Tod was written chronologically on the basis of oral tradition preserved by bards (*bhāṭas* and *cāraṇas*) of Rajasthan (first published in 1829) which has been corroborated by written records also. J. Kennedy has correctly stated that "The true history of India is hidden under a thick veil of Brahminical or bardic fiction".[18] The institution of bards, which was hereditary, existed not only in Rajasthan but also in Gujarat, Kānyakubja in Uttar Pradesh, Jejākabhukti or Bundelkhaṇḍ and other parts of Madhya Pradesh, Kashmir, mysore and the Deccan. The historical value of Indian bardic literature of both ancient and medieval period has been acknowledged by a number of scholars.[19]

The *Paramardi Rāso* (a poem generally called *Mahotsavakhaṇḍa*), an anonymous, is a biography of Paramardi (AD 1165-1206), the Candella sovereign of Jejākabhukti (Bundelkhaṇḍ), east of Rajasthan and south of the Yamunā. He belonged to Candrātreya dynasty. The said work was composed originally in Jejākabhukti sometime after 1182 or 1192 but not later than 1203. It was later modified and incorporated in the gradually growing *Pr̥thvīrāja Rāso* corpus. It exists in different recensions. We learn from this work that Candravarman, the first Candrātreya king, built eighty-five temples at Kharjūravāhaka (Khajurāho), one of the most important cities in the Candella kingdom. He built a capital for himself named Mahotsava (Mahobā). It appears that these events took place in the first half of the ninth century AD. He and his successors ruled over the kingdom with its capital at Mahotsava.

An accurate historical account of a reverse the king Paramardi sustained in the war of 1182 at the hands of Pr̥thvīrāja Cauhān is given in the *Paramardi Rāso* or *Mahotsavakhaṇḍa.* We are told that the war occurred as a result of one of Pr̥thvīrāja's expeditions when some of his troops were crossing territory of Candella kingdom on their way home and became involved in a squabble with of Paramardi's men. Paramardi's resulting attack on the Cāhamāna force was an 'unchivalrous' and 'impolitic' act. His

18. *Imp. Gaz. Ind.*, 2, p. 309.

19. For details see Haimendorf, "The Historical value of Indian Bardic Literature", in C.H. Philips (ed.), *Historians of India, Pakistan and Ceylon,* vol.I, pp. 87-93.

general, Udayasiṁha, "tried to restrain him but Paramardi persisted, instigated by the mischievous advice of his brother-in-law, a Pratihāra prince who was his vassal but secretly wished to ruin him by embroiling him in war with a stronger army". After this the continuing intrigue of the Pratihāra prince forced Ālhā and his brother Ūdal, the two best generals of Paramardi, into exile. Pṛthvīrāja kept informed of the situation by the Pratihāra prince launched his expedition in retaliation against Parmārdi. The latter finding himself unable to check the former retreated, but managed to secure a temporary truce which afforded him a chance to implore his generals to return to his aid. The battle ensued between the forces of Pṛthvīrāja Cauhān and Paramardi in 1182 with very heavy losses on both sides. Ūdal and other leaders of the latter and one of the sons of the former were killed, and Ālhā was wounded. Paramardi fled to the fortress of Kālañjara and the victorious Pṛthvīrāja marched into Mahotsava. Afterwards Pṛthvīrāja sent a general to capture Kālañjara, and Paramardi was taken prisoner, but Ālhā's son, Indal, suddenly attacked the Cāhamānas with forces and freed his king. The city of Mahotsava eventually fell under the occupation of Pṛthvīrāja. Paramadi died in shame soon afterwards, but inscriptions of the Candella kings do not bear testimony to this fact rather show that Paramardi escaped complete annihilation, and afterwards recovered the lost ground. He was in possession of his capital Mahotsava again within two years at most and ruled another twenty years until he died. It was the heroism of Ālhā, Ūdal and Indal which saved their king and his kingdom.[20] The original poem was composed to celebrate their marvellous feats of action, to commemorate the courage and valour displayed by Paramardi against his political adversary or to preserve the memory of the event that took place in 1182. The said work supplements the information supplied by Cand in his *Pṛthvīrāja Rāso*. Jejākabhukti seems to have maintained its own tradition of historiography.

Oral tradition has preserved in the Bundelī dialect of Hindu an epic known as the *Ālhā Rāso* which is supposed to have been composed by Jagvik or Jagnaik Rao, Paramardi's messenger. It supplies more information than the *Paramardi Rāso* about Paramardi. He has been called a magnanimous hero. There is some historical basis for this assesment of his character. It gives more detail of the intrigue of the Pratihāra prince. It gives a vivid description of the first battle between the Cāhamāna king Pṛthvīrāja and the Candella king Paramardi resulting in a victory for the latter, Ālhā and Ūdal inflicting heavy losses on the former. We are further told that the war was resumed for a different cause, and Pṛthvīrāja's kingdom was invaded by the forces led by Paramardi's

20. Warder, *op. cit.*, pp. 80-83.

son, who was killed during the expedition. Several more battles followed and finally the Candella kings were defeated after Ūdal's death and the city of Mahotsava fell in the hands of victors. Paramardi could not bear the disgrace and went on fast which led to his death and Mahotsava ceased to be the capital of Jejākabhukti.[21] The indication given in the work about a great event towards the end of Paramardi's reign was stubborn resistance he offered to Qutb-ud-din Aibak in 1203 during the siege of Kālañjara. Finding it not possible to stand with the odds which were altogether against him, Paramardi capitulated, but he died before fulfilling any of the terms imposed on him, according to the evidence available in standard historical works.

The *Surathotsava* of Someśvara (AD 1179-1262) contains the life-sketch of Bhīma II (AD 1178-1241), one of the later Cālukya monarchs of Gujarat. The author describes, of course, allegorically the vicissitudes of fortune of Bhīma II. In AD 1178, soon after his accession, Gujarat had to face a Muslim invasion led by the Sultan of Ghor. The Sultan (Muhammad Ghori) attacked Anhilwāḍa (modren Paṭan), then the capital of Gujarat, but was repulsed by the brave Rājpūt hero, Bhīma Dev, in a hard-fought battle. The next important event during the reign of Bhīma was Qutb-ud-din's invasion of Gujarat. The latter captured Anhilwāḍa in AD 1197, but his occupation was only temporary. Besides, Gujarat also suffered from the inroads of the king of Mālawā and the Yādava ruler of Devagiri. Lavaṇaprasāda, the Vaghelā minister and feudatory of Bhīma II, established himself in an almost independent position in southern Gujarat, thereby reducing the latter's jurisdiction to its northern part. Thus, the reign-period of Bhīma was very eventful.

A Critical Evalution of Biographical Writings

The preceding biographical works have, no doubt, great historical value. They belong to a class of literature called *kāvya*. This explains the reason why their authors could not avoid the use of metaphor and imagery and coalescing of facts and fictions in their writings. They have presented biographical histories by adopting *kāvya* style of writing which is characterised by literary ornamentation, high-flown expression and poetic embellishments. They actually followed the literary tradition of historiography. As most of the works were written by the poets in the courts of their respective patrons, it was but natural for the former to bestow praise on the latter and to glorify their deeds, extol their virtues and exalt their glory to keep them gratified. However, the main object of

21. Warder, *op. cit.*, pp. 80-83.

the authors of the biographical works was not the glorification of kings but to portray a true picture of their lives and times by applying their literary skill and ingenuity. The biographical writings are by and large eulogistic in nature and panegyric in tone but not deviod of historical contents. There are, of course, some exaggerations in authors' presentation of subject-matter but not distortions of historical truth. They have preserved all important historical facts in their respective works. All contemporary significant historical events have been incorporated in them. The biographical works on the whole are full of valuable historical information. That is why they are often called 'historical epics' which include mostly prose works. The works which were written independently without any royal patronage are free from laudatory expression. The works in general contain apart from biographical details other historical material.

> "The ancient biographies are . . . of very great importance to the modern student, because history is presented in them not as a chart of events but as a detailed map in which the events are located with reference to contemporary values. We do not simply get a narration of events but their interpretations according to the culture of the time as well. These interpretations may appear grotesque to the modern historian as history viewed from the modern angle would have been to the ancient thinkers. . . . These historical biographies can well be utilised for reconstructing the history of the past, provided we carefully study the nature of the idealising agents and the contemporary methods of historical organisations and inferences."[22]

Many events and incidents narrated in some biographical works have been corroborated by inscriptions and other faithful records. Most of the facts regarding *digvijaya* (conquests) of the kings recorded in works have found support from contemporary epigraphical records and other valuable sources. Genealogies of kings and patrons given in some works have also been found reliable. All these go to prove the historicity of the works concerned. The biographers of famous kings and other historical personages were definitely endowed with a historical sense. The biographical works of historical character also bear testimony to the gradual progress in historical conception. Among the biographical writers of ancient and early medieval India there were few who critical of their own men and liberal to the enemies of their patrons which is a distinct proof of the

---

22. V.S. Pathak, "Ancient Historical Biographies and Reconstruction of History", in *Problems of Historical writing in India* (Proceedings of the Seminar held at the India International Centre, New Delhi, 21-25 January, 1963), pp. 20-21.

objective treatment of the subject. Admitting all these facts we cannot deny that the tradition of writing genuine historical biography had not fully developed in ancient India.

The biographical tradition of historiography despite all its shortccomings has its own value. "Ancient Indian biographies, like their counterparts in other countries, are by no means perfect. By modern standards they fall short of the desired ideal. By and large their authors appear to have been believers in the 'Great-Men theory of History', being ardent admirers of their patrons. Rarely they have succeeded in unfolding the full courses of the lives of their patrons and have seldom explored the quirks and crannies of their personalities. Yet viewed as a whole, their works have enabled us to know many things about the lives and careers of eminent personalities of ancient and early mediaeval India and occasionally to recapture in our imagination all that they had lived and died for."[23]

23. Dasgupta, *op. cit.*, p. 24.

8

The Writing of Chronicles and Vaṁśāvalīs

Here mention may first be made of the *Rājataraṅgiṇī* (a chronicle or history of kings of Kashmir) by Kalhaṇa,[1] a distinguished Kaśmīrī historian of the twelfth century AD. He was the son of Campaka, a minister of king Harṣa (AD 1089-1101). He adorned the court of king Jayasiṁa (AD 1127-59), the son of Sussala II. It was during his reign that he composed his great work. According to all available evidences, he began his work in AD 1148 and completed it in 1150. His *Rājataraṅgiṇī* became the most famous of all the ancient royal chronicles of Kashmir.

Kalhaṇa was gifted with all qualities of a true historian. He occupies the highest place among the ancient historians of India. With his appearance on the scene ancient Indian historiography took a new turn.

Kalhaṇa utilised the works of eleven chroniclers of Kashmir who preceded him as sources of his information for composing his work. The eleven chronicles (*rājakathās*) used by him include the oldest extensive original works containing the royal chronicles (of Kashmir) condensed or abridged by Suvrata in the form of a handbook of the history of Kashmir (I.11) the *Nṛpāvalī* or *Rājāvalī* (List of Kings) of Kṣemendra (AD 1028-63), who graced the court of king Ananta Deva (I.13), the *Pārthivāvalī* (List of kings in twelve thousand verses) of Helārāja (I.17), the work (name not known) of Padmamihira containing the list of eight kings who preceded Aśoka (I.18), and the work (name unknown) of Śrīchavillākara (also called Śrīcchavillaka) containing the list of five princes from Aśoka to Abhimanyu out of fifty-two (lost ones) (I.19 & 20). In addition to the chronicles, he consulted also a Purāṇic record which is the *Nīla Purāṇa* of Nīlamuni. From this source he obtained the list of four kings, viz., Gonanda and his three successors (I.16). While acknowledging the aforesaid works Kalhaṇa observes:

1. Ed. by Durga Prasad (Bombay, 1892); Eng. tr. by M.A. Stein, 3 vols. (Westminster, 1900, rept. Delhi, 1961); R.S. Pandit (Allahabad 1935, rept. Delhi, 1968) and J.C. Dutt, 2 vols. (Calcutta 1879 & 1887, rept. Delhi. 1997).

> "I have examined eleven works of former scholars which contain the chronicles of the kings, as well as the Purāṇa containing the views of the sage Nila." (I.14)

He critically examined the existing historical records on Kashmir before wielding his pen. In fact, he adopted a critical method of historical research. Of all the works utilised by him for his purpose only the said Purāṇa is now available and the rest have passed into oblivion. We do not possess any information about the use of the earliest historical *kāvya*, the *Bhuvanābhyudaya* of Saṅkula of Kashmir (*c.* AD 850), which describes the local battles, by him.

Kalhaṇa made a thorough use of royal charters, edicts, records of land-grants, the contemporary documents, coins, inscriptions and other archaeological evidence, and with the help of these he corrected errors occurring in the earlier works. He has himself stated that by looking at the ordinances (*śāsana*) of former kings, at the inscriptions recording the grants and erection and consecration of temples and other monuments, at the laudatory inscriptions (*praśasti-paṭṭa*), and the written records (*śāstra*s), all worries arising from errors have been overcome and doubts have been set at rest (I.15). Like a serious historian or researchers of today he used all the relevant sources available to him for composing a chronicle of Kashmir.

The principles Kalhaṇa followed for carrying out his historical investigation also merit our attention. His strict adherence to the exposition of facts can best be qualified in his own words : "That virtuous (writer) alone is worthy of praise who, free form love or hatred, restricts his language to the exposition of facts" (I.7). He tells us that the discovery of truth was his sole object. He discarded all bias and prejudice which is duty of a true historian. He laid stress on the fact that while writing a history of the past one has to pronounce his judgements like a judge. The mission of a historian, he says, is to "make vivid before one's eyes pictures of a bygone age". (I.4). He further says about the methodological technique he adopted for writing the history of the past: "How great a cleverness is required in order that men of modern times may complete the account given in the books of those who died after composing each the history of those kings whose contemporary he was ! Hence in this narrative of past events, which is difficult in many respects, my endeavour will be to connect." (I.8-10) He had, no doubt, clear understanding of fundamental principles of historiography. His impartiality, honesty and objectivity find reflection in the statement of facts recorded in his work.

The *Rājataraṅgiṇī* (in Sanskrit containing nearly 8000 verses) is divided into eight books called *taraṅga*s. It embraces the history of Kashmir from the time of the first

Hindu king Gonanda to AD 1149, the 22nd year of the reign of the last illustrious king Jayasiṁha. It contains the genealogies and chronology of kings of various dynasties that ruled Kashmir during this period. The achievements of all important kings and the details of all important events which took place during their times have been highlighted by the author in his work.

Of fifty-two kings who are said to have ruled Kashmir in the early phase, the list of only seventeen which includes Gonanda I and his successors and some other kings has been provided in Book I. Kalhaṇa could not find the names of thirty-five kings as their records are lost. The same Book contain the list of twenty-one kings who succeeded Gonanda III. Book II contains the list of six princes from Pratāpaditya I to Aryyarāja who belonged to Āditya dynasty. From Book III it appears that there was restoration of Gonanda dynasty and ten princes of this dynasty from Meghavāhana to Bālāditya reigned in Kashmir. These three Books contains more or less a traditional history from the time of the great battle of Kurukṣetra or beginning of the *Kali-yuga* to the end of the sixth century AD which is based on *itihāsa-purāṇa* tradition. Some kings are, of course, mythical but there are some kings like Aśoka and his son Jālauka, Kaniṣka and other whose historicity is well established. Their activities are also well recorded in Kalhaṇa's work. However, there is anachronism in the genealogical list furnished in Book I. And the chronology of some of the kings mentioned in the said three Books is not reliable.

Of all the early kings mentioned in the first three Books Aśoka is the most important. We are told by Kalhaṇa that in his time Kashmir formed part of the Maurya empire. He built there many *stūpas* and monasteries, and founded the city of Śrīnagara and made it capital (the ruins of which have been found at a distance of about ten miles from modern Śrīnagara). He also 'pulled down the wall of an old Hindu temple and built a new wall to it'. In his time Buddhism was the prevailing religion. After Aśoka's death, one of his sons, Jālauka, became king of Kashmir. He drove back the *mlecchas* (Scythians ?) from there and further extended his conquests to the eastern side of Kanauj. He professed the Śaiva sect of Hinduism. During his time Śaivism found many supporters, and Brāhmaṇical supremacy was established. But during the reigns of Kaniṣka and one of his successors, Huviṣka Buddhism became once more a popular religion. Kashmir was never under the political sway of the Guptas. The Hūṇa chief, Mihirakula, is said to have usurped the throne of a Kashmir ruler, who was his contemporary, sometime in the early sixth century AD and excercised his authority over a limited territory in the valley.

The information porvided by Kalhaṇa in Books IV-VIII covering the period from early seventh century AD to about the middle of the twelfth century are more trustworthy than what we find in the earlier three Books from both historical and chronological points of view.

Book IV contains the history of seventeen kings from Durlabhavardhana to Utpalapīḍa who belonged to the Karkoṭa (also called Karkoṭaka) dynasty. Durlabhavardhana, the descendant of Nāga Karkoṭa or Karkoṭaka, founded this dynasty. He appears to have ruled from *circa* AD 598 to 634. His reign was chiefly distinguished by this encouragement of religion, the temples he founded, the endowments he bestowed upon the brāhamaṇs, and some other benevolent works he undertook for the general welfare of the people. He won the friendship of Harṣavardhana by presenting him a prized tooth-relic of the Buddha for installation in a shrine at Kanauj. The most powerful ruler of the line was Lalitāditya (AD 724-60), the third son of Durlabhaka *alia*s Pratāpaditya. Lalitāditya has been described as an efficient administrator, valiant warrior, great conqueror and patron of arts and culture. The author of the said work has given a faithful account of his *digvijaya* (conquest). He subjugated Yaśovarman of Kanauj (in AD 773 or in about AD 740) and invaded Karṇāṭa, then subject to a queen named Ratta, who submitted to the invadeer but was later restored to her dominions. He also subdued the coast and the islands opposite the banks of the Kāverī, and reduced seven Koṅkaṇas. He occupied Avantī and Kamboja, conquered a portion of the Punjab, launched his campaigns in Tukhāristān (the upper Oxus valley) and Daradadeśa (Dardistān, north-west of Kashmir), carried his arms to the land of the Bhauṭṭas (Tibetans) and advanced to the realms of Uttarakuru. After having accomplished his task he returned to his own dominion and proclaimed himself the sovereign ruler of Kashmir. Next he went for revamping of whole administrative structure. He set-up various new administrative departments and appointed officials of all ranks for the good governance of the kingdom. He founded a number of cities which include Lalitapura and Parihāsapura. In the city of Parihāsapura he built temples for Brāhmaṇical gods — Bhūteśa (Śiva) and Parihāsa Keśava (Viṣṇu). In this city he erected stone-image of Garuḍa, and constructed a colossal figure of the Buddha and a figure of Hari. In Huṣkapura he erected an image of Mukta Svāmin and temple of Jyeṣṭha Rudra. He built Buddhist *vihāra*s at Huṣkapura and other places. His most famous construction was the Mārttaṇḍa temple of the Sun whose ruins still testify to its former magnificence and splendidness. Jayāpīḍa (AD 779-810), one of the successors of Lalitāditya, was another illustrious monarch of Kashmir. The author has given detailed description of his military enterprises and other activities. He is said to have defeated and dethroned a king of Kanauj who may be identified with Vajrāyudha or Indrāyudha.

His expeditions against Pauṇḍravardhana (north Bengal), then the residence of Jayanta, king of Gauḍa, who submitted to the victor, and his conflict with king of Nepal are prolixly narrated in the author's work. One of the principal works of his reign was the construction of the fort of Jayapur and its embellishment by a temple of Śiva and by a Brāhmaṇical college. He was a great patron of learning, and his court was adorned by many literary celebrities and geniuses like Udbhaṭa, Vāmana and Dāmodaragupta. In hot pursuit of his passion to amass the wealth Jayāpīḍa adopted such measures which became fatal to his subjects. He levied heavy exactions on all ranks of people, and particularly oppressed the brāhmaṇas by taking back the endowments which he and his predecessors had bestowed upon them. He was followed by a number of weak and incompetent rulers. Their mutual conflict over the issue of possessing real sovereignty of Kashmir coupled with political convulsions led to the gradual decline of the power of the Karkoṭakas. About the middle of the ninth century their glory had totally eclipsed and they were supplanted by the Utpalas. Utpalapīḍa, the last monarch of the Karkoṭa dynasty, was deposed and Avantīvarman, the son of Sucavarman and founder of the Utpala dynasty, succeeded.

The narrative of fifteen princes from Avantīvarman to Śūravarman II belonging to the Utpala or Varman dynasty has been provided in Book V. The accession of Avantīvarman did not take place without opposition and he had to undergo many cnflicts with his own cousins and even with his brothers before his dominion was established. by his valour, prudence, sagacity and wisdom aided by the wise counsel of minister, Sura or Suyya, to whom he was indebted for his crown, he overcame all opposition, restored order and tranquillity, ascended the throne in AD 855 and remained the undisputed sovereign of Kashmir till the end of his reign. "He was not in a position to embark upon any schemes of conquest as the kingdom had suffered greatly from economic and political troubles during the reigns of the later Karkoṭkas". He, however, took some steps to tone up the administration, establish internal security, mobilise resources and restore the health of state economy. He took some bold steps to curb effectively the power and influence of the Ḍāmaras, "a turbulent class of rural aristocrats". The minister of the king undertook some works of public utility. He constructed channels for irrigation which increased the fertility of the land resulting in the higher agricultural production. This led to the economic prosperity of the kingdom. During the reign of Avantīvarman many towns and temples were constructed which increased the grandeur of the kingdom. The king himself built temples and bestowed upon them the endowments. He also gave liberal grants in charity to brāhmaṇas. It is said that they also received the Agrahāras,

Khaduya and Hastikarṇa, from Sūravarman who was nominated by the king Yuvarāja. The city, Avantīpura, was founded by the king at Viśvakeśvara Kṣetra in which he also erected a temple and dedicated it to Avantīśvara or Śiva whose worship he had adopted in place of the Vaiṣṇava tenets in which he had been initiated. He also erected here three statues of the same deity under the names of Tripureśvara, Bhūteśa and Vijayeśa. But in the last phase of his life he again became the votary of Viṣṇu and popularised the Vaiṣṇava faith. The adoration of deities of Hindu pantheon during his time was on the increase. The King's minister built a town, Surapura or Suyyapura on the banks of Vitastā (Jhelum). The modern town of Sopur still preserves the name of the minister. The king also extended his patronage to literary figures amongst whom the most prominent was Ānandavardhana. Avantīvarman after having ruled for 28 years passed away in AD 883.

After the death of Avantīvarman, the reign of Kashmir passed into the hands of his on, Śaṅkaravarman. The latter reversed the peaceful policy of his father and kept himself engaged in wars and conquests. He invaded Darvābhisāra (the region between the Vitastā or Jhelum and the Candrabhāgā or Cenāb), extended his sway to Trigarta region (Kāngrā) after subduing its king, Pṛthvīcandra, and defeated the Gurjara (i.e., Gujarat of Pakistan) chief Alakhāna and his ally Lalliya Shahi seizing the treasures and kingdom of the former and leaving him only Taccadeśa. Śaṅkaravarman also siezed certain territories, conquered earlier by Mihira Bhoja, from Mahendrapāla I Pratihāra, and transferred them to the Thakkiya chief. In order to replenish the treasury which became depleted becasue of his military operations, and also to satiate his desire to accumulate wealth, Śaṅkaravarman subjected his people to every king of extortion. He levied heavy tolls and taxes, exacted undue proportions of the produce of the land, and let out to farm those lands which were the property of temples. He levied fees even on religious festivities and ceremonies. This oppressive taxation resulted in the gradual impoverishment of the people. Learning also suffered under his rule for want of patronage. He diverted the attention of his subjects by engaging them in military expeditions. He is said to have led an army to the north where he subdued the people along the Indus. He entered the Uraśa (Hazārā) region where he was shot in the neck with an arrow by a mountaineer which resulted in his death. Thus, Śaṅkaravarman after having reigned for 18 years died in AD 902.

Śaṅkaravarman was succeeded by his son, Gopālavarman. The only notable event during reign of the latter was the defeat his minister Prabhākaradeva inflicted on a rebellious Shāhī king of Udbhāṇḍapura (Ohind, a few miles north of Attock) who may be identified with Alberuni's Samand (Śāmantadeva). His coins have also been found in large numbers in Afghanistan and the Punjab which are of the bull and horseman type and bear the legend "*Śrī-Sāmantadeva*" on the obverse. We also learn that the victor (Prabhākaradeva) placed Kamaluka on the Shāhī thorne but he was later deposed because of being disobedient and unfaithful to the royal authority in Kashmir. It is noteworthy that in those days the Punjab and the territory beyond the Indus as far as Kabul were ruled by the Hindu princes of the Shāhiyā dynasty. Gopālavarman after having ruled for two years died in AD 904. The author has narrated all the events in detail which took place in the succeeding period. We further learn that the last king but one, Unmattāvantī (AD 937-39), was 'worse than wicked'. He slew his father and starved all his half-brothers to death. After his death, with the brief reign of Śūravarman II the the Utpala dynasty came to an end in AD 939.

In Book VI, the author has provided the history of ten kings in the lines of Yaśaskara and Parvagupta. We are informed that after Śūravarman II, Yaśaskara (son of Gopālavarman's minister, Prabhākaradeva), was elected by the brāhmaṇas as king. During his benevolent reign of nine years (AD 939-48) a new era of peace, progress and prosperity commenced in Kashmir. His son and successor, Saṁgrāma, was killed in AD 949 by the minister Parvagupta who unsurped the throne himself. The most prominent and powerful ruler in this line was Diddā, granddaughter of Bhīma Shāhī and daughter of Siṁharāja, a chief of the Lohara (in the Puñch state). It is said that "She was an ambitious and energetic woman, and for nearly half a century-first as queen-consort of king Kṣemagupta (AD 950-58), then as regent, and lastly as ruler (AD 980-1003) — she was the dominant personality in the politics of Kashmir". During this period there were constant court-intrigues which were suppressed by her with an iron hand. And in spite of the opposition of Ḍāmaras (land-owning nobles) and the brāhmaṇas she maintained her position and exercised authority with the assistance of Tuṅga, a Khasa of low origin, for whom she had immense affection.

The history of six princes from Saṁgrāmarāja to Harṣa belonging to so-called the Lohara dynasty is contained in Book VII. Saṁgrāmarāja *alias* Kṣamāpati, nephew of Diddā and brother of the Lohara prince, Vigraharāja, ascended the throne in AD 1003 and continued to rule till 1028. Saṁgrāmarāja proved to be a weak king, and during the earlier part of his reign Tuṅga was virtually the ruler in the state. Kalhaṇa tells us that the latter went along with army to help the Hindu Shāhī king against the aggression of a Turuṣka (Muslim) named Hammīra, who, however, utterly routed the combined Hindu army. Tuṅga was murdered and thereafter Kaśmīrī soldiers fled back before conquering the Turuṣkas. And 'Shāhīrājya' was annexed to the realm of Turuṣkas. Here Kalhaṇa speaks of Trilocanapāla (the Hindu Shāhī king of Lahore), who was defeated by Sultan Mahmud of Ghazni in AD 1021 despite being helped by his ally from Kashmir, and of the Pujab which was annexed to the Ghazni empire. The historical accuracy of author's statement pertaining to this episode is well tested. We are also told that during the reign of Anantadeva (AD 1028-63) seven *mleccha* kings had entered Kashmir but were beaten back by Rudrapāla, the powerful Kaśmīrī general. Barring brief intervals of good government, the subsequent history of Kashmir is mainly a long tale of tyranny, misrule and fiscal oppression. Harṣa (AD 1089-1101), who began his political career as an able administrator, military leader, great conqueror, and "liberal patron of the softer arts of music and poetry, later degenerated into a profligate, cruel-hearted, and irreligious man". He is said to have conquered Rajāpura (Rajori). He employed Turuṣka generals in the army, and went on plundering the temples and defiling the images. At last, the powerful Ḍāmaras with chiefs, Ucchala and Sussala I, raised the banner of revolt against his excessive taxation and oppression, and consequently chaos and anarchy prevailed in the kingdom. Ucchala defeated Harṣa and his son Bhoja in a single battle, burnt the capital and after having killed the former in AD 1101 seized the throne of Kashmir. The political spectacle, howver, changed, but the people almost began to groan under the weight of civil wars, misgovernment, and machinations of the aristocracy.

Kalhaṇa seems to be balanced in his value-judgements. He describes the periods of glory and misery, and greatness and weakness of rulers. He has highlighted both the bright and dark sides of the character of some kings. For instances, he describes Harṣa (the patron of his father) as tyrannical, but, on the other hand, counts his bravery as one of his good qualities. He prasied Lalitāditya for his valour, benevolence and many other qualities but did not hesitate to criticise him for his betrayal of the king of Gauḍa. These are some of the instances which constitute a testimony to his objective treatment of subject.

The last and the eighth Book contains the history of seven kings from Ucchala (AD 1101-11) to Jayasiṁha (AD 1127-59), the last illustrious sovereign. The author has provided an eye-witness account of the events which took place about the middle of the twelfth century AD.

Kalhaṇa has presented the narratives of the kings of Kashmir from the early seventh century AD to his own time maintaining his perfect historical sense. The history of this period is not only authentic but also in proper chronological order.

On the whole, the reigns of the kings whose history is known cover a period of 2,330 years up to the time of Kalhaṇa.

The *Rājataraṅgiṇī* is a native chronicle of Kashmir. One of the characteristic features of this chronicle is that it contains information not only about kings but also about contemporary society, economy, religion and culture. It contains valuable information about the religious toleration, the prevalence of three popular cults of Hindusim, Śaiva, Śakti and Vaiṣṇava, and co-existence of Brāhmaṇism and Buddhism, in Kashmir. Thus, it is important for the study of dynastic, political, socio-economic and cultural history of ancient Kashmir, R.C. Dutt has rightly pointed out that the historical value of this chronicle can best be judged by its contents.[2] J. Hutchison opines that "Kashmir is the only country (state) in India of which we posses a written and detailed history of the Hindu period to literary labours of poet-historian Kalhaṇa".[3] A.L. Basham is also of the view that ". . . No similar chronicles were composed elsewhere. . . ."[4] He observes: "Though every important Hindu court maintained archives and preserved genealogies of its rulers, Kashmir is the only region in India in which a tradition of historical writing is known to have existed in pre-Muslim times."[5]

As a matter of fact, the tradition of historical writing not only existed in Kashmir but also in other parts of India. Tod has correctly stated that "It is now generally regarded as an axiom that India possesses no national history. . . . But the *Rajatarangini* clearly demonstrates that regular historical composition was an art not unknown in Hinduistan".[6]

V.A. Smith has also acknowledged that "this work is nearest to the European notion of a regular history". The historical value of the work has been estimated by different scholars in different ways. This chronicle can undoubtedly be considered a valuable historical record. The statement of some scholars that this is the only work which can be called a history is not worthy of acceptance. In fact, this is the best of all ancient Indian historical works.

Kalhaṇa's name stands the foremost in the galaxy of chroniclers or historians of

2. "A Note on Kalhaṇa's *Rājataraṅgṇī*", in H.H. Wilson, *The Hindu History of Kashmir*, p. 159; "An Introductory Essay on the History of Kashmira", in J.C. Dutt, *op. cit.*, II, XXIX.
3. J. Hutchison and J. Ph. Vogel, *History of the Punjab Hill States* vol. I, p. 1.
4. *The wonder that was India*, p. 45.
5. Cf. C.H. Philips (ed.), *Historians of India, Pakistan and Ceylon,* vol. I, p. 57.
6. *AAR*, introduction, p. xiii.

Kashmir school. A true conception of history and the correct method of writing were not altogether unknown in ancient India. However, it was he who set several new landmarks in the history of historical writing in ancient India. He was the first Indian to understand the basic principle of historiography in the real sense of the term. The principles he laid down for writing history were far in advance of his age. He made a critical and objective apporach to the study of history. He was the first to emphasise the need of a thorough critical examination of all past records useful for the purpose for producing a genuine historical work. A new age of critical historiography began. The first serious attempt at scientific presentation of history was made by him. And in that sense he is often called the father of scientific historiography in ancient India, though we cannot deny the fact that to some extent he adopted the literary style of writing as is evident from the earlier part of his work. However, his comparison with Herodotus, Thucydides or any Greek historian is unwarranted. The history writing in ancient India passing through several stages reached the height of its progress in the time of Kalhaṇa. He, no doubt, made significant contribution to the development of historical writing in ancient India. His work is marked by high standard of accuracy. Its value can be judged even by the modern standard of historiography. He was the forerunner of many Indian historians in the realm of debunking the truth from falsehood. M.A. Stein has also observed that "Honesty in a historian has not unjustly been called a forerunner of critical judgement in regard to contemporary history. Kalhana has manifestly endeavoured to be fair and impartial. May we not assume that the same feeling has helped to guide him rightly also in the opinions he formed of the past?"[7]

Kalhaṇa was the source of inspiration for future historians of India. His historical principles and laws were first followed by the Kaśmīrī chroniclers of the medieval age.

J.N. Sarkar has unequivocally called Kalhaṇa a "historian".[8] According to him, ". . . the standard set by Kalhana was not reached by any other Hindu historian of the medieval period, just as the lines chalked out by Ibn Khaldun do not appear to have been worked out by any other Arabic writer".[9]

The tradition of composing chronicle in Kashmir was further continued in medieval period by the future successors of Kalhaṇa.

7. *Rājataraṅgiṇī*, ed. I, introduction, p. 32.

8. "Thoughts on the Study of Indian History", General President's Address, 37th Session, IHC (Calicut, 1976), p. 11, *PIHC*, p. 9.

9. "Ideas of history in Medieval India", *QRHS*, IV, 1-2, pp. 1-21.

The *Kīrtikaumudī* (in Sanskrit) of Someśvara (AD 1179-1262)[10] is one of the important chronicles of Gujarat. In the introductory portion of his work, the author, Someśvara, has presented a brief history of Cālukya dynasty of Anhilwāḍa (identified with modern Paṭan in Gujarat) from its founder Mūlarāja I (AD 941-95) to king Mūlarāja II (AD 1176-78). The said work provides possibly the best history of the Cālukyas up to the period. It deals with dynastic history in which we come across the facts about different historical personalities and other interesting details. It contains valuable information regarding different members of the Cālukya house of Gujarat. The details provided in the work about the later history of Gujarat is equally valuable. The author gives an account of the Vaghelā (originally called the Vyāghrapalliya) dynasty of Gujarat. He has chronicled all the important events which took place during the times of the Vaghelā kings who were the later Rājapūt rulers of Gujarat. It may be noted here that about 1179 the main line of the Cālukyas at Paṭan suffered a setback and that of Arṇorāja Vaghelā or Dholka came into prominence. Lavaṇaprasāda, the Vaghelā minister and feudatory of Bhīma II (AD 1178-1238), one of the later Cālukya monarchs of Gujarat, established himself in an almost independent position in southern Gujarat, thereby reducing the latter's jurisdiction to its northern part. Gradually, the Vaghelās took Anhilwāḍa and extended their sway over the whole of Gujarat. The brāhmaṇa scholar and poet, Someśvara, enjoyed the patronage of Vastupāla (AD 1220-42), a minister of king Vīradhavala (AD 1219-39) of Vaghelā branch of Cālukya family. The latter, son of Lavaṇaprasāda, was ruler of Dholka. The author of the said work has described in detail the life and character of his patron, Vastupāla (a Jain of the merchant class). We are told that Vastupāla was a valiant warrior. He defended with his army the kingdom against the attacks of the allied forces of the kings of the Deccan. The author in his work, called 'a historical epic', has dwelt at length on the glorious deeds of Vastupāla. The inscriptions on the stone-walls of the Jain temples at Mounts Ābu and Girnāra were composed by Someśvara in praise of Vastupāla. These temples (constructed by Vastupāla himself) with inscriptions stand as monuments of his glory.

Someśvara in his *Kīrtikaumudī* (IV, stanzas 43-53, 55-63) has provided and interesting account of an invasion of Gujarat by a Yādava ruler of Devagiri (modern Daulatābād), Siṅghaṇa (AD 1210-47), in the time of Lavaṇaprasāda and his son Vīradhavala. The Yādava prince (who was hostile to the Cālukyas of Gujarat) attacked with vast army. The Yādavas overran Gujarat. Lavaṇaprasāda taking the Yādava forces invincible submitted and concluded a treaty of alliance with Siṅghaṇa.

---

10. Bombay, 1883.

The whole narrative in the *Kīrtikaumudī*, which is a local chronicle of Gujarat, appears factual except for some exaggerated statement in traditional fashion about the earlier Cālukya kings.

Someśvara was a poet as well as a historian. He occupies an important place among the historians of Gujarat School. He, of course, made some contributions to the development of historical writing in Gujarat. A number of chronicles were further composed in Gujarat in medieval period.

The naive chronicle of Sindh which is popularly known as *Cacanāmā* (or *Chachnama*)[11] also deserves mention here. It is an ancient history of Sindh from the Hindu period down to the Arab conquest. It was originally writtern in Arabic by an anonymous Muslim historian of Sindh incorporating some older sources for the Buddhist and brāhmaṇa rulers of the sixth and seventh centuries AD and adding an account of the Arab invasion early in the following century. It is difficult to six the exact year of the composition of the original Arabic work. However, we have every reason to believe that the work was written not very long after AD 712, the year which marks the Arab conquest of Sindh. From the internal evidence of the narrative it appears that the work must have been writtern before AD 753. Later, in AD 1216, it was translated into Persian by Muhammad Ali bin Abu Bakr Kufi. The work gives a brief account of Sindh and its inhabitants. It contains the details of all important incidents which took place in the course of Arab invasion of Sindh in the early eighth century AD. It throws light on the political condition of Sindh at the time of its conquest by the Arabs. It gives a fairly accurate picture of the circumstances that led to Muhammad bin Qasim's invasion of Sindh and the causes of his success and defeat of the Hindus.

In the sixth and early seventh centuries AD, the kingdom of Sindh with its metropolis at Alor (near modern Rohri), a large and well fortified town adorned with magnificent places, was under the rule of kings of the Rāi family of śūdra origin. The five kings of this family ruled the kingdom altogether for 137 years during the period. At the beginning of the seventh century AD the reigning of sovereign was Rāi Siharas, a believer in Buddhism. He was succeeded by his son, Rāi Sāhasi II, the last ruler of the family. He was deposed by his brāhamaṇa minister Caca (generally spelled as Chach), who put his royal master to death, usurped the throne and founded the brāhmaṇa dynasty in AD 641. He was a great king. During his long reign of forty years he extended the frontiers of the

11. Eng. trans. in H.M. Eliot and J. Downson, *The History of India as told by its own Historians*, vol. I (Allahabad, year of publication not given).

kingdom and held sway over them. After the death of Caca his brothers Candar succeeded him. He patronised in Buddhist monks and promulgated their doctrines. But he dies soon after and a dispute arose for the throne between his son Duraj and the eldest son of Caca named Dāhir. Eventually, Duraj was defeated and ousted, and Caca's two sons, Dāhir and Daharsiah, divided the kingdom. On Daharsiah's death Dāhir became the sole ruler of Sindh. On the eve of the Arab conquest, Sindh was very much weakened owing to political instability and internal strife.[12]

It is further related in the *Cacanāmā* that Muhammad bin Qasim, an able general, marched with a strong army to invade Sindh in AD 712. At the time of this invasion the famous Hindu King, Dāhir, was ruling Sindh with its capital at Alor. Debal (modern Karachi), a port town of Sindh, was the first to near the brunt of attack. It was a colossal blunder on the part of Dāhir to remain inactive at his capital. He could not foresee the disastrous consequences of this invasion for himself as well as for his kingdom. He did not make any serious attempt to stem the tide of the progress of the invading army nor did he send any reinforcement to Debal which had a slender garrison of 4,000 troops as against the mighty invading army numbering over 25,000. The troops of Qasim besieged the town of Debal which was well protected by a strong stone-wall. The troops stationed at Debal for its protection fought bravely but they were hopelessly outnumbered. "During the course of the siege a Brahmana from the chief temple deserted to the Arabs and informed Muhammad that as long as the red flag, to the base of which a talisma (a charm consisting of a magical figure cut, and supposed to preserve the bearer from injury or sudden death) was tied, remained flying at the top of the temple, the town could never be taken." The people of the town were asked to choose between Islam and death. They preferred the latter to the former. The carnage, destructions and depredations that followed continued for three days. All the males of seventeen years and above were put to death and their women and childern were made slaves. Temples were desecrated and demolished and mosques built in their places. And finally Debal was conquered. From the chronicler's account of the subject it appears that a huge booty fell into the hands of the victor.[13]

Further, Muhammad bin Qasim and his troops crossed the Indus by a bridge of boats and attacked Rawar. Several pitched battles were fought between the troops of both the sides. A fierce battle which took place on 20 June, 712, resulted in the defeat

---

12. *The History of India as told by its own Historians*, vol. I., pp. 138-55.
13. *Ibid.*, pp. 155-69.

and death of Dāhir. Thereafter the women of Sindh led by Dāhir's widow, Rānī Bāī, made an attempt to expiate for the sins of their men-folk. The Rānī put up a heroic defence within the fort of Rawar and her garrison numbering about 15,000 rained stones and missels on the invading army causing them great damage. She left no stone unturned to push back the invader. But when she lost all hope of success she burned herself on the funeral pyre along with her women followers to save her honour and chastity. She became precursor of women if Rājapūtānā so far as this practice (*jauhar*) is concerned. The fort of Rawar was untimately capturerd. Another round of battle was fought at Brāhmaṇābād (a city of brāhmaṇas at a distance of about 47 miles to the north-east of Haidarābād) between the remnants of Dāhir's troops numbering more than 8,000 and the troops of the enemy with casualities on both sides. Jai Singh, Dāhir's son, finding resistance useless retired to Chitrur. And thereafter Qasim with the help of his troops occupied Brāhmaṇābād with its treasures and Rānī Lāḍī, another widow of Dāhir, and the two maiden daughters of the latter, Sūryā Devī and Parmal Devī. The graphic description of the whole occurrences has been provided in the said local chronicle of Sindh. Alor (also called Aror), the then capital of Sindh, was the next target of invader's attack. This capital town was then held by another son of Dāhir. He along with the residents of the capital fought bravely against the invader and stoutly defended the town and abandoned it only when further resistance proved to be of no avail. With the capitulation of the fort of Alor the subjugation of Sindh became complete. The conqueror took in his possession Dāhir's territory with all its dependencies. And thus the Hindu kingdom of Sindh fell into the hands of the Arabs.[14] After the death of Muhammad bin Qasim his successors made continuous efforts to expand their territory but they failed to achieve their objective.

The *Cacanāmā* is a principal source of our information for the study of early medieval history of Sindh.

The tradition of preserving historical literature in the forms of chronicles and *vaṁśāvalī*s was maintained also in Oḍradeśa (modern Orrisa). Archives were kept in the temples and some have survived such as those of the famous Jagannāth temple at Purī. These were primary sources for the compilers of chronicles, *vaṁśāvalī*s and other historical works. The famous chronicle, *Mādalā Pāñjī*, in prose style in Oriyā language was compiled from the Purī archives. This chronicle is believed to have been begun on the order of the king of Gaṅga dynasty, Anantavarman V Choḍagaṅga, at the beginning

14. *The History of India as told by its own Historians*, vol. I, pp. 170-211.

of the twelfth century AD and kept up to date since then. Manuscript copies of it are kept by various priests attached to the temple and they sometimes vary in detail. Anantavarman was called Choḍagaṅga because he was the son of Rājarāja Gaṅga by his Coḷa wife, Rājasundarī, daughter of Rājendra Choḍa. Choḍagaṅga ruled over Kaliṅga from AD 1077 to 1147. The Gaṅga family rose to the zenith of its power and height of its glory under him. Tradition ascribes to him the building of the famous temple of Purī. He is a said to have extended the bounds of his realm. The said chronicle contains valuable information about he rule of Gaṅga dynasty over Kaliṅga. It records at some length the significant events which took place during the rule of the Gaṅga kings. Its *Rājacaritra* section deals with the life and achievements of kings of Gaṅga dynasty. From the account furnished in the chronicle it appears that Anantavarman V was invited from the south by a certain brāhmaṇa official and then ruled over the whole kingdom. The building activities of some Gaṅga kings and also their organisation of the revenues of Kaliṅga are recorded in the chronicle. Anaṅgabhīma II at the end of the twelfth century was one of the greatest builders of temples and magnificent palaces. He conducted a new survey of the whole kingdom and reorganised the revenue administration. His speech on this subject addressed to the nobility is preserved in the chronicle. He proposed to build a new temple at Purī and their agreement is recorded.

The palm-leaf manuscripts or chronicles preserved in the archives of the temple of Jagannāth at Purī contain historical narratives about the lives of the rulers of Orissa right from the establishment of the Gaṅga dynasty and their military expeditions, battles, coquests, achievements, etc. The date and authorship of the chronicles are controversial. However, the materials and themes incorporated therein are important for the study of individual rulers of different dynasties and their mode of administration, economic policies, benevolent activities and success and failures. The chronicles are valuable documents regarding the royal dynasties of Orissa.

The *vaṁśāvalī*s (historical records of dynastic genealogies or genealogical histories) were compiled and maintained with great care.

In Orissa, the tradition of compiling the *vaṁśāvalī*s began in the ancient period and continued till the fifteenth or sixteenth century. A number of *vaṁśāvalī*s were written and revised with some additions during the period. These records contain lists of the kings and the length of their reigns and the dates of important events. The Eastern Gaṅgas of Kaliṅga maintained the *vaṁśāvalī* records which are full of details of their kings. The *Gaṅgavaṁśānucarita* in Sanskrit (preseved at Purī) is based largely on the

Mādalā Pāñjī and partly on the earlier writings. It was, in fact, revised by Vasudevaratha in lattter half of the fifteenth century after the Gaṅga dynasty was supplanted by the Gajapati dynasty but under the patronage of a local ruler belonging to a branch of the Gaṅga family. This Sanskrit composition works up the matter of a chornicle in artistic form. But, actually it is a *vaṁśāvalī*. This *rājavaṁśāvalī* is a history of the Gaṅga dynasty. According to the testimony of this record, the Eastern Gaṅgas ruled Kaliṅga for nearly a thousand year (AD 496-1435). The names of the kings of the Gaṅga dynasty who preceded and succeeded Anantavarman V are given therein with details of achievements of some of them. The details available in the chronicle, *Mādalā Pāñjī*, and the *vaṁśāvalī* about the Gaṅga kings up to about the middle of the twelfth century are almost similar. Some later additions are there in the latter. We are informed that about the middle of the thirteenth century Narasiṁha I had emerged as a popular legendary figure in Kaliṅga. 'He was a great general and builder of the splendid temple of the Sun at Konarka.' Anaṅgabhīma (AD 1211-38), a benevolent ruler, Bhānu, Kapilendra (AD 1435-66) a nobleman of Solar ancestry, and other rulers find mention in the said *vaṁśāvalī*. The names of rulers of the Gajapati dynasty and their deeds were further added to earlier genealogical details therein. Kapilendra's son and successor, Puruṣottama (AD 1466-97), is noted chiefly for his military exploits in the south as far as Tamil Deśa. His son and successor, Pratāparudra (AD 1497-1533), was a staunch follower of Caitanya cult of Vaiṣṇavism. He was patron of Caitanya who arrived at Purī in 1510 and stayed there for eighteen years or so. A fanciful story is narrated about the decision the king Pratāparudra took to suppress Buddhism in Kaliṅga. After his death his sons were murdered by the minister Govinda Vidyādhara who proclaimed himself king.[15]

The tradition of compiling and preserving the *vaṁśāvalī*s in Nepal (i.e., "Jambūdvīpe Bhāratakhaṇḍe Nepālrājye") was handed down from generation to generation or age to age. It is difficult to determine the antiquity of this tradition with precision and accuracy. Some *vaṁśāvalī*s in full still exist but parts of some old ones seem to have been lost. These records contain genealogies and chronology of kings of various dynasties with a few details, both mythical and historical. The lists of kings and the dates of their succession and duration of their reigns given therein are of exceptional value. The *vaṁśāvalī*s which have survived till date are all based on ancient collections with new versions. These include a *vaṁśāvalī* in Sanskrit (anonymous) probably written in AD 1350, the *Gopālarāja Vaṁśāvalī*,

15. Warder, *An Introduction to Indian Historiography*, pp. 133-38; for *Vaṁśāvalī* of Orissa see also *JASB*, vol. VI, pt. II, 1837, pp. 756ff; for chronology and History of Orissa see *As. Res.*, vol. XV, 1822.

a composite work in three parts, partly in Sanskrit and partly in old Newārī, apparently put together and supplemented in AD 1390 (preserved in the Darbar Library Kāṭhmāṇḍu, discovered by C. Bendall in the course of his journey in Nepal in 1884-85) and the *Parbatiyā Vaṁśāvalī* which was originally written in *parbatiyā* with an admixture of Sanskrit and Newārī.[16] The *Parbatiyā Vaṁśāvalī* in particular saw its different recensions. According to its Buddhist recension, it was translated in 1867 by Munshi Shiva Shankar Singh (attached to British Residency who lived in Nepal for almost thirty years) and Pandit Shri Gunananda (a native of Nepal residing at Paṭan whose ancestors for many generations have been compilers of this history).[17] The *vaṁśāvalī* texts (also called local chronicles) are authentic reocrds on the early history of Nepal to the twelfth century AD. Their earlier portion, no doubt, represents the coalescence of both myth and history but the dynastic accounts and other details which follow from the sixth century BC onwards are purely historical. The Gopāla dynasty founded by Nemuni first ruled over Nepal for about 521 years. This dynasty was supplanted by the Kirāta dynasty. According to the *vaṁśāvalī* tradition, 29 Kirāta kings ruled in the valley of Nepal. Their rule virtually commenced towards the beginning of the *Kali-yuga* and continued uninterruptedly until the beginning of the first century AD. It was during their rule that the Buddha and Aśoka made historic visits to Nepal. The latter is said to have founded the town of Lalitapaṭan and built four Buddhist shirnes there. After the appearance of the later Licchavis on the political stage of Nepal in the first century AD their sturggle with the Kirātas ensued for power and political supremacy which continued till the end of the third century AD. This period marked the beginning of the decline of the Kirātas' rule but not the disappearance or downfall of the Kirātas. According to the most reliable versions of the *vaṁśāvalī*s, in the early centuries of the Christian era Nepal was virtually ruled by the Licchavi dynasty. Jayadeva I is generally regarded as the real founder of this dynasty. The Licchavis ruled over Nepal from the first century AD down to the end of the eighth century. Candragupta II married the Licchavi princess, Kumāradevī, and brought under his sway all the frontier ruler of Nepal. During the period from the fifth century AD to the seventh century Nepal witnessed the vicissitude of its

---

16. Pt. Baladeva Prasad Mishra, *Nepal Kā Itihāsa* (Bombay, 1904), p. 45; Pt. Bhagawanlal Indraji, *Some considerations on the History of Nepal*; for his writings on the *Vaṁśāvalī*s of Nepal see *Ind. Ant.*, vol. XIII, pp. 411ff; Warder, *op. cit.*, pp. 88-94; D.R. Regmi, *Ancient Nepal* (Calcutta, 1969), p. 41; *Gopālarāja Vaṁśāvalī*, ed. by Regmi in his *Nepal: Medieval Period*, vol. III, pp. 112ff, 158ff; K.P. Jayaswal, "Chronology and History of Nepal, 600 BC to 800 AD", *JBORS*, vol. XXII, pt. III, 1936, pp. 157-264.

17. *History of Nepal*, ed. by Daniel Wright (Cambridge, 1877, rept. Kāṭhmāṇḍu, 1972) is totally based on the translation of the *Parbatiyā Vaṁśāvalī*.

political fortunes. According to the *vaṁśāvalī* tradition, a new Gupta dynasty was founded by Jayagupta. This dynasty ruled in Terāi area up to Janakapura, the earlier capital of the Videha Kingdom, from AD 500 to 625. The Licchavi and Gupta dynasties ruled over Nepal simultaneously. But their relationship was very hostile of which the Kirātas took advantage and attempted revive their position. Towards the close of the sixth century AD Aṁśuvarman, the minister of the Licchavi king, Śivadeva, founded the Ṭhākurī dynasty and ruled in the valley of Nepal for at least forty-five years. It was during his time that Nepal came under the suzerainty of Tibet. There was restoration of the Licchavi rule. After Mānadeva I, one of the most prominent Licchavi rulers, the Kirātas again tried to restore the fallen fortunes of their dynasty. But they were defeated by the Guptas. The Ābhiras, who were the feudal chiefs during the Licchavis' rule, also ruled for sometimes between the fifth and eighth century AD. But they were defeated by Aṁśuvarman. The Kirātas were finally overthrown by the Ābhira Guptas in the seventh century AD — the period which marked the end of the dynastic rule of the Kirātas in Nepal. We further learn the Nānyadeva, the Karṇāṭa chief of Tirhut, established his hegemony over Nepal sometime in the first half of the twelfth century.

It has been rightly said that "We are also under deep obligation to a great band of Indian writers — most of whose names are unknown to us — who have rendered eminent service to the cause of history chief among these are the compilers of the Vansavalis or genealogical rolls of the ancient rulers. From remote times it has been the custom in the royal and noble families of India to keep a careful record of their pedigree in a document called Vansavali which possesses an accuracy of historical record".[18]

The existence of historical chronicles in Kashmir, Gujarat, Orrisa and Sindh and the *vaṁśāvalī*s in Nepal testifies to the fact that the royal archives containing such records were maintained there. The chronicles and *vaṁśāvalī*s are very faithful records for the study of dynastic histories concerned.

The local chronicles and *vaṁśāvalī*s were futher composed in different parts of India in medieval period.

18. Hutchison and Vogel, *op. cit.*, pp. 2-3.

9

Historical Writings in South India

SOUTH India has had its own tradition of historiography. This tradition first began in Tamil Deśa in the age of the third Saṅgam. The three successive Saṅgams (academies of learned writers, poets and scholars) existed in three different cities. The authors of the Saṅgam age enjoyed liberal patronage of the kings. The seat of the third Saṅgam was the city of Madurā (present Madurāi), a centre of learning and capital of the Pāṇḍyas. The Pāṇḍya kings patronised the poets who produced poems on kings and their wars and other important historical events. The poets belonging to the age of the third Saṅgam made notable contributions in the field of historical writing. It must be noted here that the third Saṅgam on the whole covers the first three centuries of the Christian era, but it was the second century AD which marked the beginning of the tradition of historical writing in Tamil Deśa.

A number of works were produced in the second century AD by the poets of the third Saṅgam some of which are, of course, very important from a historical point of view. The earliest available work of considerable historical value composed in the second century AD in Tamil is the *Eṭṭuttogai* ("eight collections") which contains some poems of historical interest. It is a treasure-house of useful information about the life and culture of the Tamils of the early age. Of these eight, *Puranānụ̄ru* and *Padirruppattu* supply in the form of poetry valuable historical information. They deal with kings and their wars and other activities. *The Puranānūru* covers especially the Pāṇḍyas of Madurā and the Coḷas who ruled the tract to the north of them with their capitals at Uragapura (Uraiyur, near Trichinopoly) and Kāveripaddanam (Puhār). It is very helpful for collecting information about the political exploits of the kings of these two dynasties during the period. The *Padirruppattu* provides material for a more continuous dynastic history of two main lines of the Ceras (Keralas) on the west coast ruling from Tondi and Vañci early in the second century AD. According to this work, the Kongu region, i.e., the district of Coimbatore, was also ruled by the Ceras in the second century AD. It is also contains a reliable genealogy of the Cera kings of the Saṅgam age. Udiyanjeral was one of the prominent Cera kings who was succeeded by his son, Nedunjeral Adan. Seven other chiefs of this line are described in another group of poems. Another important ruler who is dealt with is Senguttuvan, the son of Nedunjeral Adan, Shose glory was sung by another poet named Paranar. The biographical accounts of Cera kings in the *Padirrupattu* highlighting especially their achievements are of exceptional value. Kapilar, a brāhmaṇa poet of the third Saṅgam, sang the glories of Cera prince, Selvakkadungo Vali Adan, who ruled in the second century AD. There are scattered references to historical subjects in the other collections of the aofresaid eight. The authors of the poems seem to be contemporary with the kings whose deeds they celebrate. In fact, the works of court-poets contain histoircal facts with poetic exaggeration.

The two other available historical classics of the third Saṅgam are the *Pattuppāṭṭu* ("ten idylls" or an anthology of ten poems, descriptive in nature) and the *Padineṇkizhk Kaṇakku* (an anthology of "eighteen minor works"). The former was composed in the second century AD and the latter in the second and third centuries AD.

Some parts of *Pattuppāṭṭu* relate to the Coḷa, Pāṇḍya and Cera kings. Of the ten poems, the two — *Porunārrārruppaḍai* by poet Muṭattāmakkaṇṇiyar and *Paṭṭinappālai* by poet Uruttiraṅ Kaṇṇanār — are very important. In both these poems, the Coḷa monarch, Karikāla (also called Karikālan), who ruled in the second century AD, finds mention. In the *Porunārrārruppaḍai*, he is described as having defeated the Pāṇḍya and the Cera kings and a number of minor chieftains allied with them in the battle of Veṇṇi (Kovil-Veṇṇi, near Tanjore). It is said that the Coḷa kingdom gained greatly both in territory and in influence during his reign. The old capital of the Coḷas was Uragapura, as noted before, and he founded his new capital named Kāveripaddanam. He seems to be the greatest of all the early Tamil kings known to us from the works of the Saṅgam period. In the *Paṭṭinappālai*, we find a remarkable description of the deeds of this Coḷa king especially of his economic reforms. Of the ten poems, the other two, *Maduraikkāñchi* (the longest one) by poet Māṅgudi Marudanār and *Neḍunalvāḍai* by poet Nakkirar, are devoted to the activities of the Pāṇḍya rulers of whom Neḍunjeliyan was the most famous. He ruled over the kingdom in the second century AD with his capital of Madurā. He is hero of both the poems. He is described particularly in the former as having achieved a glorious victory over the two kings of the Coḷa and Cera dynasties and also five other chieftains in the famous battle of Talaiyālaṅgānam (modern Talai-alam-Kādu, Tanjore district). Being a poet himself he was a great patron of learning. The above-mentioned four poems do contain biographical references but they are very scanty. The second ten of the said anthology was composed by Kummattur Kannanar on the Cera king Neḍunjeral Adan. The poet had focused on Neḍunjeral's war with the Coal ruler Valpah Tadakkai Peruvirarkilli in which both of them died.

The *Kalavazhi-nārpatu* (one of the said eighteen poems) by Poygaiyar is on one of the early Coḷa kings, Koccenganān or Senganān, describing a battle with a Cera king. The date of the event and of the poet who appears as a contemporary has not been established. The event and the poet both may resonably be assigned to the third century AD.

The *Śilappadikāraṁ* and the *Maṇimekalai*, the two epics composed in the age of the third Saṅgam, are of great historical importance.

The *Śilappadikāraṁ* was written by a Buddhist monk named Ilaṅgovaḍigal (also called Ilaṅko Adikal), brother of Cera king, Senguṭṭuvan, in the second century AD. The exploits of Senguṭṭuvan have been immortalised in the Tamil classic by his own monk-brother. Among the Cera kings in Kerala Senguṭṭuvan figures prominently. He appears to have been powerful potentate. He is said to have won several victories against the Coḷas and the Pāṇḍyas who were his political adversaries. He was a contemporary of the Coḷa king Karikāla and the Pāṇḍya king Neḍunjeliyan. This epic as well as the colophons added to the poem *Padirruppattu* (one of the eight collections, already mentioned here before) establish the contemporaneity of Senguṭṭuvan (*c.* AD 173-90), Karikāla and Gajabāhu I of Ceylon and thereby solve the problem relating to their chronology. Both these sources also confirm that Koṅgudeśa formed pact of the Cera kingdom in the second century AD.

The Tamil Saṅgam works provide us with some information regarding the kingdom of the Coḷas. Both legendary and historical figures appear in them. The works testify to the rule of several Coḷa princes. It is one of the baffling problems to settle their chronology and order of succession. The most prominent among the Coḷa rulers who are celebrated in the works of the third Saṅgam, including the *Śilappadikāraṁ*, are Ilanjeṭcenni and his son and successor, Karikāla, and Senganān.

The most celebrated Pāṇḍya king praised in several poems for his heroism is Neḍunjeliyan. In the *Śilappadikāraṁ,* he appears to have greatly increased the prestige and strength of the Pāṇḍyas by overpowering a formidable league of his enemies at Talaiyālaṅgānam. The prominent Pāṇḍya kings whose glories were sung by the poets of the third Saṅgam were Neḍunjeliyan and his remote ancestor, Mudukudumi. The Pāṇḍya kingdom and its capital Madurā are elaborately described in the poems of the Saṅgam age. Many kings, who were contemporaries of Neḍunjeliyan, and their achievements have also been touched upon by the poets of the Saṅgam age. From the epic it appears that the Pāṇḍyas belonged to the Lunar dynasty.

The *Maṇimekalai* by a Buddhist poet named Sittalai Sāttanār, who is supposed to have been a merchant from Madurā and contemporary and friend of Ilangovaḍigal (author of the *Śilappadikaram*), is also not devoid of historical contents. The author mentions the legendary expeditions of the Cera King Senguṭṭuvan as far as the Ganges and the Coḷa realm. His prologue also refers to the Coḷas as a solar dynasty. The works shows the ascendency of Buddhism but tolerance of other region, viz., Jainism, Ājīvakism and Lokāyata. It yields valuable information about ancient Tamil society.

The Tamil Saṅgam works of the second and third centuries AD including the epics and other anthologies throw light on many obscure aspects of contemporary political history of the Coḷas, Ceras and Pāṇḍyas. They yield us valuable information about the frequent wars which took place among the Coḷa, Cera and Pāṇḍya kings during the period for political supremacy and expansion of the frontiers of their respective kingdom and the resultant chages in the boundaries of their territories. We also learn from the works of the third Saṅgam that there were several chieftains who either owed allegiance to these kings and fought for them or maintained and independent existence ruling over small principalities. There were also feudatories of one or the other of these kings. The glories and prosperity of the capital towns of chieftains and those of the extensive Coḷa and Pāṇḍya kingdoms have been sung by the poets of the third Saṅgam in their respective poem with some historical accuracy. The works contains trustworthy information about other aspects of the life of the Tamils in the early centuries of Christian era.

There are some historical references in the Saṅgam classics to commercial intercourse of the Coḷas with the Greeks (called Yavanas) and the Romans which can further be confirmed by the evidences furnished in the *Periplus* by an unknown Greek merchant of the first century AD and the *Geography* of Ptolemy who flourished about the middle of the second century AD. The Coḷas carried on their trade with these two foreign countries during the period from their famous port, Kāveripaddanam (Kāveripaṭṭanam), situated at the mouth of the Kāverī river. There are some other historical material in the classics of the third Saṅgam relating to the socio-economic life of the Tamils.

The Saṅgam literature appears to be partly historical. It is very useful for the purpose of reconstructing socio-economic, political and religious history of the Tamils of the Saṅgam age. The works of the Saṅgam period despite containing historical truths possess all the defects of court poetry. While critically estimating the historical value of the classical works of the third Saṅgam we find that they are deficient in internal evidence of chronology and coherence and continuity in the presentation of the subject-matter. There are biographical information, though sketchy and scanty.

Some works which include mainly the biographies of quasi-historical nature were produced between the eleventh and thirteenth century AD. The historiography of the Coḷas during the period deserves special mention here. The *Rājarājacarita* or *Rājarājavijaya* on a great Coḷa monarch, Rājarāja I (*c.* AD 985-1014), and the *Kulottuṅgacolacarita* by one Tirunārāyaṇa on the Coḷa ruler, Kulottuṅga I (*c.* AD 1070-1118), were the two importanct biographical works but unfortunately they fell into oblivion after the collapse of the Coḷa dynasty. Both these works are believed to have been contemporary with their heroes. Jayagoṇḍan (better known as Jayaṅkoṇḍān) who flourished in the time of Kulottuṅga I (or in *c.* AD 1100) wrote the *Kaliṅgattupparani* (a Tamil war poem) which describes at length the victory of Kulottuṅga I over the Eastern Gaṅga king Anantavarman Chodagaṅga (*c.* AD 1077-1147) of Kaliṅga in second Kaliṅga war which took place in about AD 1112. It also gives us a lot of useful information about the Coḷa genealogy. The work was written towards the end of the reign of said Coḷa king to celebrate his victories. By this time the practice of writing *praśasti* or composing song in praise of the king and genealogy of the king and achievements of his predecessor had become popular. Oṭṭakkūttan graced the courts of the three successive Coḷa emperors, Vikrama (*c.* AD 1118-33), Kulottuṅga II (*c.* AD 1133-47) and Rājarāja II (*c.* AD 1147-62) and composed poems on all of them. These include a war poem (*parani*) on Vikrama (about his Kaliṅga war) and peace poems (*ulās*) on all three. The *ulās* provide accounts of the achievements of the kings and of their predecessors with some exaggerations. The *Vikrama-Śolan-Ulās* not only highlights the deeds of Vikrama and the events which took place during his reign but also records and few interesting points bearing on earlier Coḷa history including the legend of Karikālan and an account of expedition of Kulottuṅga I deep into the realm of western Cālukya. The *Kuottuṅga-Śolan-Ulās Rājarāja-Śolan-Ulās* are on Kulottuṅga II and Rājarāja II who were immediate successors of Vikrama. The power of the Coḷas appears to have rapidly declined under them. Besides these three *ulās*, Oṭṭakūttan wrote also a *Pillaittamil* on Kulottuṅga II which is populary known as *Kulottuṅgan-Pillaittamil*. The historical significance of *parani*, *ulās*, and *pillaittamil* cannot be questioned. These are basically biographical works which can be utilised for the study of the history of the Imperial Coḷas. The *Colavaṁśacaritaṁ* (whose author's name is not known to us) is more or less a dynastic history of the Coḷas. It contains the description of sixteen Coḷa kings of the Solar race who ruled the kingdom with its capital at Tanjāvur (Tanjore). The authencity of the information contained in some of the works, particularly about the wars and conquests of the kings, can be proved by the inscriptional records of the Coḷa period.

The *Bṛhadīśvarmāhātmya* (a *Sthala Purāṇa*) in Sanskrit of the later period also describes the history of the sixteen Coḷa kings and their capital Tanjore. The *Maduraittalavaralaru* (in Tamil) describes the history of the great Madurā temple. The *Nandikkalambakam* (a poem in Tamil) is on the Pallava king, Nandīvarman III (*c.* AD 844-66), who ruled the kingdom with its capital at Kāñcī. The work was composed by his court-poet (anonymous) to celebrate the victory of his royal patron over the Paṇḍyas who at the beginning of his reign tried to conquer his kingdom. Nandīvarman after having defeated the Pāṇḍyas, who were the traditional opponents of his house, recovered the territories conquered by them. But towards the close of his reign he was defeated by the Pāṇḍyas, and died soon after, sometime in AD 866. The said work is only evidence of historical writing on any Pallava king so far as ancient period is concerned.

The *Avantīsundarīkathā* of Daṇḍin (*c.* AD 635-700), who flourished at the court of Narasiṁhavarman II, the Pallava king of Kāñcī, towards the end of the seventh century AD (695-700), throw valuable sidelight on the history and culture of south India during the sixth and seventh centuries.

The *Periyapurāṇam* (in seventy-two cantos) of Sekkilār or Sekkizhār (twelfth century) is important for social and religious history of Tamil Deśa from the seventh to the twelfth centuries AD. The author in his work describes the lives of sixty-three Śaiva saints called Nāyanmāras (of the seventh and eighth centuries) who belonged to different castes and classes and also social customs and religious beliefs and practices of the people during the period. The religious works appearing from about the seventh century AD like *Devāram*, *Tiruvācakam* and *Tiruvaymol* are important for Śaivism, Vaiṣṇavism, Jainism and Buddhism.

The Tamil literature is, no doubt, of great value as a source for the early hostory of Tamil Deśa.[1]

1. For historiography in Tamil Deśa (Ancient period) see also Warder, *An Introduction to Indian Historiography*, pp. 100-7; J.P. De Souza and C.M. Kulkarni (ed.), *Historiography in Indian Languages*, pp. 88-96, 254-56; S.N. Padmanabhan, "Historical Biographies in Tamil Literature", in Sen (ed.), *Historical Biography in Indian Literature*, pp. 315-26; K.G. Sesha Aiyar, *Cera kings of the Sangam Period* (London, 1937); V.R.R. Dikshitar, *Studies in Tamil Literature and History* (London, 1930); *The Śilappadikāram* by V.R.R. Dikshitar (Oxford, 1939); *Maṇi-Mekhalai in its Historical Setting* by S.K. Aiyangar; S.K. Aiyangar, *The Beginnings of South Indian* →

The tradition of historical writing in Karṇāṭa Deśa (Karṇāṭaka) seems to have been maintained right from ancient times. The *Mayūravarmacarita* (in prose in verse consisting of eight chapers) of unknown date and authorship is a biographical history of king Mayūraśarman (also called Mayūravarman), who founded the Kadamba dynasty of Jayantīpura (Banavāsī) in Karṇāṭaka about the middle of the fourth century AD. It is an established fact that he set-up an independent kingdom with its capital at Banavāsī and ruled in the third quarter of the fourth century AD. It is striking to note that some of the legends mentioned in the work concerning the king stands in comparison with a more sober account found in an inscription of the time of his great grandson (latter half of the fifth century AD). The work was presumably composed by a contemporary writer of the king or by someone else towards the close of the fifth century AD. The *Parijātaharan* (in ten cantos) of Karivāja, a court poet of Kāmadeva, one of the later Kadamba princes, is another important work. The poet in his work informs us that this king ruled over the province of Haṅgal (Dhārwāḍa district), Banavāsī and Puligere. He was a feudatory of the later western Cālukya king Someśvara IV (*c*. AD 1181-1219), and began to rule about AD 1182. The city of Haṅgal was besieged by the Hoysala king Vīra-Ballāla II (*c*. AD 1173-1220) and after some vicissitude the Kadambas were completely subjugated and their territory annexed. The latter history has not been covered in the details provided in the work.

The Kannaḍa work, *Vaḍḍārādhane* of Śivakoṭi, which is said to have been written in *c*. AD 920, throws light on social, religious and administrative condition in Karṇāṭa Deśa in the ninth and early tenth centuries AD. The work also contains nineteen Jain stories reflecting upon the doctrine of Jainism.

The biographical works (in Kannaḍa) of three celebrated Jain poets, Pampa, Ponna and Ranna, of the tenth century AD deserve special notice.

Pampa, the most eminent among the ancient Kannaḍa poets, wrote *Ādi Purāṇa* and *Vikramārjuna Vijaya* (also known as *Pampa Bhārata*) in 941 or 942 under the patronage of Arikeśarī II (or Vemulavada), a feudatory ruler of the Rāṣṭrakūṭa king Indra III (*c*. AD 914-22). In his first work, Pampa relates the history of R̥ṣabha the first Jain *tīrthaṅkara*. His second work is indeed *Arikeśarī Vijaya* since he highlights his heroic deeds. Pampa was not only a court poet but also a general of Arikeśarī. As a fighter he took part in

→ *History* (Madras, 1918); K.A.N. Śāstrī, *The Colas*, vol. I (Madras, 1925); vol. II, pt. I (Madras, 1937); *The Pāṇḍyan Kingdom* (London, 1929); R. Gopalan, *History of the Pallavas* of *Kāñcī* (Madras, 1928).

many battles of his patron. He was highly impressed by his patron's bravery, magnanimity and benevolent character. He was an eye-witness to the brave deeds and other marvellous feats of action of Arikeśarī in the battles. In compliance with the wish of his patron to get all the significant events of his life recorded, he composed the work as a memoir of the former. He identifies Arikeśarī with Arjuna, the hero of the *Mahābhārata*. The work contains several details of military organisation, weapons and warfare, etc. In the beginning of the work, the author gives the genealogy of Arikeśarī which is his pedigree for the last seven preceding generations. Its accuracy can be tested on the basis of the inscriptional records of the time. He has furnished a reliable account of various campaigns of Arikeśarī in which he also took part. He tells us that Arikeśarī was a valiant warrior and actively participated in the campaigns of his imperial lords, the Rāṣṭrakūṭas. He gives "Certain interesting details regarding the northern campaign of Indra III, in which Arikeśarī had taken part. Later, Arikeśarī fought with king Govinda IV (*c.* AD 923-36), son of Indra III and gave refuge to one Bijja, who had come to Vemulavada to save his life from the wrath of Govinda. He finally refused to accept suzerainty of Govinda, led a war against him and secured the Rāṣṭrakūṭa throne to Baddega, the brother of Indra".

The poet also informs us about the matrimonialities between the two families, those of Arikeśarī and the imperial Rāṣṭrakūṭas. He has thrown sidelight on the contemporary society. He has portrayed the vivid picture of the existing social system. He refers to the caste system but disapproves its rigidity. The Brāhmaṇical sacrifices also received his notice. The woman occupied a honourable position in the society. The institution of *gaṇikās* had flourished. The prostitution also appears to have existed. Its condemnation by Arikeśarī is well attested by the poet. He has touched upon many other aspects of contemporary history. He has provided a genuine historical account of the incidents which took place during the period. The facts are recorded without any exaggeration. The evidence adduced in the work about important events of Arikeśarī's time is corroborated by his Vemulavada inscription dated AD 927 and Parabharani copper-plates of his grandson, Arikeśarī III, dated AD 966.[2]

Ponna, the court poet of the Rāṣṭrakūṭa king Kṛṣṇa III (*c.* AD 939-68), wrote *Bhuvanaika Rāmābhyudaya* which contains, besides the events of his patron's time, many contemporary historical details. His other work, *Śānti Purāṇa*, deals with the

2. See H.V.S. Murthy, "Historical Biography in Kannada Literature", in Sen (ed.), *op. cit.*, 342-44; De Souza and Kulkarni (ed.), *op. cit.*, pp. 125ff.

traditional story of Śāntinātha, sixteenth Jain *tīrthaṅkara*. Ranna, who flourished towards the end of the tenth century, continued the tradition of his two predecessors. He was the court poet of the Western Cālukya ruler of Kalyāṇī, Satyāśraya (*c.* AD 997-1008), the son of Tailapa II (*c.* 973-97). He wrote *Sāhasabhīma Vijaya* in *c.* AD 1000 to glorify the achievements of his patron, Satyāśraya. The poet in his work mentions that Satyāśraya took part in the wars his father fought with the Śilāhāras of Koṅkaṇ and the Gurjaras futher north. These campaigns as recorded by the poet are supported by the contemporary inscriptions. The poet identifies his patron with the hero Bhīma and gives him the tiltle Śāhasa Bhīma. The work is of some help to us for tracing the relationship between the early Western Cālukyas of Vātāpī (Bādāmī) and the later Western Cālukyas of Kalyāṇī. We are told by the poet that the latter descended from the former, but this is doubted by some scholars. 'This connection was, however, known to Ranna, but the genealogy that he gives in his wok differs materially from what we get in the inscriptions that come slightly later.'[3] The poet also throws some light though in an incidental manner on contemporary social life. His other work, *Ajit Purāṇa* (composed in 993) deals with the history of Ajita, the second Jain *tīrthaṅkara*.

Pampa and Ranna in their respective works, *Vikramārjuna Vijaya* and *Sāhasabhīma Vijaya*, "the two earliest historical biographies in Kannaḍa literature",[4] deal with the life and achievements of their patrons. The works of these two authors inspired the later writers to carry forward the tradition of composing biographies of historical personages.

Durgasiṁha, the court poet of the Cālukya king of Kalyāṇī, Jayasiṁha II Jagadekamalla (*c.* AD 1016-42), wrote *Pañcatantra* in 1031 which throws a good deal of light on the social, religious and political life of the people during the period. Nāgacandra, popularly known as Abhinava Pampa, wrote *Mallinātha Purāṇa* about the beginning of the twelfth century AD describing the life of Mallinātha, the nineteenth Jain *tīrthaṅkara*. About AD 1140, Karnaparya wrote, besides other works, *Neminātha Purāṇa* depicting the life of Neminātha, the twenty-second Jain *tīrthaṅkara*. Achaṇṇa, a Jain poet of the twelfth century AD, wrote *Vardhamāna Purāṇa* which is a biography of Vardhamāna Mahāvīra, the last (twenty-fourth) Jain *tīrthaṅkara*. In AD 1222, Pārśva Paṇḍita wrote *Pārśvanātha Purāṇa* which deals with the life and achievements of Pārśvanātha, the twenty-third Jain *tīrthaṅkara*. Janna wrote *Anantanātha Purāṇa* on the life and teachings of Anantanātha, the fourteenth Jain *tīrthaṅkara*. These Kannaḍa works have considerable historical value. Many other works on Jain *tīrthaṅkaras* were further composed in the

3. Murthy, *op. cit.*, p. 344; see also De Souza and Kulkarni, *op. cit.*

4. Murthy, *op. cit.*

thirteenth and fourteenth centuries.

Cāmuṇḍarāya, a devout Jain and minister and general of the Western Gaṅga king, Rājamalla IV (*c.* AD 977-85), wrote *Triṣaṣṭi-lakṣaṇa-mahāpurāṇa*, popularly known as *Cāmuṇḍarāya Purāṇa* (in prose), in 978 which contains full biographical accounts of all the twenty-four Jain *tīrthaṅkaras*. This work is very important for the history of Jainism. It also depicts the lives of sixty-three *śalākā-puruṣas* (great men). It is worthy of note that the Western Gaṅgas (so-called to distinguish them from the Eastern Gaṅgas of Kaliṅga) ruler over a large part of Mysore, called after them Gaṅgavāḍī. They were great supporters of Jainism.

The Hoysala historiography also deserves our notice. The Hoysalas for all practical purposes ruled Mysore and adjacent lands with Dvārasamudra (Halebid) as their capital. Their rule virtually began in the early part of the eleventh century AD and continued till about the beginning of the fifth decade of the fourteenth century AD. It appears that they had preserved some records of historical importance with them. They described themselves in their records as *"yādavakulatilaka"* or "kṣatriyas of the lunar race". Vidyācakravartin III, a court poet of Vīra-Ballāla III (*c.* AD 1291-1342), while giving the genealogy of the Hoysala kings in the first canto (historical introductory) of his epic poem, *Rukmiṇīkalyāṇa* (in sixteen cantos), has also associated them with the Yādava *kula* or family.

There were three poets bearing the name Vidyācakravartin in the courts of the Hoysala Kings. Vidyācakravartin I, the court poet of Vīra-Ballāla II (*c.* AD 1173-1220), was author of many poetic inscriptions, engraved on stone during the reign of his patron.

The *Gadyakarṇāmṛta* of Vidyācakravartin II is an incomplete biography (*ākhyāyikā*) of the Hoysala king, Someśvara (*c.* AD 1234-62), as it does not cover the entire details of his reign. The reason why the author could not incorporate all the events of the life of the king in his work is not known to us. The events described in the biography took place during the reign of his father, Narasiṁha II (*c.* AD 1220-34). The author calls himself 'a new Bāṇa' and closely follows the model of *Harṣacarita*. He describes in detail the battle that took place at Śrīraṅgam (called Mahendramaṅgalam) between Narasiṁha II and the Pāṇḍya king, Māravarman Sundara (*c.* AD 1216-38), about a year before Someśvara's accession to the throne in AD 1234. The author says that the rivalry between the Pāṇḍya king and the Coḷa king, Rājarāja III (*c.* AD 1216-52) (then a vessel of the Hoysala emperor) resulted in a battle between the Pāṇḍya and the Hoysala kings. What the author says is a historical truth. As narrated by the author, the Pāṇḍya king Sundara invaded the Coḷa territory and defeated Rājarāja III. The latter fled and tried to reach the central Hoysala territory (described in the work as Kuntala) for seeking the protection of Narasiṁha but was intercepted by the Kādava chieftain, Kopperuñjinga (called Nijahu) of the Pallava ancestry and an ally of Sundara, and then captured and imprisoned in the fortress of Jayantamaṅgalam (Sendamaṅgalam, South Arcot district). On hearing this news the Hoysala prince Narasiṁha II hurriedly marched down into the Tamil territories and sent his army to Jayantamaṅgalam who defeated and slew the Kādava chief and set Rājarāja III free and then attacked the Pāṇḍya army at Śrīraṅgam (the place of the battle) and routed them. Thereafter the peace was concluded, and the Pāṇḍyas as well as the Coḷas became the tributary vassals to Narasiṁha II (also called Kuntaleśvara) who thus sought to establish a balance between the two main Tamil dynasties and maintain his hegemony or hold his sway over the whole region. The fall of the Pāṇḍyas and the revival of the Coḷas as recorded in the work are corroborated by the inscriptions of the Hoysalas. The author further relates that Someśvara was married to a princess Devikā, granddaughter of a king of Gurjara (Vallabha king of Gujarat). The ceremony was performed after Narasiṁha's victory. Someśvara was installed by his father as a ruler of the central part of the Tamil region strategically situated between the Pāṇḍya, Coḷa and Kādava domains. It appears that he began to rule from 1233, a year before he became the virtual emperor after the death of his father. The author concludes his biography with the attainment of royal fortune by Someśvara.[5] This biographical work appears to have been composed either much ahead of the end of Someśvara's reign or note much later than his accession. The information available in the standard works on ancient Indian history and the epigraphic records of the Hoysalas relating to the events concerned go to prove the historical accuracy of the statements of the author of the work. This is the reason why this work is regarded as historical.

"Works on Hoysala history continued to be written for centuries after the dynasty came to an end apparently based on various surviving records and on tradition." The *Hoysalarājavijaya* and *Hoysalarājakulavaṁśa* are the two notable examples of such work. This shows the continuity in historical tradition of Karṇāṭa Deśa. The *Sthala Purāṇas* describe the places of historical significance including those which formed parts of the Hoysala empire during the imperial rule.

5. See also Warder, *op. cit.*, pp. 116-18; M. Krishnamachariar, *HCSL*, pp. 477-78.

Āndhra Deśa is one of those parts of south India which has had the distinction of preserving the records of historical value from very early times.

The kings of different dynasties ruled different parts of Āndhra Deśa in ancient times and later. The Sātavāhanas were the first to rule it. They ruled in the Kṛṣṇā-Godāvarī region from the first century BC to the close of the first quarter of the third century AD. The dynasty of the Sātavāhana was supplanted by that of the Ikṣvāku founded by Cāṁtamūla or Śāntamūla I. He ruled in the lower Kṛṣṇā valley in the second quarter of third century AD. The records of his son, Vīrapuruṣadatta, have been found at the three famous Buddhist sites, Amarāvatī, Jagayyapeṭa and Nāgārjunakoṇḍa, which are very important for the history of the Ikṣvāku family in general and growth of Buddhism in particular. This is the earliest evidence of preservation of historical records in Āndhra Deśa.

A Śaiva poet, Nannecoḍu (*c*. AD 1150), in his *Kumāra Sambhavamu* (in twelve cantos in the form of *campu*, i.e., partly in prose and partly in verse) has presented a historical account of struggle of Vijayāditya II (*c*. AD 799-847) and Vijayāditya III Guṇaga (*c*. AD 848-92), the two Eastern Cālukya kings of Veṅgī (modern Peddavegi near Ellore), with the Rāṣṭrakūṭa king, Amoghavarṣa I (*c*. AD 814-78), for political supremacy. Vijayāditya II is said to have fought 108 battles in course of his prolonged struggle with the Rāṣṭrakūṭas, the Gaṅgas, and other contemporary powers extending over twelve years. He achieved victories against the Rāṣṭrakūṭas towards the close of his career. Ultimately the Rāṣṭrakūṭa king, Amoghavarṣa, defeated the Eastern Cālukya army and reasserted his supremacy over Veṅgī. The traditional hostilities between the Eastern Cālukyas and the Rāṣṭrakūṭas further continued during the time of Vijayāditya III, the most powerful ruler of the dynasty. Vijayāditya III obtained a glorious victory over the combined forces of Rāṣṭrakūṭa king Kṛṣṇa II (*c*. AD 875-911 or 878-914) and Kalacūri 'Śaṅkaragaṇa' (Kokalla I of Tripurī, father-in-law of the latter) at the battle of Kiraṇapura (Bālāghāṭ), burnt Achalapura (Ellichpur), and overan the Rāṣṭrakūṭa kingdom. The work also deals with Vīraśaivism, the popular form of religion in Āndhra in twelfth century. The historicity of the information supplied by the author of the work is well proven. Nannaya's *Mahābhāratamu* written in AD 1030 in *campu* style at the instance of his patron Rājarāja Narendra, the Eastern Cālukya monarch of Veṅgī (*c*. AD 1018-60), is another literary work of historical importance. It gives a vivid and true picture of contemporary Āndhra Deśa. It gives the genealogy of the Eastern Cālukyas with a description of their capital Veṅgī.[6] These two works in Telugu are authentic sources of information regarding socio-

6. See also De Souza and Kulkarni, *op. cit.*, pp. 60-61.

religious and political history of Āndhra Deśa during the period. They are of invaluable aid for the historians.

The tradition of historiography further continued during the Kākatiya period. The Kākatiya ruler, Prola II (also called Prolarāja), himself used to preserve records of important happenings. One of his records is dated in the Cālukya-Vikrama *Saṁvat* 42 = AD 1117-18, which is the date of his accession. The seat of Kākatiya government at that time was Anmakoṇḍa (Hanamkoṇḍa). From the time of Gaṇapati (1198-99) onwards Oruṅgallu (Warangal) continued to be the capital of the Kākatiyas till the end of their rule in 1323. One of the Śaiva poets, Pālakuriki Somanātha (*c*. 1200- 40) of the Kākatiya period, was the author of twenty-five works. He wrote in Telungu, Kannaḍa and Sanskrit. His two major works, *Basava Purāṇamu* and *Paṇḍitārādhyacaritra*, are the biographies of the two Śaiva prophets, Basaveśvara and Paṇḍitārādhya, respectively. The works are important for the religious history of Āndhra Deśa during the twelfth and thirteenth centuries. The *Raṅganātha Rāmāyaṇam* in Telungu by Gona Buddha Reḍḍi (*c*. 1200-50) is a work of considerable importance for the history of the 'Gona Haihaye' dynasty in Teleṅgānā, subordinate to the Kākatiyas.

The historiographical tradition in Kerala began in the eleventh century AD with the composition of *Muṣikavaṁśa* (a dynastic history of the Muṣikas) by Atula.

The *Muṣikavaṁśa* (an epic consisting of fifteen cantos) was composed by the poet Atula in the time of Śrīkaṇṭha, his contemporary and the last king of the Muṣika dynasty. It is one of the historical works of early south India. The poet in his work narrates the history of the kings who ruled over the Muṣika kingdom in the northern part of Kerala. Rāmaghaṭa was one of the prominent rulers of this dynasty. Several cantos are devoted to his life and achievements. He is said to have killed Mādhavavarman, the king of Magadha, in a battle and married his daughter Bhadragenā. He installed the son of Mādhavavarman on the throne of Magadha. Rāmghaṭa had two sons. The elder Vatu was made king of Māhiṣmatī (called Haihaya Deśa) and the younger Nandana king of the Coḷa kingdom. A brief description of all the kings from Nandana down to Īśānavarman II appears in Canto XI. But in absence of their synchronisms it is not possible to get an absolute chronology for the more historical part of Atula's work mentioning a few notable events such as wars with the Pallavas, the founding of temples, etc. There seems to be a historical basis for most of the events described in this canto. The records and traditions of the temples which cherished the memories of certain kings as their founders also appear to have been the sources of information for Atula. He may have utilised them along with the dynastic lists preserved in the royal archives for the purpose concerned. Canto XII appears more historical than the earlier ones. It deals with the activities of fifteen kings of the dynasty in a continuous and more detailed manner. Īśānavarman II married a princess of the Kalacūri family ruling in the Dāhala region on the upper Narmadā and also claiming descent from the ancient Haihayas. "It does not seem likely that he could interfere much in Kalacuri politics, with the Rāṣṭrakūṭa empire dominating the vast region between the two small kingdoms, yet Atul credits him with an expedition there to instate his father-in-law. He was then enagaged in a war with the king of Kerala (i.e. the central region of Kerala, round Vānci or Mahodaya of early medieval period) who was his borther-in-law, but eventually the two were reconciled and concluded peace. Aftereards Isānavarman married a Coḷa princess who produced an heir to the throne."

From the time of king Validhara (Īśānavarman's grandson via the Kalacūri princess) the dynasty switched over to the matriarchal system of succession, characteristic of medieval Kerala. Validhara repulsed an invasion by the Gaṅgas (of Talkāḍ or Talavanapura in the Mysore district of Karṇāṭaka) from beyond the mountains which formed his inland frontier. We are further told that his nephew Vikramarāma protected the famous Buddhist temple at Mūlavāsa from the waves of the ocean by erecting a sea wall. Of Jayamāni II it is noted that there was religious toleration in the kingdom of the Muṣikas during his reign. The poet elucidates that there was perfect harmony among the followers of opposite doctrines. Cantos XIII and XIV describe the events which took place during the reign of Valabha II, rephew of Jayamāni III. In Canto XIV, it is clearly stated that Jayamāni sent Valabha II as heir-apparent with an army to join the king of Kerala in opposing the advance of Coḷa king towards Kerala. It is most likely that the Coḷa king referred to in the text was Rājendra I (*c*. AD 1014-44). While marching to the south, Valabha learnt of Jayamāni's death and of usurpation of the throne. Valabha II was succeeded by his younger brother, Śrīkaṇṭha, whose prosperous reign is described in the fifteenth and last canto of the work.[7] The credit goes to the author of the work for saving the history of the Muṣika kingdom from passing into obscurity by recording and preserving it.

In Kerala, except the *Muṣikavaṁśa* no other historical work worth the name was ever composed in ancient period as far as our knowledge goes.

The preceding works as a whole are very useful for throwing light on various phases and facets of ancient and early medieval history of South India.

7. Warder, *op. cit.*, pp. 110-12, *HSCL*, p. 170.

10

Traditional Chronology

CHRONOLOGY is an inseparable part of history. The former is not only an eye but also the backbone of the latter. Highlighting the importance of chronology in the context of historiography, P.K. Gode said: 'Wrong chronology produced wrong history and want of chronology produced no history.'[1] While dealing with history of historical writing in ancient India we cannot keep aside the chronology. The ancient Indians had maintained both historical and chronological traditions. Different systems of chronology seem to have been followed by the Hindus, Buddhists and Jains. The statement made by Sir Willian Jones in 1788 that the chronological system of the Hindus is neither authentic nor systematic[2] is no longer valid. John Bentley, while writing on the eras and dates of the ancient Hindus in 1796, also observed that "the confusion and darkness that prevade the Hindu chronology" may precisely be attributed to the "Ignorance of modern Hindus who are not able to discern the difference between the several eras and modes of dating which were made use of by their ancient historians. Brahmans and poets in recording past events have blended the whole together into one mass of absurdity and contradiction. It is not easy to describe the meaning of all the different modes of dating formerly in use".[3] His observation was obviously an attempt to prove that the chronological method applied by the ancient Hindu historians of India is not easy to be understood because of its certain intricacies. But his attempt proved to be a failure. It is unworthy of credence that "the chronology has been disturbed by the scholars of the Brāhmaṇical historical schools". The statement of celebrated American Sanskrit scholar, W.D. Whitney, that "All dates given in Indian literary history are pins set up to be bowled down again"[4] is

---

1. Cf. S.R. Tikekar, *On Historiography*, p. 52
2. "On the Chronology of the Hindus", *As. Res.*, vol. 2 (Delhi, 1979), pp. 111-12; see also Buhler, "Hindu Chronology", in *En. Br.*, vol. 13 (211th edn.), pp. 499-500.
3. "On the Principal Eras and Dates of the Ancient Hinuds", *As. Res.*, vol. 5 (Delhi, 1979), p. 315.
4. Cf. Winternitz, *HIL*, vol. I, p. 25; Tikekar, *op. cit.*

also not tenable. There is, however, some scope to reexamine the authencity of traditional chronology.

There were three traditions of chronology — Purāṇic, Buddhist and Jain.

We shall first begin with Purāṇic tradition. The regnal years of the kings of various dynasties of the post-Bhārata war period or so-called *Kali* age and the total duration of each dynastic rule are given in the Purāṇas (*Vāyu*, *Viṣṇu*, *Matsya*, *Brahmāṇḍa* and *Bhāgavata*) which are helpful for chronological computation to fix the dates of the end of one dynasty and the beginning of the other and determine the reign-periods of the rulers and the dynasties.

The length of reign of all twenty-two kings of the Bṛhadratha dynasty who ruled over Magadha are given separately in the Purāṇas[5] with some variations. After having accepted the figures which appear reasonable we find that they altogether ruled approximately for 638 years. The length of reign of all five kings (from Pradyota to Avantīvardhana) of Pradyota dynasty who ruled Avantī kingdom are also given in the Purāṇas. They are said to have ruled for 138 years.[6] According to our calculation, they ruled either for 100 or 102 years (*c*. 513-413 or 411 BC).

The regnal years of kings of following six Magadhan dynasties are also given in the Purāṇas with total duration of rule of each dynasty.

The length of reign of all ten kings belonging to the dynasties of Bimbisāra and Śiśunāga are given with variations. It appears that they altogether ruled for 303, 360 or 362 years.[7] The total duration of their rule has gone high because of some bombastic or inflated figures. And this is the reason why it is not taken as trustworthy. It is generally believed that they ruled for not more than two hundred years. The nine Nandas are said to have ruled for 40 or 100 years.[8] In reality, only two of them, the first (Mahāpadmananda, the founder of the dynasty) and the last (Dhanananda) were the reigning kings. We can reasonably assign twenty-two years to them, and accordingly *c*. 343-321 BC can be taken as their reign-period. According to Purāṇic tradition, a period of 1050 years had elapsed between the birth of Parīkṣit and the coronation of Mahāpadmananda[9] which is sheet-

5. *Vy*., 99, 294-308; *Vṣn*., IV, 23, 1-13; *Mts*., 271, 18-30; *Bmd*., 3, 74, 107-21; *Bhāg*., IX, 22, 46-49.
6. *Vy*., 99, 308-14; *Vṣn*., IV, 24, 1-8; *Mts*, 272, 1-5; *Bmd*., 3, 74, 121-25; *Bhāg*., XII, 1, 2-4.
7. *Vy*., 99, 314-21; *Vṣn*., IV, 24, 9-19; *Mts*., 272, 5-3; *Bmd*., 3, 74, 127-33; *Bhāg*., XII, 1, 5-7.
8. *Vy*., 99, 321-28; *Vṣn*., IV, 24, 20-24; *Mts*., 272, 14-21; *Bmd*., 3, 74, 139-44; *Bhāg*., XII, I, 8-11.
9. *Vy*., 9, 415; *Vṣn*., IV, 24, 104; *Mts*., 273, 36; see also *Bmd*., 3, 74, 225-30; *Bhāg*., XII, 2, 26-32.

anchor of ancient Indian chronology. This figure is applied in various ways to fix the date of Great Bhārata battle. For instance, some scholars taking *c* 350 BC as the date of coronation of Mahāpadmananda fix (1050 + 350) 1400 BC as the date of the battle.

Max Müller's statements that "Everything in Indian chronology depends on the date of Chandragupta. . . . All the dates before him are to be considered only as hypothetical",[10] and the observation made by E.M. Elphinstone in 1839 that in ancient Indian history no date before the invasion of Alexander the Great (*c.* 326 BC) can be fixed with absolute certainty[11] contain some substratum of truth. V.A. Smith also for sometime went on harping on the same tune,[12] but later he himself admitted that "The researches of multitude of scholars and antiquarians have rendered it possible to fix the considerable number of dates in pre-Alexandrian period (extending from *c.* 600 BC to 326 BC) with approximate accuracy as well as to reconstruct the obscure history of ancient India . . . with the help of literary tradition".[13]

There is no denying fact that all the dates in ancient Indian history of pre-Bimbisāra period are either hypothetical or tentative but the dates of some kings of pre-Maurya dynasties of Magadha fixed on the basis of Purāṇic length of their reigns are reliable. It is true that the date of coronation of Candragupta Maurya can be taken as the starting point for calculating the Indian chronology.

The Purāṇas have provided authentic chronology of the Mauryas, Śuṅgas and Kaṇvas on the basis of which the reign-period of each individual ruler of these three dynasties as well as the total duration of each dynastic rule can be worked out.

Of the ten Mauryas, nine were the actual rulers whose regnal years are given almost uniformally in the Purāṇas. Candragupta is said to have ruled for 24 years (*c.* 321-297 BC), Bindusāra for 25 years (*c.* 297-272 BC), Aśoka for 36 years + 4 years before he was crowned and thus total for 40 years (*c.* 272-232 BC), Kuṇāla for 8 years (*c.* 232-224 BC), Daśaratha (or Bandhupālita) for 8 years (*c.* 224-216 BC), Samprati (or Indrapālita) for 10 years (*c.* 216-206 BC), (Śāliśuka, according to some Purāṇas, did not reign as the crown did not devolve upon him), Devavarman (or Somaśarman) for 7 years (*c.* 206-199 BC), Śatadhanvan for 8 years (*c.* 199-191 BC) and Bṛhadratha (the last king) for 7 years (*c.* 191-

10. *HASL*, pp. 245, 268.
11. E.B. Cowell (ed), *The History of India*, 9th edn. (London, 1911), p. 11.
12. *EHI*, p. 1.
13. *EHI*, pp. 4, 10-11.

184 BC). They are said to have ruled for (133 + the said 4 years) 137 years (*c.* 321-184 BC)[14] which is perfectly accurate.

Puṣyamitra, the founder of the Śuṅga dynasty, is said to have reigned for 36 years (*c.* 184-148 BC), Agnimitra for 8 years (as a viceroy at Vidiśā during the lifetime or period of his father), Vasujyeṣṭha (or Sujyeṣṭha) for 7 years (*c.* 148-141 BC), Vasumitra for 10 years (*c.* 141-131 BC), Odraka for 2 years (*c.* 131-129 BC), Pulindaka for 3 years (*c.* 129-126 BC), Ghoṣa for 3 years (*c.* 126-123 BC), Vajramitra for 9 years (*c.* 123-114 BC), Bhāgavata for 32 years (*c.* 114-82 BC), and Devabhūti for 10 years (*c.* 82-72 BC). These ten Śuṅga kings (all brāhmaṇas) altogether reigned for (120-8) 112 years (*c.* 184-72 BC)[15] which is absolutely correct.

The Vasudeva, the founder of the Kaṇva dynasty, is said to have reigned for 9 years (*c.* 72-63 BC), Bhūmimitra for 14 years (*c.* 63-49 BC), Nārāyaṇa for 12 years (*c.* 49-37 BC) and Suśarman for 10 years (*c.* 37-27 BC). The four Kaṇva kings (also brāhmaṇas) reigned exactly for 45 years (*c.* 72-27 BC).[16]

The reliability of Purāṇic tradition of chronology in respects of the Maurya, Śuṅga and Kaṇva dynasties can hardly be doubted. The length of reigns of the kings of these three dynasties and total duration of their rule as given in the Purāṇas are generally accepted by the historians of ancient India. Pargiter, while throwing light on early Indian traditional history and chronology as recorded in Purāṇas, observes that the Purāṇas "furnish details of dates to an extent that even in days of historical records may be surprising, for they mention even months and days in their computation. Whatever those ancient authors did or wrote, they did it with sincerity and accuracy, 'truth' being the basis of accuracy. Our educational institutions are saturated with the teachings of modern scholars on the untruth of these puranic accounts, but it is still hoped that time will come when truth will triumph and display a real orientation of ancient Indian history".[17]

The regnal years of each individual ruler of the Āndhra or Sātavāhana dynasty is also given in the Purāṇas with little variations. The total duration of reigns of 30 kings

---

14. *Vy.*, 99, 331-36; *Vṣṇ.*, IV, 24, 29-32., *Mts.*, 272, 22-26; *Bmd.*, 3, 74, 145-49; *Bhāg.*, XII, I, 12-15.
15. *Vy.*, 99, 336-42; *Vṣṇ.*, IV, 24, 33-37; *Mts.*, 272, 26-33; *Bmd.*, 3, 74, 150-55; *Bhāg.*, XII, I, 16-18.
16. *Vy.*, 99, 343-47; *Vṣṇ*; IV, 24, 38-42; *Mts.*, 272, 32-37; *Bmd.*, 3, 74, 155-60; *Bhāg.*, XII, I, 19-21.
17. "Earliest Indian Traditional History", *JRAS*, 1914, p. 267; see also his "Ancient Indian Genealogies chronology", *JRAS*, 1910, pp. 26ff.

of this dynasty (from Simuka to Pulumayi IV) comes to 456 or 460 years.[18] It is further stated in some Purāṇas that a period of 836 years intervened between Mahāpadmananda and the last Āndhra king, Pulumayi.[19] According to this chronological data, the Āndhras' rule began 376 years after the Nanda and lasted for 460 years (376 + 460 = 836). There is a great controversy among the authorities on ancient Indian history with regard to the date of beginning and end of this dynasty. Some scholars relying on the Purāṇic testimony that the Āndhras ruled for about four centuries and a half assign the beginning of their power to the last quarter of the third century BC and its end to the first quarter of the third century AD. The generally accepted view is that their rule began sometime in the first century BC and continued till about the the end of the first quarter of the third century AD. Whatever may be the fact regarding the duration of their rule, the Purāṇic regnal years of some kings of proven historical identiy are consistent with their inscriptions found in western India (Mahārāṣṭra).

The chronological data about various kings and dynasties of the post-Sātavāhana period supplied in the Purāṇas in an incidental or interspersed manner are not very credible. According to a tradition preserved in the *Bhaviṣya Purāṇa*, the seven Gupta kings reigned for 245 years. But the fact remains that in the imperial Gupta line there were twelve or thirteen kings (from Śrīgupta to Bhānugupata) who altogether reigned for 235 years (*c.* AD 275-510).

The Buddhist tradition of chronology is no less significant than the Purāṇic one. The chronology of Magadhan rulers from Bimbisāra to Aśoka is of special importance.

According to Pāli commentary, *Sāmantapāsādikā*, Bimbisāra's son, Ajātasattu (Ajātaśatru), reigned for 24 years. The Buddha is said to have passed away in the eighth year of his reign. Udāyi Bhadda reigned for 16 years, Anuruddha and Muṇḍa jointly for 18 years, Nāgadāsaka for 24 years, Śiśunāga for 18 years, Kālāsoka for 28 years and his ten sons, including Nandīvardhana, altogether for 22 years, the Nandas for 22 years, Candagutta (Candragupta) for 24 years and Bindusāra for 28 years.[20] Aśoka is said to have reigned without coronation for four years.[21]

18. *Vy.*, 99,, 348-58; *Vṣṇ.*, IV, 24, 43-50; *Mts.*, 273, 1-17; *Bmd.*, 3, 74, 160-70; *Bhāg.*, XII, I, 22-28.
19. *Vy.*, 99, 416-17; *Mts.*, 273, 37; *Vṣṇ.*, IV, 24, 105-7; *Bmd.*, 3, 74, 230-36.
20. *Sāmantapāsādikā*, I, pp. 72-73.
21. *Ibid.*, p. 41.

The chronology in the two Pāli chronicles, *Dīpavaṁsa* and *Mahāvaṁsa*, is little different form that in the said commentary.

According to the *Dīpavaṁsa*, Bimbisāra reigned for 52 years, Udāyi Bhadda for 16 years and ten sons of Kālāsoka for 22 years. Candragupta Maurya is said to have ascended the throne of Magadha 162 years after the death of Buddha (i.e., 483—162 = in *c*. 321 BC) and ruled for 24 years (i.e., till 297 BC).[22] We are also told that Aśoka was formally crowned as a king 218 years after the death of the Buddha (i.e., 483—218 = in *c*. 265 BC).[23] The chronology given in this chronicle is apparently a broken one.

According to the *Mahāvaṁsa*, Bimbisāra ruled for 52 years (*c*. 543-491 BC) and his son, Ajātasattu, for 32 years (*c*. 491-459 BC). In the eighth year of the reign of the latter Buddha died (i.e., in 483 BC). Ajātasattu's son and successor, Udāyi Bhadda, ruled for 16 years, Anuruddha and his son Muṇḍa for 8 years, Nāgadāsaka for 24 years, Śiśunāga for 18 years and his son Kālāsoka for 28 years and ten sons of the latter, including Nandīvardhana and Mahānandin, altogether for 22 years. These ten kings in the line of Bimbisāra and Śiśunāga altogether ruled for 200 years. The nine Nandas are said to have reigned for 22 years. Candragupta Maurya reigned for 24 years and his son Bindusāra for 28 years.[24] This chronicle also states that Aśoka's coronation took place 218 years after the death of the Buddha (i.e., in 265 BC).[25] There is another evidence to show that his coronation did not take place until *c*. 269 BC.[26]

Max Müller has correctly stated that there are "more than one system of Buddhist chronology", but his view, that "none of them can be considered authentic with regard to the times previous to Asoka . . .",[27] is untenable.

It is significant to point out that there is neither synchronism in the Purāṇic and Buddhist genealogical lists of kings of Bimbisāra and Śiśunāga dynasties nor parallelism between the two chronologies with regard to the regnal years of kings of these two dynasties and duration of their rule. In fact, the Buddhist chronology in respects of these two dynasties and the Nanda dynasty is more reliable than the Purāṇic one. According to Buddhist chronology, the ten rulers belonging to the dynasties of Bimbisāra

---

22. *Dip*., III, 50-60; V, 97.
23. *Ibid*., III, VI, 1.
24. *Mhv*. (ed.), II, 28-32; IV, 1-8; V, 14-15; trans., pp. 12, 15, 21, 163f, 168f.
25. *Ibid*., V, 21.
26. *Ibid*., (trans.), p. 28.
27. *HASL*, p. 235.

and Śiśunāga reigned altogether for 200 years (*c.* 543-343 BC), and the nine Naṇḍas for 22 years (*c.* 343-321 BC), which are corrective to the Purāṇic duration of their rule given before. Candragupta Maurya has been assigned 24 years (*c.* 321-297 BC) as a length of his reign which perfectly agrees with Purāṇic chronology. By striking a compromise between the two traditions of chronology — Purāṇic and Buddhist — we can fix the reign periods of two other Maurya rulers. Bindusāra and Aśoka. According to Buddhist historical tradition, Bimbisāra ruled for 28 years (*c.* 297-269 BC), and Aśoka ascended the throne in 269 BC and ruled for four years as a uncrowned king and then further ruled after being formally crowned as a king in *c.* 265 BC. In the Purāṇic tradition, Bindusāra is said to have reigned for 25 years (*c.* 297-272 BC) and Aśoka for 36 years (after his coronation). In case of Bindusāra, it is the Purāṇic length of reign which is acceptable and not the Buddhist one. Taking Aśoka's rule 4 years before and 36 years after his coronation we find that he ruled exactly for 40 years (*c.* 272-232 BC), as noted before.

The chronological traditions of the Jains appear somewhat different from those of the Hindus and Buddhists. The Jain chronology is not very systematic. It is rather fragmentary. It has, however, some considerable value.

> ". . . the ancient Jainas seemed to have a love for dates and exactness which is evident from their numerous pontifical genealogies and dynastic chronologies, the dated colophons of their works and of the latter's successive manuscript copies, the historical and even prehistorical traditions recorded with corresponding dates and periods in later works, and from their inscriptional records which reach back to the 5th century BC."[28]

K.P. Jayaswal once remarked that "among the Hindus the Jainas alone have preserved a complete and admirable chronology for the two and a half thousand years or so after Mahāvira's death".[29] Bühler also speaks very highly of the historical value and authenticity of Jain traditions.[30]

There are some Jain records of dynastic chronology. The regnal years of individual rulers and total length of reigns of some dynasties are given therein.

---

28. J.P. Jain, *The Jaina Sources of the History of Ancient India*, (100 BC – AD 900), p. 3.
29. *JSS*, I, 4, p. 21 cf. *ibid.*
30. "On the Authenticity of Jain Traditions", in *The Indian Sect of the Jains* (trans. Burgess, London, 1903), pp. 21-23 cf. Jain, *op. cit.*

According to Jain tradition, simultaneously with the *nirvāṇa* of Mahāvīra, Pālaka, the son of king Caṇḍa Pradyota of Ujjayinī, was crowned. In both Digambara and Śvetāmbarra tradition, he is said to have ruled for 60 years. The former tradition is recorded in Yativṛṣabha's *Tiloyapaṇṇati* (IV, 95-96) and Jinasena's *Harivaṁśa* (60, 487-88) and the latter in an old Prākṛt text, *Titthogāli-painna* (vv. 620-21), the *Tapāgaccha Paṭṭāvalī* (v. 1-2) and some other *Paṭṭāvalīs* (*Paṭṭāvali-Samuccaya*, p. 197). The *Tīrthoddhāra-Prakaraṇa* also contains the same regnal years. We are also informed that in the period of 60 years allotted to Pālaka, Kuṇika (Ajātaśatru) and Udāyi were ruling at Pāṭaliputra (*Paṭṭāvalī-Samuccaya*, p. 17. The contemporaneity of Pālaka of Avantī and Ajātaśatru of Magadha can be established also on the basis of Purāṇic chronology.

Hemacandra of Śvetāmbara school is in perfect agreement with all other Jain scholars in stating that the rule of Nanda dynasty commenced 60 years after the death of Mahāvīra. He further says, that this dynasty ruled for 95 years (*Pariśiṣṭaparvan*, VI, 243). From the *Tapāgaccha Paṭṭāvalī* (v. 2) and the *Tīrthoddhāra-Prakaraṇa* it appears that the rule of this dynasty ended 155 years after the *nirvāṇa* of Mahāvīra. Thus, the first king (Mahāpadmananda) of this dynasty began his rule in (477–60) 417 BC. He and his descendants continued to rule Magadha till the last king was deposed by Cāṇakya 155 years after the death of Mahāvīra which comes to (477–155) 322 BC. They ruled from 417 BC to 322 BC which covers a period of 95 years (417–322 or 155–60).

Hemacandra differs from all other Jain scholars, Digambara or Śvetāmbara earlier or later than himself, so far as the date of Candragupta Maurya's accession to the throne of Magadha is concerned. According to him, he became king 155 years after the *nirvāṇa* of Mahāvīra (*Pariśiṣṭaparvan*, VIII, 339). Basing the calculation on the dates of Mahāvīra's *nirvāṇa* as given by him we find that his accession took place in (480–155) 325 BC, (477–155) 322 BC, (468–155) 313 BC or (467–155) 312 BC. Another Jain tradition recorded in the *Vicāraśreṇī* (cf. *Prabandhacintāmaṇi*, composed in 1306 by Merutuṅga, a scholar of Śvetāmbara school) places his accession 255 years before the Vikrama era (57 BC) which dates back to 312 BC. Some ancient Jain scholars are of the opinion that his accession took place either 210 or 215 years after Mahāvīra *nirvāṇa* (527 BC) which comes to (527–210) 317 BC or (527–215) 312 BC. Some of the *Paṭṭāvalīs* give 219 years as the interval between Mahāvīra's *nirvāṇa* (544 BC) and the accession of Candragupta Maurya on the basis of which (544–219) 325 BC is sometimes fixed as the date of the beginning of latter's rule which is note correct at all. All the dates accept 322 BC are unworthy of acceptance. 317, 313 or 312 BC should be taken as the dates of extension of his rule and not its beginning. It is true that in three different traditions — Purāṇic, Buddhist and Jain — the date of his accession is calculated in different ways which varies from 322 BC to 312 BC. But generally 322 or 321 BC is accepted by the historians of ancient India as the date of his ascendency.

The Mauryas are said to have ruled for 108 years (*Tapāgaccha-Paṭṭāvalī*, v. 2; *Tīrthoddhāra-Prakaraṇa*) or 160 years (*Titthogāli-Painna*, v. 621; *Paṭṭāvalī-Samuccaya*, p. 197) whcih is irreconcilable with Purāṇic duration of their rule.

Puṣyamitra (the founder of the Śuṅga dynasty) is said to have ruled for 30 years (*Tiloyapaṇṇati*, IV, 96-97; *Harivaṁśa*, 60, 489; *Tapāgaccha Paṭṭāvalī*, vv. 2-3) or 35 years (*Titthogāli-painna*, vv. 621-22), and his successors, Vasumitra and Agnimitra for 60 years (*Tiloyapaṇṇati*, IV, 96-97; *Harivaṁśa*, 60, 489) and Bālamirta and Bhānumitra also for 60 years (*Titthogāli-painna*, vv. 621-22; *Paṭṭāvatlī-Samuccaya*, p. 197; *Tapāgaccha-Paṭṭāvalī*, vv. 2-3).

The Gaddabha, Gaddabhila or Gardabhilla dynasty ruled (over Ujjayinī) for 100 years (*c.* 74 BC-AD 26) as appears form the *Tiloyapaṇṇati* (IV, 97), the *Harivaṁśa* (60, 490), the *Titthogāli-painna* (v. 622) and the *Paṭṭāvalī-Samuccaya* (p. 197).

According to the *Tiloyapaṇṇati* (IV, 86 & 93), the Śakas' incursion onto Ujjayinī took place 461 years after Mahāvīra's *nirvāṇa*, i.e., in (527–461) 66 BC. It is furhter recorded in the *Tapāgaccha-paṭṭāvalī* (v. 3) and the *Vicāraśreṇī* of Merutuṅga that they ruled for 4 years (*c.* 61-57 BC). The Kṣatrapa of Ujjain, Caṣṭana, has been called Bhacchaṭṭhanān (Bhadra-Caṣṭana) in the Jain tradition. Caṣṭana of Ujjain is probably identical with Ptolemy's Tiastenes of Ozene. The Śakas are said to have ruled (western India) altogether for 242 years (*Tiloyapaṇṇati*, IV, 93, 97-98; *Harivaṁśa*, 60, 490-91) which can be accepted without any hesitation. Nahavāhana (Nahapāna) of Śaka nationality was Kṣaharāta ruler of Saurāṣṭra and Mahārāṣṭra. He is said to have ruled for 40 years, i.e., from AD 26 to 66 (*Tiloyapaṇṇati*, IV, 97; *Harivaṁśa*, 60, 490; *Titthogāli-painna*, v. 622; *Paṭṭāvali-Samuccaya*, p. 197; *Tapāgaccha-paṭṭāvalī*, v. 3).

The Muruṇḍas (kinsmen of the Kuṣāṇas, also mentioned in some of the Purāṇas) are said to have ruled for 40 years (*Tiloyapaṇṇati*, IV, 96; *Harivaṁśa*, 60, 489). It is a fact of history that they had ruled a great part of central India for sometime in the first half of the third century AD.

The traditions preserved in the *Tiloyapaṇṇati* and the *Harivaṁśa* bear witness to the fact that the Gupta rule virtually commenced at the expiry of 242 years of Śaka rule which gives us (78 + 242) AD 320, which marked the beginning of the rule of Candragupta I. The Guptas are said to have ruled for 231 years (*Tiloyapaṇṇati*, IV, 98; *Haivaṁśa*, 60 491) or 255 years (*Tiloyapaṇṇati*, IV, 94). The period of 231 years is in near approximation to the truth. This period covers 190 years of reigns of the early imperial Guptas in the line of Candragupta and 41 years of reigns of the three later Gupta rulers of Magadha in the line of Kṛṣṇagupta.

Kalkirāja called Kalki was a Hūṇa chief who is asid to have ruled for 42 years (*Harivaṁśa*, 60, 492; *Tiloyapaṇṇati*, IV, 94). It is difficult to say as to who the said Hūṇa chief was?

The chronologies given in the *Dhavala* of Vīrasena (AD 780), the *Jayadhavala* of Jinasena Svāmī (AD 837), the *Uttara Purāṇa* of Guṇabhadra (AD 898), the *Trilokasāra* of Nemicandra (AD 973) and other Digambara works are almost identical with those in the *Tiloyapaṇṇati* and the *Harivaṁśa*. The chronology, which is given in the *Tapāgaccha-Paṭṭāvalī* (60 years of Pālaka's rule, the end of the Nandas' rule 155 years after the death of Mahāvīra, 108 years of the Mauryas' rule, 30 of Puṣyamitra, 60 of Balamitra and Bhānumitra and 40 of Nahavāhana), is preserved in the *Vicāraśreṇī* of Merutuṅga. The *Prabhāvakacarita* of Prabhācandra (AD 1277), the *Vividha Tīrthakalpa* of Jinaprabha Sūri (AD 1332) and other Śvetāmbara works are also important for the chronology of the rulers and the dynasties mentioned above.

The Jain literature is rich in chronological data. But the data need a careful examination keeping in view some discrepancies. The chronology given in the Jain traditions is not complete either in the case of kings or in the case of dynasties. In some cases the total length of reigns may not prove to be exact. But certain reign-periods after the proper calculation of the data cencerned have been found correct. The chronology of the rulers and the dynasties, particularly of Magadha and Ujjayinī, is useful for various purposes.

There were definitely some chronologists among the *purāṇakāras*, Buddhists and Jains as appears form the chronological data furnished by them. The chronological records were preserved by them. Their chronological conceptions are well reflected in the dates of the past events they have preserved. A critical combination of Purāṇic, Buddhist and Jain chronology provides us the solid basis for chronological reconstruction of Indian history from the sixth century BC to the early third century AD. By effecting compromise between different systems of chronology we can obtain positive result.

Macdonell's view, that the ancient Indian Sanskrit literature "suffers from an entire absence of exact chronology . . . and definite dates do not begin to appear in the Indian history till about 500 AD",[31] can outrightly be rejected.

J.W. McCrindle's statement, that there is not a single chronological landmark in early Indian history of pre-Candragupta period,[32] can also be disposed of.

The traditional chronology is to certain extent reliable. And it has, no doubt, some historical value.

The information supplied by the classical (Greek and Roman) writers regarding the traditional chronological belief of the Indians in the fourth century BC also deserve our notice. The Greek ambassador Megasthenes, during his five years' stay (*c.* 303-298 BC) at the court of Candragupta Maurya in Pāṭaliputra gathered information from various sources about the history and chronology of India down to his time. He informs us that the Indians counted 153 kings who had preceded Sandrakottos (Candragupta) and reigned for a period of 6042 years. This information has been brought to light by Arrian (second century AD) in his *Indika* (I, IX).[33] Solinus (third century AD)[34] has also quoted Megasthenes' statement as recorded in Arrian's *Indika*. According to Pliny (frist century AD), the reigns of 153 Indian kings down to the time of Alexander the Great extended over 6451 years and three months.[35] The Purāṇic genealogies and chronology of pre-Candragupta period are greatly supported by the classical evidence.[36] McCrindle observes: "It is not known from what sources Megasthenes derived these figures, which are extremely modest when compared with those of Indian chronology."[37] "Pliny and Arrian were indebted for . . . details to Megasthenes, who evidently endeavoured to bring the chronology of the Brahmans into some degree of correspondence with that of his countrymen."[38]

No discussion of traditional Indian chronology will be complete without including in it some of the historical eras and their chronological significance.

31. *HSL*, p. 10f.
32. *AIMA* (London, 1877), p. 7, fn.
33. *AIMA*., p. 203.
34. *History*, 52.5.
35. *Nat, Hist*., VI, 17 (21) cf. McCrindle, *AICL* (Westminster, 1901, rept. Delhi, 1984), p. 108; R.C. Majumdar, *CAI* (Calcutta, 1981), p. 340; see also R.C. Jain, *EAB* (Vārāṇasī, 1970), p. 203.
36. See also F. Wilford, "Chronology of the Hindus", *As. Res*., V (Delhi, 1979), pp. 291-92.
37. *AIMA* (supra), p. 203, fn.
38. *AIÇL*, p. 108, note 1.

The eras were introduced in ancient India to mark the historic events and to preserve the memory thereof and were used to fix the date of accession of kings and the beginning and end of the dynastic rule, to determine the reign-periods of rulers and so on. The eras were extensively used in ancient Indian inscriptions to record the important events that took place during the reigns of kings.

Here we shall first begin with the Mahāvīra era. Vardhmāna Mahāvīra occupies an important place in the history of ancient India. According to the popular tradition of the Jains, 527 BC, the date of his *nirvāṇa*, marked the commencement of Mahāvīra era. The date "is one of the earliest landmarks in the chronology of ancient India, while it is the very sheet-anchor of Jaina chronology".[39] There are some positive evidences in favour of this date. The Digambara tradition recorded in the *Tiloyapaṇṇati* (IV, 1499) of Yastivṛṣabha (*c.* AD 176), the *Dhavala* of Vīrasena (*c.* AD 780), the *Harivaṁśa* (60, 549 and 551) of Jinasena (*c.* AD 783) and the *Trilokasāra* (v. 850) of Nemicandra (*c.* AD 973), and the Śvetāmbara in the *Titthogāli-Painna* (v. 623 cf *Paṭṭāvalī-Samuccaya*, pp. 197 and 537) and the *Vicāraśreṇī* of Merutuṅga (*c.* AD 1306) show that there is an interval of 605 years and five months between Mahāvīra's *nirvāṇa* and the commencement of the Śaka era (*c.* AD 78) which comes to (605–78) 527 BC. Another class of Jain tradition gives the same date in terms of the Vikrama era. "The Prākṛt *Paṭṭāvalī* of the Nandī Saṁgha, which is one of the oldest Digambara *Paṭṭāvalī*s, the equally old Śvetāmbera *Tapāgaccha-Paṭṭāvalī*, Haribhadra's *Āvaśyakavṛtti* (*c.* AD 775), the *Tīrthoddhāra-Prakaraṇa* and several other works unanimously state that Mahāvīra died 470 years before the commencement of the Vikrama era (*c.* 57 BC)". The date is further confirmed by the traditional belief of the Jains themselves, as recorded in some of their works, that Mahāvīra died 461 years before the first entry of the Śakas into the Ujjayinī region in 66 BC. The statement recorded in some of the Pāli texts that the Buddha survived Mahāvīra by many years also proves that the latter died 44 years before the former's death in 483 BC. The age of Mahāvīra at the time of his death is stated to have been "71 years, six months and seventeen days". He was born on "30 March 599 BC". His renunciation on "11 November 570 BC" and enlightenment "on 26 April 557 BC" were two of the important events in his life. And his *nirvāṇa* took place on 15 October 527 BC. The earliest use of this Mahāvīra era is found in the *Paum-cariu* (also called *Padma-carita*) of Vimalasūri who gives his date as ME 530 (AD 3).[40]

39. Jain, *op. cit.*, p. 32.

40. For details see Jain *op. cit.*, pp. 36-54.

Hemacandra (a Śvetāmbara scholar of twelfth century AD) in his *Pariśiṣṭaparvan* has given different dates of Mahāvīra's *nirvāṇa*, as mentioned before, and accordingly fixed the dates of the accessions of some kings and the beginning and end of rule of some dynasties. He has stated that Candragupta Maurya ascended the throne in ME 155 and the Nanda dynasty began in ME 60. His calculation is entirely based on the dates different from 527 BC. But in one of his works, *Triṣaṣṭiśalākāpuruṣacarita* (X, 12, vv. 45-46), he says that the accession of Kumārapāla (the Cālukya monarch of Gujarat) took place in ME 1669 = AD 1142 which is evidently a proof of his acceptance of the date 527 BC.

Mahāvīra was a contemporary of Buddha and Bimbisāra but not Ajātaśatru. A Śvetāmbara tradition states that Mahāvīra attained *nirvāṇa* in the 16th year of the reign of Kuṇika (Ajātaśatru) which corresponds with 475 BC. Such contradictory statements are there in some Jain and other sources which sometimes create confusion in our mind about the date concerned. However, on the weight of the internal as well as external evidence 527 BC can be accepted as the date of Mahāvīra's *nirvāṇa* and the commencement of Mahāvīra era. We find that Candragupta Maurya ascended the throne of Magadha 205 or 206 years after Mahāvīra's *nirvāṇa* (i.e., in 322 or 321 BC). The date 527 BC does not affect the Mauryan chronology. The said era has been used mostly by the Jain writers of ancient and medieval periods.

The popular Buddhist tradition places the Buddha's *nirvāṇa* in 483 BC. This is the date which marked the beginning of the Buddha era. It coincides with the eighth year of Ajātaśatru's reign which proves that he ascended the throne of Magadha *c.* 491 BC.

The other two eras — Vikrama and Śaka — are very important from both historical and chronological points of view.

According to Jain historical tradition, Mahendrāditya, king of Ujjayinī (ME 453 – 466 = 74-61 BC), was the father of Vikramāditya. The Śakas entered Ujjayinī in ME 461 = 66 BC which marked the commencement of the first Śaka era. After having consolidated their position they defeated Mahendrāditya in 61 BC and thereafter occupied Ujjayinī and ruled over it until they were vnquished and expelled in ME 470 = 57 BC by the Mālava people led by Vikramāditya. After the expulsion of the Śakas the latter was crowned as a king. In order to commemorate this event or his victory over the Śakas Vikramāditya introduced a new era called Vikrama or Mālava. Merutuṅga has explicitly stated in his *Vicāraśreṇī* that "Vikramāditya and his dynasty ruled for 135 years, and 605 years after Mahāvīra's *nirvāṇa* (i.e., in AD 78) came the Śaka king who displaced the dynasty of Vikramāditya". On the authority of this Jain writer it is believed that the Śakas after 57

BC again rose to power, reoccupied Ujjayinī and reasserted their authority. In order to celebrate it and to supersede the Mālava era they started a new era of their own, i.e., the second Śaka era of AD 78. Some scholars regard Caṣṭana, a Kṣatrapa of Ujjayinī, as the founder of the Śaka era of that year. But this goes against the truth, for his earliest known date is the year 52 in Śaka era = AD 130. The Kuṣāṇa king, Kaniṣka, is generally credited with having founded the Śaka era in AD 78. But his chronological position still remains uncertain. With regard to the year of his accession the choice lies between AD 78 AD and AD 125. Different other dates have also been suggested by the historians of ancient India. No definite date of his accession can be suggested with absolute certainty and accuracy. And we, therefore, do not take him as the originator of this era. Nor is there any ground to believe that an era founded by him in AD 78 was afterwards called the Śaka era "in consequence of its long use by the Śaka princes of western India". It is traditionally believed that, it was Śālivāhana of Ujjain who conquered a group of the Śakas exactly 135 years after Vikramāditya (i.e., in AD 78) and celebrated his victory by commencing a new era called 'Śālivāhana Śākābda'. But the fact remains that an era of AD 78 founded by the Śakas after having reoccupied Ujjain was later changed to Śālivāhana Śaka Samvat.

The two principal and very popular eras, Vikrama and Śaka, have been in use in terms of chronology since ancient times.

Another important era was the Gupta era which began in AD 319 with the accession of the imperial Gupta ruler, Candragupta I. But, according to the Jain works, *Tiloyapaṇṇati* and *Harivaṁśa*, this era began in AD 320. And this is the reason why some scholars assign AD 319-20 to the commencement of the era.[41] This era has been used in some inscriptions of the Gupta and post-Gupta period. Equally important was the Valabhī era of AD 319-20 introduced in Saurāṣṭra (Kāṭhiāwāḍ). Both the eras were used for chronological purpose. The mention of the Cālukya chiefs of Saurāṣṭra in one of the Ūnā charters bearing the Gupta-Valabhī date 574 = AD 893 as feudatories of Mahendrapāla Pratihāra is an instance of their use in inscription by combining them together.

The traditional and historical eras of the Hindus also received the notice of Alberuni (AD 973-1048), who visited India during the time of Mahmud of Ghazni (AD 997-1030), learnt Sanskrit, studied Purāṇic and other ancient Indian literature and produced a scholarly work, *Tahkik-i-Hind* (An Enquiry into India), in AD 1030. His description of the eras of Vikramāditya, Śaka, Valabha, Gupta and Harṣa is of utmost importance. He has

41. See also Sen (ed.), *Historians and Historiography in modern India*, pp. 37-39.

unequivocally stated that "the epoch of the era of Śaka or Śakakāla falls 135 years later than that of Vikramāditya" .... "The epoch of the era of the Guptas falls like that of the Valabha (the ruler of the town of Valabhī) 241 years later than the Śakakāla" which comes to AD 319. The Harṣa era of AD 606 was used in Mathurā and Kanauj. The Vikrama era was used in western and southern parts of India. All these eras, according to him, were used as cardinal points to fix the chronology which he calls "historic chronology".[42]

One of the most important eras of ancient India was the Laukika era, which was in use in Kashmir and its neighbourhood in the eleventh and twelfth centuries AD. The 24th year of this era corresponds with the year 1070 of the Śaka era (AD 1148).[43] Kalhaṇa, a Kaśmīrī historian of the twelfth century AD, used this era for his chronological computation. He has supplied the chronology of the kings of Kashmir belonging to various dynasties in this era adjusting it with other two eras — the Kali and Śaka or Śālivāhana — which can further be adjusted with the Christian era. His perfect sense of history and chronology is well reflected in Books IV-VIII of his work, *Rājataraṅgiṇī*. He has fixed the reign periods of all the kings who ruled the kingdom of Kashmir from about the end of the sixth century AD to about the middle of the twelfth century AD and the total duration of each dynastic rule with perfect accuracy. The reign-periods of seventeen kings of the Karkoṭaka dynasty from Durlabhavardhana to Utpalapire are given in Book IV. The rule of this dynasty is said to have begun in AD 598 and come to an end in AD 852. The reign-periods of fifteen princes of Utpala or Varman dynasty from Avantīvarman to Śūravarman II are given in Book V. The rule of this dynasty commenced in AD 855 and ended in AD 939. The reign-periods of ten princes from Yaśaskara to Diddā belonging to mixed dynasties are given in Book VI. The rule began in AD 939 and came to an end in AD 1003. The reign-periods of six kings of the Lohar dynasty from Saṁgrāmarāja alias Kṣamapati to Harṣa are given in Book VII. The rule of this dynasty commenced in AD 1003 and ended in AD 1101. The reign-periods of all seven kings from Ucchala to Jayasiṁhadeva figure in Book VIII. In this Book, Kalhaṇa begins the chronology with AD 1101, which marks the commencement of the rule of Ucchala and ends with AD 1149, which marks the twenty-second year of the reign of Jayasiṁha.[44] The dynastic chronolgy

42. *Alberuni's India*, Eng. trans. of the Arabic text by E.C. Sachau, II, pp. 1-11; see also Alberuni's *Chronology of Ancient Nations*, trans. by Sachau, pp. 6, 368, note.

43. See also Colebrooke, "The Saptarṣi Era". *As. Res.*, IX (1st published 1811, rept. Delhi, 1979) pp. 323 ff.

44. *Kings of the Kashmir*, Eng. trans. of *Rājataraṅgiṇi* by J.C. Dutt (supra), I, Appendix, XXI-XXIII, II, XLV.

provided by him in the said Books of his work requires no modification. The dates given by him have been found correct and used by the historians of ancient India in their respective works while dealing with history of Kashmir.

The eras which are not of historical or chronological significance have not been included in the discussion here.

11

Historical and Chronological Sense
General Review

SCHOLARS, including the historians, Indologists and orientalists, are divided in their opinion about the historical and chronological sense of the ancient Indians, particularly the Hindus.

It has often been said that the ancient Indians had no sense of history and chronology. Alberuni was the first to remark that "The Hindus do not pay much attention to the historical order of things, they are very careless in relating the chronological succession of their kings, and when they are pressed for information and are at a loss, not knowing what to say, they invariably take to tale-telling".[1] This remark was made by him in AD 1030 in his work *Tahkik-i-Hind*. It is striking to note that the genealogies of kings of different dynasties in the Purāṇic records, which were the principal sources of information for him for writing his book as admitted by himself, are in proper historical and chronological order, of course, with a few exceptions. It is paradoxical that he calls his own work "a simple historic record of facts",[2] but the sources on which it is based are spoken of as unhistorical. He presents the picture of Indian civilization as painted by the Hindus themselves. He has himself tried to fix the chronology of some historical events with the help of the chronological data furnished by the Hindus in different works, as it appears from his book.

S.R. Sharma in an attempt to justify Alberuni's statement writes that his "version on the lack of historical sense of Indians is largely justified by the paucity of historical works properly so called in our country coming down from ancient times. Material from which history can be constructed is undoubtedly available in abundance but very little of

1. Sachau, *Alberuni*'s *India*, II, pp. 10-11.
2. *Ibid.*, Preface, p. 7.

it shares the character of regular history".[3] But on the other hand, A.K. Majumdar asserts that "... we can't admit that the Hindus had incapacity for writing history and our ancestors have not bequeathed to us any reliable historical work for early period. They knew the simple art of writing history".[4]

L.J. Trotter and W.H. Hutton have remarked that "... the old Hindus produced ... not one historian of even the smallest mark".[5] Any sensible historian will never accept such kind of absurd remark. Some scholars have levelled the charge against the ancient Hindus that they "wrote no formal history at any period".[6] They did not have capacity to write history. "Though genuine materials once abounded in India yet we find no national history of the Hindus".[7] H. Beveridge opines that "With the exception of a work on Kashmir, the literature of India has failed to furnish a single production to which the name of history can in any proper sense of the term be applied".[8] These biased remarks made within conceptual framework have inscreasingly given rise to misgivings in the minds of many. However, the subjective elements should not be allowed to influence and overshadow our objective judgement.

A. A. Macdonell is of the opinion that "History is the one weak spot in Indian literature. It is, in fact, non-existent. The total lack of historical sense is so characteristic that the whole course of Sanskrit literature is darkened by the shadow of this defect, suffering as it does from an entire absence of exact chronology. In the first place early India wrote no history because it never made any. . . . Secondly, the Brahmans whose task it would naturally have been to record the great deeds . . . have felt but little inclination to chronicle historical events".[9] This is nothing but a total rejection of truth.

Nothing can be more farther from the truth than the statements that ancient India was without history and historians. The ancient Indians had "a distaste for history". The details of past events did not interest them and, therefore, they did not record them.[10]

---

3. *The Making of Modern India*, p. 308.
4. *EHIDS*, 1, p. 6.
5. *History of India from the Earliest times to the present Day*, p. 39.
6. J.N. Farquhar, *An Outline of the Religious Literature of India*, p. 3.
7. Fleet 's paper on Epigraphy, *Imp. Gaz. Ind.*, II, p. 21.
8. *A Comprehensive History of India*, vol. I, p. 18.
9. *HSL*, pp. 10-11.
10. P. Masson-Oursel & C. *AIIC*, Foreword by Henri Berr, XI-XII, XIV, p. 22.

J.W. McCrindle (a popular authority on ancient India by the classical writers) holds that "The Indians themselves did not write history. They produced, no doubt, a literature both voluminous and varied, . . . but within its vast range history is conspicuous by its absence. Their learned men were Brahmans whose modes and habits of thought almost necessarily incapacitated them for the task of historical composition . . . they allowed events, even those of the greatest public moment, to pass unrecorded, and so to perish from memory".[11] And Sanskrit literature is deficient in history and chronology.[12] But his views cannot be accepted as they run contrary to the truth. R.G. Bhandarkar's observation, that "India has no real history. . . . The historical curiosity of the people was satisfied by legends what we find of a historical nature in the literature of the country before the arrival of the Mahomedans",[13] can also be disposed of. He like many other scholars considers only Kalhaṇa's *Rājataraṅgiṇī*a historical work.

It is really very unfortunate that some Indian and foreign scholars have fallen into the grip of confusion about the historical value of ancient Sanskrit literature. The confusion has been made worse confounded by some recent writings on historiography in the context.

It is not correct to say that only the ancient Greeks, Romans, Chinese, Persians, Egyptians, Babylonians, Assyrians and Sumerians maintained the historical records. The Indians in the ancient past were not historians and had no political history like them.[14] It is further said that "The Hindus have no history and no authentic Chronology . . . and there is no certain date in the wide range of their literature except what is imported from Greek history".[15] In fact, each country had its own tradition of historical writing and each tradition has its value. The value of historiographical tradition in ancient India should be judged independently and not by comparing with that of other countries.

Quite a few historians of ancient India have opined that in all the large and varied literatures of the brāhmaṇs, Buddhists and Jains there is not a single work which can be

11. *AICL*, introduction, p. XII.
12. *IIA*, introduction, p. 6.
13. *Early History of the Dekkan down to the Mahomedon Conquest*, introduction, I-IV.
14. See Maurice Phillips, *The Teaching of the Vedas*, pp. 14-15; D.D. Kosambi, *The Culture and Civilisation of Ancient India in Historical Outline*, pp. 9-10; Jawaharlal Nehru, *The Discorvery of India* (Delhi, 1974), p. 102; also its 1st Hindi edn. (Delhi, 1947) p. 114.
15. Maurice Philips, *op. cit.*

compared to the *Histories* of Herodotus, historical work of Thucydides or the *History* of Polybius of Greece or the *Annals* of Livy or Tacitus of Rome.[16] But this is not because the ancient Indians had no history. E. J. Rapson remarks : "We know from other sources that the ages were filled with stirring events; but these events found no systematic record. Of the great foreign invasions of Darius, Alexander the Great and Seleucus no mention is to be discovered in any Indian work. The struggles between native princes, the rise and fall of empires, have indeed not passed similarly into utter oblivion. The memory is to some extent preserved in epic poems, in stories of the sages and heroes of old, in genealogies and dynastic lists. Such in all countries are the beginnings of history; and in ancient India its development was not carried beyond this rudimentary stage."[17] He further observes that the literature of brāhmaṇas, Buddhists or Jains are deficient as records of political progress. And "By their aid alone it would be impossible to sketch the outline of the political history of any of the nations of India before the Muhammedan conquest".[18]

It will be futile and unproductive exercise to draw a demarcation line between the historical writings in ancient India on the one hand and in ancient Greece and Rome on the other from the standpoint of degree of importance. All these three ancient countries were the repositories of historical wisdom. James Tod has rightly pointed out that "Those who expect from a people like the Hindus a species of composition of precisely the same character as the historical works of Greece and Rome commit the very egregious error of overlooking the peculiarities which distinguish the natives of India from all other races, and their intellectual productions of every kind. Their history like their Philosophy, their poetry and their architecture are marked with traits of originality".[19] He speaks very higly of historical sense and historical works of all kinds of ancient Indians. He further adds that historical records including the Purāṇic ones and other works of a mixed historical character existed in ancient India.[20]

---

16. E.J. Rapson (ed.), *CHI*, I *Ancient India*, p. 51; Rapson, *Ancient India from the Earliest Times to the first century* AD, p. 8; J. Allan, Wolseley Haig and H.H. Dodwell, *The Cambridge Shorter History of India*, p. 1; R.S. Tripathi, *History of Ancient India*, p. 1; Kosambi, *An Introduction to the study of Indian History*, p. 1; H.C. Raychaudhuri, *PHAI*, p. 1.

17. *CHI*, I, p. 51.

18. *Ibid.*, pp. 51-52.

19. *AAR*, I, introduction, XIV-XV.

20. *Ibid.*, XIII-XVII.

The said ancient Greek and Roman historians produced only political histories,[21] whereas the ancient historians of India touched upon all aspects of history — social, economic, political, religious and cultural. Both ancient Indian and classical tradition of historiography have relative value. Max Müller is absolutely right in stating that history provides a comprehensive knowledge of all that happened in the past.[22] "There is history in the large and history in the small; each has its value, but their values are different".[23]

It is worthy of note that in every country and in every age the body of history has been shaped by the events of the contemporary age which were not identical at all. The events became the theme of historical writing or subject for historians to deal with. The historian makes history and the subject makes historian. "Instead of the historian choosing the subject, the subject chooses the historian."[24] Sometimes history is produced by a historian and sometimes historian is produced by an event. "The historian, before he begins to write history, is the product of history."[25]

As in ancient India so in ancient Greece and Rome history developed as a branch of literature. To the Greeks and Romans also history was an art and not "a critical science". Very few of them were ciritcal historians. It is not the fact that the classical historians concerned produced purely scientific histories. In fact, they made both scientific and artistic approach to the study of history. They too like the ancient historians of India adopted the literary style of writing. They have been called "literary artists" by the authorities on classical historiography. Even Herodotus, "the father of history" has been discribed by them as "a great artist" and "story teller". It is a fact to reckon with that he has also mixed up history with myths and legends. All ancient historians, whether of India, Greece or Rome, were much more concerned with the artistic presentation of the truth than the creation of regular and scientific history.[26] Greece was not the first home of historical composition as generally believed by the scholars. It is equally not correct to say that the Greeks first learnt the art of writing history. The history acquired its

21. See also B.B. Chakravorty, *Itihāsa of Bhāratavarṣa from the Bhāratīya Viewpoint* (up to Gupta period), pp. 25-26, 81-82.
22. *India; What can it Teach us*? (London, 1883), pp. 25-27.
23. L. Gottschalk, *Understanding History — A Premier of Historical Method*, p. 10.
24. Collingwood, *The Idea of History*, p. 27.
25. Carr, *What is History?*, p. 40.
26. For details see Stephen Usher, *The Historians of Greece and Rome*, Introduction, IX, XI, pp. 4, 7, 45-46; J.W. Thompson, *A History of Historical Writing,* vol. I, pp. 21-26, 76f; Rowse, *The Use of History*, pp. 112-13; H.E. Barnes, *A History of Historical Writing*, p. 29; J.T. Shotwell, *The History of History*, I, p. 185.

meaning and purpose and received the treatment in both ancient India and Greece concurrently. The contemporaneous growth of historical sense and development of historical writing in both the countries cannot be denied. And, thus, it will be unfair to highlight the importance of one and discard or depreciate the value of other.

We do not find ourselves in agreement with E.J. Rapson that if "any ancient Indian literature, Brāhmaṇa, Jain, or Buddhist" is compared with Greek and Latin classics, it will be found that "in none of them has the art of historical composition been developed beyond its earliest stages".[27] He further observes that "Its sources — heroic poems, legendary chronicles, ancient genealogies — are indeed to be found in abundance. From the literatures and from the monuments we learn the names, and some of the achievements, of a great number of nations who rose to power, flourished, and declined in the continent of India during the twenty-two centuries before the Muhammedan conquest; but not one of these nations has found its historian". The literatures of ancient India "supply materials by means of which it is possible to trace the daily life of the people, their social systems, their religion, their progress in the arts and sciences, with a completeness which is unparalleled in antiquity; but events are rarely mentioned, and there is an almost total absence of chronology. Dynastic lists with, in some instances, the length of the different reigns are certainly to be found; but these in themselves supply no fixed point for the determination of Indian chronology".[28]

In above observations we find both acceptance and distortion of truth. His all statements are correct except that ancient India had no historian; and in ancient Indian literature historical events are not recorded and chronology is totally absent. The statements of J. Allan, Wolseley Haig and H.H. Dodwell are also of mixed nature. Ancient Indian literature in comparison to European literature, according to them, is of little value from historical and chronological points of view. They state that the two great epics are of little importance for political history. The Purāṇas, whose authors may be compared to "medieval chroniclers, are mainly legendary and mythological collections". But they "contain certain amount of genealogical matter, the historical significance of which it is very difficult to estimate. The only professedly historical work, the late twelfth century chronicle of Kashmir, contains a certain amount of historical information. . . . Bana's *Harshacharita*, a pseudo-biographical work, contains disappointingly little of historical value and belongs to literature rather than history. . . . The historical data

27. *Ancient India from the Earliest times to the first century* AD, p. 8.
28. *Ancient India from the Earliest times to the first century* AD, pp. 8-9.

that can be gathered from Sanskrit and Pāli literature cannot be despised, but interpretation is often difficult and there is an entire lack of chronological data. It is with the help of synchronisms given by . . . mainly Greek and chinese writers that the chronology of Indian history has been built up."[29]

As already stated, the Purāṇas are very authentic records of dynastic genealogies and chronology, Bāṇa's *Harṣacarita* is a historical biography and forms part of historical literature; the chronicle of Kashmir contains a bulk of valuable historical information; Purāṇic and Buddhist literatures are not deficient in chronological data and it is on the basis of this data that the chronology of ancient Indian history has been partly built up.

Some balanced and rational judgements have been pronounced on the subject under review. Affirming the historical sense of the ancient Indians and their historical writings, Maurice Winternitz (a German Scholar) writes: ". . . . One must not believe as it has so often been asserted that the historical sense is entirely lacking in the Indians. In India too there has been historical writing and in any case we find in India numerous accurately dated inscriptions which could hardly be the case if the Indians have had no sense of history at all. It is only truth that the Indians in their writing of history never knew how to keep fact and fiction strictly apart, that to them the facts themselves were always more important than their chronological order, and they attached no importance at all especially in literary matters to the question of what was earlier or later. Since the fifth century after Christ inscriptions too begin to give us information about the dates of many writers. . . ."[30] He further asserts that there is an abundant wealth of historial information in ancient Indian literature, which forms a necessary complement to the classical literature of ancient Greece and Rome.

A.B. Keith is perfectily right in stating that "To the old complaint that India has not historians and no historical sense it has recently been objected, doubtless with a measure of truth, that there is certain amount of writing and a number of facts attesting a degree of sense for history. In view of the antiquity and the developed character of Indian civilization it would indeed by ridiculous to expect to find India destitute of historical sense. . . ."[31] But his statements, that "despite that abundance of its lierature, history is so miserably represented, and that in the whole of the great period of Sanskrit

29. *Op. cit.*

30. *HIL*, vol.I, pp. 29-30.

31. *HSL*, p. 144.

literature there is not one writer who can be seriously regarded as a critical historian",[32] are not absolutely correct. He, however, admits that some historical and semi-historical works were produced in ancient India. The Purāṇic genealogies, the *paṭṭāvalīs* of the Jains and the works of the Buddhists, according to him, are of considerable historical value. The biographical works of Vākpatirāja Padmagupta, Bilhaṇa and others (already mentione before) in his estimation are of greater historical value. The *Chronicle of Kings of Kashmir* in his opinion like that of others is nearest approach to history. And its author, Kalhaṇa, is called by him "a true historian", who, according to him, is not a suitable match for Herodotus. We are in perfect agreement with him that the historians of Kashmir made substantial contributions to the growth of historiography of a serious nature. He points out that the national feeling, which is a powerful aid to the writing of history, was not evoked in ancient India. The political events which took place in India up to the twelfth century AD, including the foreign invasions and the struggles and wars between rival dynasties and empires, were not recorded by its historians of ancient times because of absence of such feeling.[33] The struggles and wars between native rulers do find mention in some ancient Indian historical works; but the foreign invasions could not be recorded by ancient historians of India which may be attributed to non-availability of sources concerned in India during their times and not to the absence of national feeling among them.

Prof Bühler, writing to Noldke in 1877 on the contribution of the ancient Hindus in the field of historical literature, said: "you are a little behind the age with your notion that Indians have no historical literature".[34] He referred to the works discovered by himself in which he found that the authors are contemporary with the events they describe Max Müller has also attested to the historical value of ancient Sanskrit literature including the *Ṛgveda*. He has categorically stated that in order to understand the civilization of ancient India one shall have to rely upon its historical literature. He also does not give his assent to the views of some scholars that India had no historical work.[35] J.T. Wheeler has rightly placed the *Ṛgveda*, the two epics and the Purāṇas under the category of semi-historical literature. He has admitted that the materials for the history of India prior to the advent of Buddhism are to be founded in these sources. He is not wrong in saying that the "Sanskrit literature, whether Vedic or Brahmanic,

32. *HSL*, p. 144.
33. *HSL*, pp. 144-48.
34. Cf. *Modern Review*, January 1955, pp. 68-69.
35. *India : What can it Teach us?* (London, 1899), pp. 5-10, 90-96.

has no historial annals in the modern sense of the word".[36]

A. Weber has correctly stated that history was a part of literature. Indian literature has both history and chronology. Old Purāṇas contain historical portions with dynasties of kings and chronology. The works of Bāṇa, Bilthaṇa and Kalhaṇa are solid proofs of historical writings. Kalhaṇa's *Rājataraṅgiṇī* is a great work from both historical and chronological points of view. The family records preserved in ancient times are trustworthy. The ancient inscriptions, grants, etc., are also of considerable historical value.[37] M.A. Stein has also recorded his agreement on the points under discussion. He concurs with the scholars who are of the opinion that the ancient Indians posseseed historical sense as well as historical works. He says: ". . . advancing research has also proved that written records of events and traditions concerning them have by no means been wanting in ancient India".[38]

A.K. Warder, a great authority on Indian historiography, has strongly advocated the historical sense of the ancient Indians. He has presented in his work abundant proofs of historical writing in ancient India. He says that it is superficial misconceptions that ancient India produced little or no historical literature. He has firmly established that there was continuity in historiographical tradition in ancient India from Vedic antiquity to the twelfth century AD.[39]

U.N. Ghoshal,[40] A.D. Pusalker,[41] R.C. Majumdar,[42] R.C. Dutt,[43] Radha Kumud

---

36. *India from the Earliest Ages* (*Hindu, Buddhist and Brahmanical Revival*), vol. III of the *History of India*, preface, VIII, pp. 5-6.

37. *HIL*, pp. 213-15.

38. *Rājataraṅgini*, trans., p. 3.

39. *An Introduction to Indian Historiography*, preface, vii, pp. 15ff; see also C.H. Philips (ed.), *Historians of India, Pakistan and Ceylon*, pp. 44ff.

40. *The Beginnings* of *Indian Historiography and Other Essays*, pp. 21-23, 50-52; see also his *Studies in Indian History and Culture*, pp. 7-8, 15-18; "History and Historians of Ancient India in the modern Age", *Indo-Asian Culture*, Indian Council for Cultural Relations, Delhi, IX, 1961 pp. 353-84.

41. "Conception of History in Ancient Indian Literature", *Our Heritage*, Calcutta, XII, 2, 1964, pp. 35-52; See also his "Sanskrit Histories and Chronicles" in S.K. Chatterji (ed.), *Cul. Her. Ind.*, V (Calcutta, 1978), pp. 283-90.

42. "Sources of Indian History", in *Vedic Age*, ed. by himself, pp. 47-52; *Ancient India*, pp.7-8; "Ideas of History in Sanskrit Literature", in C.H. Philips (ed.), *Historians of India, Pakistan and Ceylon*, vol. I, pp. 13-28.

43. *A History of Civilisation in Ancient India Based on Sanskrit Literature*, I (2000-320 BC), pp. 2-4, 109-11; see also his *Ancient India* (2000 BC-AD 800), Delhi, 1980.

Mookerji,[44] Radha Kamal Mukerjee[45] and Romila Thapar,[46] the noted authorities on ancient Indian history, have proved beyond doubt that the ancient Indians had a true sense of history and produced historical and quasi-historical works of various kinds. They have acknowledged the facts that the tradition of historical writing was manitained in ancient India; the historical tradition is preserved in the epics and Purāṇas; the historical biographies, historical chronicles and other historical treatises were composed in different parts of India; the Hindus, Buddhists and Jains made significant contributions to the evolution of historiography in ancient India.

Radha Kumud Mookerji has rightly pointed out that "History is not merely political and chronological and is not limited only to individual and datable facts and events. History is more important and interesting as a history of thought. It is social and cultural history".[47]

The author of this work begs to differ from Romila Thapar so far as the statement, that "The Indian tradition until the seventh century AD lacks any literature which can be specifically described as historical writings",[48] is concerned. It is an acknowledged fact that the most important tradition of historical writing before the seventh century AD was Purāṇic one. A lot of valuable historical information is available in the Purāṇic literature of the pre-seventh century AD. Besides, some Buddhist and Jain works composed before this century also contain historical writings. The author, however, entirely agrees with her so far as the statements, that the historical biographies and histories of kingdoms produced between the seventh and the twelfth century AD form parts of historical literature[49] and that "the Indian historical tradition, particularly in the period prior to the seventh century AD, was not concerned primarily with keeping a record of essential politcal events. . .",[50] are concerned.

It is not merely the genealogies, biographies and chronicles of kings but also other materials of history that received the attention of the ancient Indians. There were

44. *Ancient India*, pp. 4ff.
45. *The Culture and Art of Inldia*, pp. 33-34.
46. "The Tradition of Historical Writings in Early India", in her *AISH*, pp. 268-92; *The Past and Prejudice*, pp. 2-3.
47. *Op. cit.*, pp. 4-5.
48. *AISH*, p. 268.
49. *Ibid.*
50. *Ibid.*, p. 269.

different conceptions of history. There is a positive evidence to prove the recording of history in the time of Candragupta Maurya. Various state officials were appointed by him to collect the details of all important events and to put them in writing which constitued the source material of history. It is evident from the *Arthaśāstra* of Kauṭilya that it was the duty of the Gopa (an official incharge of five or ten villages) to keep a record of everything concerning a village including its agricultural products and trade and commerce. He had to show social groups, class and caste, and different professional and occupational groups. He had to register the total number of the inhabitants in each village specifying in the numbers of the brāhmaṇas, kṣatriyas, vaiśyas and śūdras, farmers, traders, artisans, labourers and slaves.[51] These materials supply invaluable data for the purpose of social and economic history of the contemporary age. Kauṭilya also testifies to the maintenance of the archives in the Maurya court (*Arth.*, II, 25).

Hiuen-Tsang's testimony of the practice of preserving historical records in India also deserves out notice. He during his stay in the country for about fifteen years (AD 629-45) noticed that its each province had its own state officials for maintaining written records of events. He has distinctly mentioned that there were separate custodians of the archives and records. The offical annals and state papers, according to him, were called collectively *'Ni-lo-pi-Cha'* or *'Ni-lo-Pi-t'u'*.[52] The *sūtas* were the first to keep the records of the genealogies of royal families preserved in some of the Purāṇas. The practice of maintaining written records continued for centuries after the Hiuen-Tsang. At the courts of kings archives were maintained for preserving the records of important happenings. The archival records were used for compiling mainly the chronicles and *vaṁśavalīs*. The existence of historical chronicles in Kashmir, Gujarat and Nepal supports the belief that the royal archives of different states contained such chronicles. The Śilāhāras princes, who ruled over south Koṅkaṇ with seat of government at Goa from the last quarter of eighth century AD to about the second decade of the eleventh century AD, maintained their own records and those of their sovereigns, the Rāṣṭrakūṭas. The western Cālukyas of Kalyāṇī (AD 997-1182) got from the dynastic archives knowledge of the earlier Cālukya dynasty of Vātāpī (Bādāmī). The palm-leaf manuscripts preserved in the archives of the temple of Jagannāth at Purī contain valuable information about the history of Orissa. There is enough evidence to show the historical consciousness on the

51. *Arth.*, trans. by R. Shama Sastry (Bangalore, 1915), pp. 178-79; ed. with Hindi trans. by Vachaspati Gairola (Vārāṇasī, 1984), pp. 241-42.
52. S. Beal (trans.), *BRWW* (London, 1906), I, p. 78; Thomas Watters, *YCTI* (London, 1904-05, Delhi, 1973), I, p. 154.

part of the ancient Indians as to preserve the records of the past events. A.L. Basham also observes that "At the courts of ancient Indian kings careful records were kept of the events of chief importance to the realm, but unfortunately these archives are completely lost to us".[53] He further adds that Kalhaṇa was the first to write the history of his native land, but his work although of great value for the study of the history of Kashmir has little to tell us about India as a whole. And no similar chronicles were composed elsewhere. It is unjust to maintain that the ancient Indians had no sense of history. The great empires which had risen and fallen in historical times did not receive their serious attention.[54]

The evidence of historical writing in ancient India produced by C.V. Vaidya is very striking: "The charge has often been brought against the Indians that they had no idea of history. . . . Works known as Histories or *Itihāsas* were known even in Vedic times. The *Mahābhārata* itself was originally a history. Historical facts, especially genealogies, were most carefully recorded at all times in ancient India. The detailed figures given by Megasthenes himself clearly prove that this was done in his time. Hiuen Tsang has recorded it as a fact that annals were carefully recorded in each state. The *Rājataraṅgiṇī* speaks of ancient histories of Kashmer. In the presernce of such evidence extending over such a long period, we cannot believe that history had no existence in India."[55]

A great nation never passes away without leaving records of its deeds and achievements. Ancient India was not bereft of such records. "Each successive age has left in its literature, an impress, a photograph as it were, of its thought and civilization; and when we bring all these photographs together. . . . We perceive at a glance the whole history of the Hindu nation and its civilization."[56]

It is also believed that some of the ancient annals and other written records were destroyed or tempered with by the Muslims in the course of their invasions of India.

The inscriptional records also reflect the historical and chronological sense of the ancient Indians. The inscriptions constitute valuable testimony to historical writings in ancient India. They are, "in fact, the earliest form of written history in prose . . . betraying the historical ideas of their authors". They give a lot of historical information with

53. *The Wonder that was India*, p. 45.
54. *The Wonder that was India*.
55. *The Mahābhārata*: *A Criticism*, pp. 58-59.
56. R.C. Dutt, "An Introductory Essay on the History of Kashmira", in J.C. Dutt, *op. cit.*, II, IV-V.

reliable dates. They supply genealogies of the reigning kings and recount their as well as their ancestors' lives and deeds, throw light on conditions of gifts and grants of lands, etc. Inscriptions engraved on stones, copper-plates, rocks, pillars, walls and coins bespeak the history of the land. The historical sense of the authors or composers of the inscriptions can in no way be doubted. The information supplied by Hariṣeṇa (a brāhmaṇa poet-laureate) in Allahabad pillar inscription (partly inverse and partly in prose) about the conquests and campaigns of his patron, Samudragupta (*c.* AD 335-75) and by Ravikīrti (the Jain poet) in Aihole inscription (dated Śaka 556 = AD 634) about the achievements of his patron Pulakeśin II, the Cālukya ruler of Bādāmī (*c.* AD 610-43), vindicates their sense of history. Vidyācakravartin, the court poet of the Hoysala monarch, *Vīra-Ballāla* II (AD 1172-1219), was the author of many inscriptions engraved on stones. Historical events were recorded in the inscriptions at the instance of the contemporary kigs so as to preserve them as records for the future. It is significant to add that Vigraharāja IV also known as Vīsaladeva (AD 1152-64) was grandfather of the famous Pr̥thvīrāja Cauhān. He ruled over the kingdom of Ajmer form AD 1152 to 1158. He was a great warrior. He captured Delhi, the capital of Tomar kingdom, in AD 1158. He was himself an accomplished poet and a parton of learning. He himself composed the *Harakeli-nāṭaka* in Sanskrit describing his conquest as a military leader and got it engraved on stone slabs portions of which have been recovered from an inscribed stone slab on the wall of a mosque named Aḍhāi-din-kā-Jhoprā at Ajmer. His court poet, Somadeva, composed *Lalitvigraharāja* which was also engraved on stone slabs. But only a part of it is row available.[57]

Most of the ancient Indian inscriptions are dated. They give the dates of the events that took place during the reigns of the kings. They specify the reign periods or length of the reigns of the kings. The inscriptions of Aśoka, king Khāravela of Kaliṅga, Rudradāman of Jūnāgarh, the Sātavāhanas, Samudragupta, Harṣa, the Pālas, Senas, Cālukyas, Rāṣṭrakūṭas, Pallavas, Coḷas and Hoysalas are important from both historical and chronologial point of view. Fleet, an authority on Gupta inscriptions, had to accept that the ancient Hindus had an ability and capability to write history.

The coins also like inscriptions give us the dates of rulers and events. Among the non-literay sources these two provide the most important materials for writing history

57. I am extremely grateful to Dr. V.S. Bhargava, retd Principal, Govt. College, Ajmer, for supplying me the infromation sought for through his letter dated 16 February 1991. For details of the *Harakeli-Nāṭaka* see *Ind. Ant.*, XIX, 1890, pp. 215-19, XX, 1891, p. 201.

of ancient India.[58] N.L. Dey observes:

> "There is no systematic history of India before the Mahomedan conquest, the facts are meagre and scattered . . . the ancient Hindus did not possess any regular history, except the *Rājataraṅgiṇi*. Historiography was perhaps too secular to be worthy of the consideration of a people so much imbued with religious ideas. The *Rājataraṅgiṇi* . . . written by Kalhana . . . is only the chronicle of the kings of Kashmir. But the ancient Hindus have left behind them innumerable works form which some idea of the civilization . . . could be deduced. The several copper-plate inscriptions, incriptions upon rocks and temples, and the various coins which are exhumed from time to time from the bowels of the earth, might also very well form a chapter of ancient Hindu history".[59]

Ancient India was not devoid of either history or historians. The hitherto existing impression created by some Indian and foreign scholars that the ancient Indians lacked in historical sense can be dispelled on the basis of the richness of historical material embodied in different kinds of literature and the inscriptions. They have displayed enough historical sense in the genealogical lists of royal dynasties, biographical works and chronicles. Some of the Purāṇas, Pāli chronicles and commentaries, and the Jain works, Kalhaṇa's work (all noted before) and the inscriptional records testify to their knowledge of chronology too.

58. See A.K. Narain, "Numismatists and Historical Writing", in C.H. Philips (ed.), *op. cit*, pp. 94-98.
59. *Civilisation in Ancient India*, pp. 5-6, 175-76.

12

Observations and Conclusions

THE ancient Indians were acquainted more with the art than science of historiography. It would be too much to expect scientific, serious or absolutely genuine histories from the authors of ancient times. The professional historians of today with few exceptions in their zeal for the truth, accuracy, objectivity and authentic chronology often neglect the study of histories contained in ancient Indian literature. It has been aptly remarked that ". . . . The modern historian of ancient India unceremoniously discards the ancient forms and ideas — the very context of ancient historical works".[1] The value of the works produced by ancient historians of India should be judged by the standard prevailing in a contemporary age and not by the modern standard of historiography. Every age had its own tradition of historiography. The prevailing attitudes in any age guide or influence the historian in the treatment of his subject.[2] The ancient concept of history and chronology was totally different from the modern one. The ancient historians of India have presented the facts whatsoever without distorting them. The tradition of presenting history within a chronological framework had not fully developed in ancient India. In ancient Indian historical writings, facts are more important than the chronology.

The tradition of historical writing in ancient India began in the time of Vedavyāsa and continued till the end of the twelfth century AD. The oldest Indian historical tradition is preserved in the *R̥gveda*. The R̥gvedic hymns about the Āryan people speak of the sense of history of those who composed them. These hymns constitute the earliest evidence of the historical sense in India. And the composition of the original *Bhārata Itihāsa* or *Bhārata Saṁhitā* and the *Purāṇa Saṁhitā* or *Itihāsa Saṁhitā* by Vyāsa in the

1. A.K. Narain, "Writing a new History of Ancient India : A Study in Problems, Sources and Methods", in *Problems of Historical writing in India* (proceeds of the Seminar held at Delhi Jan. 1963), p. 8.

2. See also Narain, *op. cit.*; Pathak, *Ancient Historians of India*, p. 148; Barnes, *A History of Historical Writing*, pp. 295-96.

Dvāpara age marked the beginnings of Indian historiography. The two main traditions of historiography in its early phase were the epic and Purāṇic. The Purāṇic tradition is relatively of greater value. The *purāṇakāras* were the first to record and preserve the dynastic genealogies and chronology — the two legitimate constituents or components of history. Their historical conception and chronological perception find reflections in the information they have supplied about the kings of different dynasties with length of their reigns. They have provided the dynastic history of India in a very systematic way up to the beginning of the Gupta rule. The details of the kingdoms and dynasties of the post-Gupta period furnished by them with some chronological data though not very systematic are also of considerable historical value. The other two important traditions of historical writing in ancient India were the Buddhist and Jain. The Buddhist and Jain scholars produced a number of semi-historical works before the seventh century AD.

Ancient Indian historiography anterior to the seventh century AD was largely based on *itihāsa-Purāṇa* tradition. However, its impact on the historical writings of the later period to a considerable extent is also discernible. The traditional concept of history went on changing with developing historical sense, prevailing historical tradition in a contemporary age and events of the time.

The period extending from the seventh to the twelfth century AD proved to be a blooming one in the history of historical writing in ancient India. A number of historical biographies were produced in different parts of India during the period. The court poet who wrote the biography of his patron highlighting his life and achievements was no less than a historiographer. There were many such court poet. The kings who patronised them also deserve the credit of giving fillip to the production of biographical works by encouraging them to undertake such works. They wanted their court poets to record both the past and contemporary events for the purpose of preserving them for the future. The biographies of many famous kings who occupy important place in the annals of ancient India were composed by their respecitve court poets during the period. Some biographies are the productions of the historical schools that flourished in the post-Harṣa period under the patronage of the Pālas of Bengal, the Paramāras of Mālawā the Cālukyas of Gujarat and Kalyāṇī and the Cāhāmanas of Śākambharī. The chronicles were also written in Sindh, Kashmir, Gujarat, Orissa and Nepal. The writing of historical biographies and of chronicles were the two significant stages in the evolution of Indian historiography. The biographies and chronicles composed during the period form important parts of historical literature. Besides these works, other historical works of various kinds were produced during the period.

The Jains made more serious approach than the Buddhists to history as evidenced by the quality of the works they produced. They have a number of historical treatises to their credit. They, however, like the Hindus made significant contributions to the development of historical writing in ancient India. The Muslim author of the chronicle of Sindh was one of the ancient historians of India.

It is not correct to say that the ancient Indians did not produce political history. The deeds of kings, the political events, including struggles between native princes for power and political supremacy, attacks and invasions, wars and conquests and rise and fall of kingdoms, etc., are described in detail especially in the biographies and chronicles of the post sixth century AD.

The tradition of historical writing in south India was no less rich than that of in other parts of the country. Various kinds of quasi-historical works were produced in south India both before and after the seventh century AD which include histories of kingdoms and dynasties, and biographies.

It is a wrong notion that except the *Rājataraṅgiṇī* of Kalhaṇa, there is no work in Sanskrit literature which merits the title of history. The fact remains that Kalhaṇa was the best of all ancient historians of India and his work was the best of all historical works produced in ancient India.

There were various schools of historical writing in ancient India. The historians of Gujarat, Rajasthan and Kashmir schools made proportinately greater contributions than those of other schools to the evolution of historiography in ancient India. The historians of these three prominent schools left indelible imprints of their writings on the historical thoughts and writings of the succeeding generations of Indian historians.

There was no poverty of historical knowledge and no dearth of historical works in ancient India. The works produced as a whole throw light on various aspects of ancient Indian history and culture. The view held by some scholars that the regular historical works on the part of the Hindus has long been a desideratum is not tenable.

The Purāṇic, Buddhist and Jain traditions of chronology and the chronology supplied by Kalhaṇa are of great value.

The ancient Indians did possess historical sense. We, of course, do admit that only few of them were endowed with perfect sense of history and were critical historians. There were both historians and historiography in ancient India. However, there was none among the ancient Indians to leave for posterity the complete history of ancient

India. The histories we have belong to different ages and different brains. "... history is what the historian makes".[3]

3. Carr, *What is History?*, p. 26; see also P. Smith, *The Historians and History* (New York, 1964).

General Bibliography

Original Sources: Texts, Translations and Commentaries

Literary Sources

THE VEDAS

Atharvaveda Saṁhitā, ed, with Sāyaṇa's comm. by S.P. Pandit, Bombay, 1895-98; trans. with comm. by R.T.H. Griffith (*The Hymns of the Atharvaveda*), 2 vols. Vārāṇasī, 1896-97; trans. by W.D. Whitney (*On the Vedas*), HOS, Cambridge, 1905, 2nd Indian rept., Delhi 1971, Calcutta, 1972; text with Hindi trans. and comm. by Dayānanda Sarasvati, Dayānanda Saṁsthān, Delhi, VS 2032; ed. with Hindi trans. and Sāyaṇa's comm. by R. Sharma Ācārya, 2 vols. Bareli, 1973, 1975.

Ṛgveda Saṁhitā, ed. with Sāyaṇa's comm. by F. Max Müller, 2nd edn., London, 1890-92; trans. by R.T.H. Griffith, Benares, 1896-97; trans. by H.H. Wilson, 6 vols., London, 1866-88; ed. with Hindi trans. and Sāyaṇa' comm. by R. Sharma Ācārya, 4 vols., Bareli, 1974-75.

THE BRĀHMAṆAS

Aitareya Brāhmaṇa, ed. and trans. by M. Haug, Vārāṇasī, 1976-77; trans. by A.B. Keith, HOS, vol. XXV, Cambridge, Mass. 1920, rept. Delhi, 1971.

Gopatha Brāhmaṇa, ed. by R.L. Mitra and H. Vidyābhūṣaṇa, Calcutta, 1872.

Śatapatha Brāhmaṇa, ed. by A. Chinnaswami Śāstrī, P. Śāstrī and R.N. Dikshita, 2nd edn., Vārāṇasī, 1984.

THE ĀRAṆYAKA

Taittirīya Āraṇyaka, ed by H.N. Apte, Poona, 1898.

THE UPANIṢADS

Bṛhadāraṇyaka Upaniṣad, ed. by O. Böhtlingk, Leipzig, 1889.

Chāndogya Upaniṣad, ed. and trans. by Swami Gambhīrānanda, Calcutta, 1983.

Upaniṣat-Saṁgraha (Containing 188 Upaniṣads), ed. by J.L. Śāstrī, Delhi, 1980.

THE SŪTRAS

Gṛhya Sūtras

Gobhila Gṛhya Sūtra, tr. by H. Oldenberg, in SBE, vol. XXX, pt. II, Oxford, 1892, rept. Delhi, 1964.

Śrauta Sūtra

Śāṅkhāyana Śrauta Sūtra, ed. with comm. of Varadatta-suta Ānartiya and Govinda by A. Hillebrandt, Callcutta, 1888.

Śāṅkhāyana Gṛhya Sūtra, trans. by H. Oldenberg, in SBE, vol. XXIX, pt. I, Oxford, 1886, rept. Delhi, 1964.

THE DHARMA-ŚĀSTRAS

Dharmaśāstra Saṁgraha, ed. by J. Vidyāsāgar, Calcutta, 1876.

Manu-Smṛti, ed. with the *Manvartha-Muktāvalī* comm. of Kullūka Bhaṭṭa and the *Maṇiprabhā* Hindi comm. of H.G. Śāstrī by G.S. Nene, Vārāṇasī, 1970.

Vaśiṣtha-Smṛti cf *Twenty Smṛtis*, ed. with Hindi trans. by R. Sharma Ācārya, 2 vols., Bareli, 1979-80.

Yājñavalkya-Smṛti, ed. by A.F. Stenzler, Berlin, 1849; H. Apte, Ānandāśrama Skt. Series, Poona, 1903.

THE EPICS

Mahābhārata, ed. with Hindi trans. by S. Dāmodar Sātavalekar and Śrutiśīla Śarmā, Pārdi (Gujarat):

Ādi Parva, 1968.

Anuśāsana Parva, 1978.

Āraṇyaka Parva, 2 vols., 1969.

Āśramavāsika Parva, 1977.

Bhīṣma Parva, 1972.

Droṇa Parva, 1975.

Karṇa Parva, 1973.

Mahāprasthānika Parva, 1977.

Mausala Parva, 1977.

Sabhā Parva, 1982.

Śalya Parva, 1973.

Śānti Parva, 2 vols., 1979-80.

Svargārohaṇa Parva, 1977.

Udyoga Parva, 1969.

Virāṭa Parva, 1969.

Vālmikī-Rāmāyaṇa, ed. by D.R. Mankad, Oriental Research Institute, Baroda, 1965; trans. by R.T.H. Griffith, London, 1870.

Ayodhyā Kāṇḍa, ed. with Hindi trans. by Akhilānanda, Amritsar, vs 2019.

Bāla Kāṇḍa, ed. with Hindi trans. of Yudhiṣṭhira Mīmāṁsaka by Akhilānanda, Amritsar, vs 2025.

Kiṣkindhā Kāṇḍa, ed. with Hindi trans. by Akhilānanda, Amritsar, vs 2021.

Uttara Kāṇḍa, cf *Vālamikī-Rāmāyaṇa Kośa* by R.K. Rai, Vārāṇasī, 1965.

Yuddha (Laṅkā) Kāṇḍa, text with Hindi trans. of Vijayapāpla, Bahālagarh, vs 2029.

PURĀṆAS

Agni Purāṇa, ed. by R.L. Mitra, Calcutta, 1873-79; trans. by M.N. Dutt, 2 vols. Cacutta, 1903-04; text with Hindi trans. of T. Jha and G.S. Tripāṭhī, Prayāg, 1986.

Bhāgavata Purāṇa, text with Hindi trans. and annotation, 2 vols., 8th edn., Gorakhpur, Samvat, 2040; ed. with Eng. trans. by C.L. Goswami, 2 pts., 2nd edn., Gorakhpur, 1982.

Bhaviṣya Purāṇa, Veṅkaṭeśvara Press, Bombay, 1910; ed. with Hindi trans. by R. Sharma Ācārya, 2 vols., Bareli, 1978.

Brahmāṇḍa Purāṇa, ed. by H.N. Apte, Ānandāśrama Skt. Series, Poona, 1895; text with Hindi trans. of T. Jha, Prayāg, 1976.

Brahmāṇḍa Purāṇa, Veṅkaṭeśvara Press, Bombay, 1913.

Brahmavaivartta Purāṇa, ed. with Hindi trans. by T. Jha, Allahabad, 1985.

Garuḍa Purāṇa, Eng. trans. by M.N. Dutt, Calcutta, 1908, rept. Delhi, 1983.

Harivaṁśa Purāṇa, ed. by N. Mukhopādhyāya, ASB, Calcutta, 1858; R. Kinjawadekar, Poona, 1936; text with Hindi trans. and comm., 4th edn., Gorakhpur, Samvat, 2044.

Kūrma Purāṇa, ed. with Hindi trans. of Shree Chaudhari Shree Nārāyaṇa Singh by Ānandasvarūpa Gupta, Vārāṇasī, 1972.

Liṅga Purāṇa, Veṅkaṭeśvara Press, Bombay, 1927.

Mārkaṇḍeya Purāṇa, ed. by K.M. Banerjee, BIS, ASB, Calcutta, 1862; ed with Hindi trans. by Dharmendra Nath Śāstrī, Meerut, 1983; trans. by F.E. Pargiter, BIS, ASB, Calcutta, 1904.

Matsya Purāṇa, Ānandāśrama Skt. Series, Poona, 1907; text with Hindi trans., 2 vols., Gorakhpur, 1985; ed. with trans. of various oriental scholars and notes of B.C. Majumdar, S.C. Vasu, H.H. Wilson, Bentley, Wilford and others by J.D. Akhtar, vol. I, SBA, Delhi, 1972.

Padma Purāṇa, ed. by V.N. Mandalika, Ānandāśrama Skt. Series, Poona, 1893-94; *Svargakhaṇḍa*, ed. by Aśoka Chatterjee Śāstrī, Vārāṇasī, 1972.

Skanda Purāṇa, ed. by Vāsudeva Śāstrī, 3 pts., Ānandāśrama Skt. Series, Poona, 1893.

Vāmana Purāṇa, ed. with Hindi trens. of G.C. Vedānta Śāstrī, Shree Chaudhari Shree Nārāyaṇa Singh and G.S. Rai by Ānandasvarūpa Gupta, Vārāṇasī, 1968.

Varāha Purāṇa, ed. by P.H. Śāstrī, BIS, ASB, Calcutta, 1893.

Vāyu Purāṇa, Ānandāśrama Skt. Series, Poona, 1905; ed. by R.L. Mitra, 2 vols. BIS, ASB, Calcutta, 1880-88; text with Hindi trans of R.P. Tripāṭhī Śāstrī, Prayāg, 1987.

Viṣṇu Purāṇa, ed. By J. Vidyāsāgara, Calcutta, 1882; text with Hindi trans. of Muni Lal Gupta, 9th edn., Gorakhpur, Samvat, 2041; trans. by M.N. Dutt, Calcutta, 1894, and H.H. Wilson, Calcutta, 1961.

Viṣṇudharmottara Mahāpurāṇa, Veṅkaṭeśvara Press, Bombay, 1912.

OTHER LITERRARY WORKS

Amarakośa of Amara Siṁha, text with the *Maṇiprabhā* Hindi comm. of H.G. Śāṣtrī, Vārāṇasī, 1957.

Arthaśāstra of Kauṭilya, ed. by R. Shamasastri, Mysore, 1909; trans. by R. Shamasastri, Bangalore, 1915; ed. with Hindi trans. by Vachaspati Gairola, Vārāṇasī, 1984.

Gauḍavaho of Vākpatirāja, ed. by S.P. Pandit, Bombay Sanskrit & Prakrit Series, No. 34, Bombay, 1887.

Harṣacarita of Bāṇa, ed. by P.V. Kane, Bombay, 1918, rept. Delhi, 1965; K.P. Parab, 3rd edn., Bombay, 1912; trans. by E.B. Cowell and F.W. Thomas, RAS, London, 1897, 2nd edn., 1929; Hindi trans. by V.S. Agrawala (*Harṣacarita: Ek Sāṁskṛtika Adhyayana*, Patna, 1964).

Kāvyamīmāṁsā of Rājaśekhara, ed with Prakāśa Hindi comm. by G.S. Rai, Vārāṇasī, 1964.

Kīrtikaumudī of Someśvara, Bombay, 1883.

Mahābhāṣya of Patañjali, ed. by F. Kielhorn, 3 vols., Bombay Skt. Series, Bombay, 1880-85.

Mālavikāgnimitra of Kālidāsa, ed. by K.P. Parab, Bombay, 1915; Eng. trans. by C.H. Tawney, Calcutta, 1875 and 1891; text with Eng. trans. of M.R. Kale, revd. by J.L. Dave and A.S. Upādhyāya, Delhi, 1985.

Maṇi-Mekhalai in its historical setting, by S.K. Aiyangar.

Mudrārākṣasa of Viśākhadatta, ed. with the *Śaśikalā* Sanskrit and Hindi comms. by S.V. Singh, Vārāṇasī, 1973.

Navasāhasāṅkacarita of Padmagupta, ed. by V.S. Islampurkar, Bombay Skt. Series, Bombay, 1895.

Nirukta of Yāska, ed. with Hindi trans. by Uma Shankar Sharma, Vārāṇasī, 1966; ed. with Durgācārya's comm. by V.K. Rajavade, Poona, 1921-26.

Pṛthvīrāja Rāso of Cand Bardai, ed. by S.S. Das, Banāras, 1904, and Pandia and Das, Banāras, 1913.

Pṛthvīrājavijaya of Jayānaka, ed. with comm. of Jonarāja by G.H. Ojha and C.S. Guleri, Ajmer, 1941; Hindi trans. in *Nāgarī Pracāriṇī Patrikā,* Kāśī, 5, 1981, pp. 133-83; Eng. abstract in *JRAS*, 1913, pp. 259-81.

Rājataraṅgiṇī of Kalhaṇa, ed. by Durga Prasad, Bombay, 1892; trans. by M.A. Stein, 3 vols. Westminster, 1900, rept., 2nd edn., Delhi, 1961; R.S. Pandit, Allahabad, 1935, rept. Delhi, 1968, and J.C. Dutt, 2 vols, Calcutta 1879 & 1887, rept. Delhi, 1997.

Rāmacarita of Sandhyākara Nandi, ed. by R.C. Majumdar, R.G. Basak and N.G. Banerjee, Rajsahi, 1939.

Śilappadikāram by V.R.R. Dikshitar, Oxford, 1939.

Vikramāṅkadevacarita of Bilhaṇa, ed. by G. Buhler, Bombay Skt. Series, No. 14, Bombay, 1875; trans. by S.C. Banerjee and and A.K. Gupta, Calcutta, 1965.

Vikramārjuna-Vijaya or *Pampā-Bhārata* of Pampā, ed. by L. Rice, Bangalore, 1898.

Yaśoharacarita of Kanakasena Vādirāja, ed T.A. Gopinatha. Rao, Tanjore, 1912.

BUDDHSIST WORKS

Canonical

Aṅguttara Nikāya, ed. R. Morris and E. Hardy, 5 vols., PTS. London, 1885-1900.

Apadāna, not yet edited.

Dīgha Nikāya, ed. T.W. Rhys Davids and J.E. Carpenter, 3 vols., PTS, London, 1890-1911, rept. 1947-60; trans. T.W. and C.A.F. Rhys Davids (*The Dialogues of the Buddha*), 3 vols., PTS, London, 1899-1921.

Jātaka, ed. V. Fausböll, 6 vols., London, 1877-97; trans. by various hands under the editorship of E.B. Cowell, 7 vols., Cambridge, 1895-1913.

Majjhima Nikāya, ed. V. Trenckner and R. Chalmers, 3 vols., PTS, London, 1888-99.

Milindapañha, ed. V. Trenckner, London, 1880; trans. from Pāli by T.W. Rhys Davids (*The Questions of King Milinda*), in SBE, XXXV, I Oxford, 1890, rept. Delhi 1969; XXXVI, II Oxford, 1894, rept. Delhi, 1969.

Saṁyutta Nikāya, ed. M. Leon Feer and Mrs Rhys Davids, 5 vols., PTS, London, 1884-1904.

Sutta Nipāta, ed. D. Andersen and H. Smith, PTS, London, 1913; ed. Rahul Sāṅkṛtyāyana, Rangoon, 1937; trans. V. Fausböll, SBE, X, II, 2nd edn., Oxford 1898.

Vinaya Piṭaka, ed. H. Oldenberg, 5 vols., London, 1879-83.

Non-Canonical

Aśokāvadāna, ed. S.K. Mukhopadhyaya, Delhi, 1963.

Avadānaśataka, ed. J.S. Speyer, 2 vols., St. Petersburg, 1906.

Buddhacarita of Aśvaghoṣa, ed. and trans. by E.H. Johnston, 2 vols., 2nd edn., Delhi 1972; trans. (cantos I-XVII) by E.B. Cowell, in SBE, XLIX, I, Oxford, 1894, rept. Delhi, 1972.

Buddhavaṁśa, ed. Morris, PTS, London, 1882; trans. B.C. Law, PTS, London, 1938.

Dīpavaṁsa, ed. and trans. H. Oldenberg, London, 1879, rept. Delhi, 1982.

Divyāvadāna, ed. E.B. Cowell and R.A. Neil, Cambridge, 1886, rept. 1976.

Lalitavistara (or *Memoirs of the Eary Life of Sakya Muni*), ed. R.L. Mitra, BIS, ASB, Calcutta, 1877; ed. S. Lefmann and A.S. Halle, 3 vols., London 1902 1908, rept. by P.L. Vaidya, Buddhist Skt. Texts Series, Darbhanga, 1958.

Mahāvaṁsa, ed. W. Geiger, PTS, London, 1908, rept. 1958; trans. W. Geiger and M.H. Bode, PTH, London, 1912, rept. 1950; trans of both *Dīpavaṁsa* and *Mahāvaṁsa* by E.M. Coomaraswamy (*The Dīpavaṁsa and Mahāvaṁsa and their Historical Development in Ceylon*), Colombo, 1908.

Mahāvastu, ed. E. Senart, 3 vols., Paris, 1882-97; trans. J.J. Jones, 3 vols. (16, 18, 19), SBB, London, 1949-56.

Mañjuśrīmūlakalpa, ed. T. Ganapati Śāstrī, 3 vols. (70, 76 & 84), Trivandrum Skt. Series, Trivandrum, 1920-25.

Sāmantapāsādikā (comm. on the *Vinaya Piṭaka*), ed. J. Takakusu and M. Nagai, 4 vols., PTS, London, 1924-38.

Sumaṅgalavilāsinī (comm. on the *Dīgha Nikāya*), ed. Rhys Davids and J.E. Carpenter, 3 vols., PTS, London, 1886-1932.

JAIN WORKS

Canonical

Ācārāṅga Sūtra, trans. H. Jacobi, SBE, XXII, Oxford, 1884.

Bhagavatī Sūtra, Āgamodaya Samiti, Surat.

Kalpasūtra of Bhadrabāhu, ed. H. Jacobi, Leipzig, 1879; trans. H. Jacobi, SBE, XXII, Oxford, 1884.

Non-canonical

Ādi Purāṇa of Jinasena III, ed. Pannālal Jain, 1st edn. BGP, Kāśī, 1951.

Harivaṁśa Purāṇa of Jinasena II, ed. Pannālal Jain, BGP, Kāśī, 1962.

Jasahara-cariu of Puṣpadanta, ed with notes by P.L. Vaidya, Karanja, 1931.

Jayadhavala of Jinasena III, BGP, Kāśī, 1947.

Kumārapālacarita (Prākṛt Dvāśrayakāvya) of Hemacandra, ed. S.P. Pandit, Bombay, 1900; P.L. Vaidya, Poona, 1936.

Kumārapālacarita of Jayasiṁha Sūri, ed. Kṣāntivijaya Gani, Bombay, 1926.

Kumārapāla-pratibodha of Somaprabhācārya, Gaekwad Oriental Series, No. XIV.

Kuvalayamālā of Udyotana Sūri, ed. A.N. Upadhye, pts I & II, revd. edn., Bombay, 1970.

Mahāpurāṇa of Puṣpadanta, ed. D.K. Jain, 4 vols., MDJG, Delhi, 1979-83; P.L. Vaidya, 3 vols., Bombay, 1937-41.

Mahāvīracarita of Gunacandra, Devchand Lalbhai Jain Series, No. 75, Bombay, 1929.

Nayakumāra-cariu of Puṣpadanta, ed. with notes by H.L. Jain, Karanja, 1933.

Nītivākyāmṛta of Somadeva Sūri, MDJG, Bombay, 1887-88.

Padma Purāṇa of Raviṣena, ed. Pannālal Jain, 3 vols., 1st edn., BGP, Kāśī, 1958-59.

Pariśiṣṭaparvan of Hemacandra, ed. H. Jacobi, 2nd edn., BIS, Calcutta, 1932.

Pārśvanāthacarita (The Life and stories of the Jain Savior Pārśvanātha), trans. M. Bloomfield, Baltimore, 1919.

Prabandhacintāmaṇi of Merutuṅga, ed. Jinavijaya Muni, Śantiniketan, 1933; Bombay, 1932.

Paṭṭāvalīs, Eng. trans. of the Digambara *Paṭṭāvalīs* by Hoernle, *Ind. Ant.*, XIX, pp. 233-42, XX, pp. 431-61, XXI, pp. 57-84; also in *Jaina Antiquary*, Arrah, XV, 2, pp. 1-7; *Jaina Siddhānta Bhāṣkara*, Arrah, I, I, p. 37; I, 2-3, p. 32; I, 4, pp. 43, 51, 71, 78, 81, 103; *Paṭṭāvalī-Samuccaya* (a Collection of Śvetāmbara *Paṭṭāvalīs*) ed. by Muni Darśanavijaya, 2 vols., Viramgam, 1933.

Tilakamañjarī of Dhanapāla, ed. Bhavadatta Śāstrī, 2nd edn., Bombay, 1938.

Tiloyapaṇṇati of Yativṛṣabha, ed. A.N. Upadhye and H.L. Jain, Sholapur, 1951.

Triṣaṣṭiśalākāpuruṣacarita of Hemacandra, trans. H.M. Johnson, I-VI, Gaikwad Oriental Series, Baroda, 1931-62.

Uttarapurāṇa of Gunabhadra, ed. Pannālal Jain, 1st edn., BGP, Kāśī, 1952, revd. edn. Kāśī, 1954.

Vardhamānacarita of Asaga, Sholapur, 1931.

Vasudevahiṇḍi of Saṁghadāsa (Dharmadāsa), Bhavnagar, 1930; *The Vasudevahiṇḍi — An Authentic Jain Version of the Bṛhatkathā*, J.C. Jain, Ahmedabad, 1977.

Yaśastilakacampu of Somadeva Sūri, ed. Sivadatta and K.P. Parab, Bombay, 1901-03.

SOME LOCAL CHRONICLES AND VAṀŚĀVALĪS

Tamildeśa

Coḷavaṁśacaritaṁ (for history of the Coḷa dynasty).

Orissa

Mādalā Pāñjī and *Gaṅgavaṁśānucarita* (based on the former) for history of Orissa since the establishment of the Gaṅga dynasty; *JASB*, vol. VI, pt. II, 1837, p. 756f (for *Vaṁsāvalī* of Orissa); *As. Res.*, vol. XV, 1822 (for Chronology and History of Orissa).

Nepal

Gopālarāja Vaṁśāvalī, in 3 pts., partly in Sanskrit and partly in old Newari compiled in AD 1390, discovered by C. Bendall in Darbar Library Kathmandu during 1884-85; ed. by D.R. Regmi, *Medieval Nepal,* vol. III, pp. 112ff, 158ff. The Chronicles and *Vaṁśāvalīs* of Nepal are important for the study of its history of ancient and early medieval period.

Parbatiya Vaṁśāvalī (Originally written in Parbatiya with an admixture of Sanskrit and Newari) by Munshi Shiva Shankar Singh and Pt. Shri Gunanand; *History of Nepal,* ed. by Daniel Wright (1st edn. Cambridge, 1877, rept. Kathmandu, 1972) is totally based on the translation of this work; *Ind. Ant.,* vol. XIII, pp. 411f (for Bhagawanlar Indraji's writing on the *Vaṁśāvalīs* of Nepal).

Vaṁśāvalī, in Sanskrit (anonymous), 2 vols., composed in AD 1350.

CLASSICAL (GREEK AND LATIN) SOURCES

Mccrindle, J.W., *Ancient India as Described by Megasthenes and Arrian* (trans. of the Fragments of the *Indika* of Megasthenes, and of the first part of the *Indika* (Chs. I-XVII) of Arrian, 1st edn., London, 1877.

———, *Ancient India as Described in Classical Literature*, Westminster, 1901, rept. Delhi, 1984.

———, *Invasion of India by Alexander the Great*, 1st edn., Westminster, 1892, rept. Delhi, 1989.

Majumdar, R.C., *Classical Accounts of India,* Calcutta, 1960, rept. 1981.

Pliny, *Naturalis Historia* (*Natural History*), ed. by C. Mayhoff, Leipzig, 1892-1909; trans., New York, 1962.

CHINESE WORK

Hiuen Tsang, *Si-Yu-Ki*, Eng. trans. by S. Beal (*Buddhist Records of the Western World*), 2 vols., 1st edn., London, 1884, rept. 1906, Delhi, 1969, and by T. Watters (*On Yuan Chwang's Travels in India*), ed. by T.W. Rhys, Davids and S.W. Bushell, 2 vols., RAS, London, 1904-05, 2nd Indian edn., Delhi, 1973.

ARABIC WORKS

Al-Biruni, *Tahqiq-i-Hind*, Eng. trans. of the the Arabic text by E.C. Sachau (*Alberuni's India*), 2 vols., 1st edn. Berlin, 1888, London, 1910, rept. Delhi, 1964, 1989.

Cacanāmā (or *Chachnama*), Originally written in Arabic by an anonymous Muslim historian of Sindh, trans. into Persian by Muhammad Ali bin Abu Bakr Kufi in AD 1216, Eng. trans. in H.M. Elliot and J. Dowson's *The History of India as told by its own Historians,* vol. I, Allahabad (year of publication not given).

Sachau, E.C. (trans.), *Alberuni's Chronology of Ancient Nations*, London, 1879.

Coins and Inscriptions

Allan, J., *A Catalogue of the Indian Coins in the British Museum, Ancient India,* London, 1936.

——, *Catalogue of the Coins of the Gupta dynasty and of Śaśāṅka, king of Gauda* (in the British Museum), London, 1914.

Cunningham, A., *Coins of Ancient India from the Earliest times dawn to the seventh century AD*, London, 1891, rept. Vārāṇasī, 1971.

——, *Coins of Medieval India*, London, 1893.

Fleet, J.F., *Inscriptions of the Early Gupta kings and their Successors*, CII, III, Calcutta, 1888.

Rapson, E.J., *Indian Coins,* Vārāṇasī, 1969.

Sircar, D.C. (ed.), *Select Inscriptions Bearing on Indian History and Civilization,* vol. I, Calcutta, 1965.

Smith, V.A., *Catalogue of the Coins in the Indian Museum, Calcutta, Coins of Ancient India,* vol. I, Oxford, 1906, rept. Vārāṇasī, 1972.

Modern Works

Acton, L., *Lectures on Modern History*, London, 1906.

Agrawala, V.S., *India as Described by Manu*, Vārāṇasī, 1970.

——, *Bhārata Sāvitrī*, vols 1 and 2, 2nd edn., Delhi, 1977, vol. 3, 1st edn., Delhi, 1968.

Agrawala, P.K. (ed.), *Itihāsa-Darśana* (Collection of Papers of the late V.S. Agrawala), Vārāṇasī, 1978.

Aiyangar, S.K., *The Beginnings of South Indian History,* Madras, 1918.

Aiyar, K.G.S., *Cera kings of the Saṅgam Period,* London, 1937.

Ali, S.M., *The Geography of the Purāṇas,* Delhi, 1983.

Allan, J., W. Haig, and H.H. Dodwell, *The Cambridge Shorter History of India,* Delhi, 1964.

Altekar, A.S., "Can we Reconstruct Pre-Bhārat war History?," *JBHU*, IV, pp. 183-223.

Arora, R.K., *Historical and Cultural Data from the Bhaviṣya Purāṇa,* Delhi, 1972.

Barnes, H.E., *A History of Historical Writing,* New York, 1963.

Barraclough, G., *History in a Changing World,* Oxford, 1955.

Basham, A.L., *The Wonder that was India,* London, 1969.

Baveridge, H., *A Comprehensive History of India*, vol. I, London, 1862, rept. Delhi, 1982.

Bentley, J., "On the Principal Eras and Dates of the Ancient Hindus", *As. Res.,* vol. 5, Delhi, 1979, pp. 315-43.

Bhandarkar, R.G., *Early History of the Dekkan down to the Mahomedan Conquest,* Delhi, 1979.

——, *A Peep into the Early History of India*, Delhi, 1978.

Bühler, G., "On the Authenticity of Jaina Tradition", in *The Indian Sect of the Jains*, trans. by Burgess, London, 1903.

——, "Hindu Chronology", in *EB*, vol. 13 (211th edn.), pp. 499-500.

Burckhardt, J., *Judgements on History and on Historians*, Oxford, 1959.

Carr, E.H., *What is History?*, Harmondsworth, 1977.

Chakraberti, C., *Classical Studies in Ancient Races and Myths,* Delhi, 1979.

Chakravorty, B.B., *Itihāsa of Bhāratavarṣa from the Bhāratīya Viewpoint (up to Gupta Period)*, Calcutta, 1995.

Chanda, R.P., *The Indo-Aryan Races*, Delhi, 1978.

Chatterji, S.K. (ed.), *Cultural Heritage of India,* vol. V, Calcutta, 1978.

Collingwood, R.G., *The Idea of History*, London, 1973.

Cowell, E.B. (ed.), *The History of India*, 9th edn., London, 1911.

Croce, B., *The Theory and History of Historiography*, London, 1921.

———, *History as the Story of Liberty* London, 1941.

Das, A.C., *Ṛgvedic India — Cultural History of India as depicted in the Ṛgveda*, 2 vols., Delhi, 1980.

Dasgupta, K.K., "Historical Biography in Sanskrit Literature" in S.P. Sen (ed.), *Historical Biography in Indian Literature,* Calcutta, 1979, pp. 3-28.

De, S.C., *Historicity of Rāmāyaṇa and the Indo-Aryan Society in India and Ceylon*, Delhi, 1976.

Devahuti, D. (ed.), *Bias in Indian Historiography,* Delhi, 1980.

———, *Harsha: A Political Study,* Oxford, 1970.

Dey, N.L., *Civilization in Ancient India,* Delhi, 1972.

Dikshita, U.S., *Maharṣi Vedavyāsa: A Historical and Cultural Biography*, Vārāṇasī, 1968.

Dikshitar, V.R.R., "The Purāṇa: A Study", *IHQ*, vol. VIII, pp. 747-67.

———, *Studies in Tamil Literature and History*, London, 1930.

Dutt, R.C., *A History of Civilization in Ancient India based on Sanskrit Literature,* vol. I (*c.* 200-320 BC), Mymensingh, 1988, rept., Delhi, 1972.

———, *Ancient India* (*c. 2000 BC-AD 800*), Delhi, 1980.

———, "An Introductory Essay on the History of Kashmira", in J.C. Dutt, *Kings of Kashmira* (Eng. trans. of the *Rājataraṅgiṇī* of Kalhaṇa), vol. II, Calcutta, 1887, rept. Delhi, 1997, pp. iii-xxx.

Farquhar, J.N., *An Outline of the Religious Literature of India*, Oxford, 1920, rept. Delhi, 1967.

Geldner, K.F., *Vedische Studiesn*, Stuttgart, 1881-1901.

Ghoshal, U.N., *The Beginnings of Indian Historiography and Other Essays,* Calcutta, 1944.

———, *Studies in Indian History and Culture*, Calcutta, 1957.

———, "History and Historians of Ancient India in the Modern Age", in *Indo-Asian Culture,* IX, 1961, pp. 353-84.

Gopalan, R., *History of the Pallavas of Kāñcī*, Madras, 1928.

Gottschalk, L., *Understanding History — A Premier of Historical Method,* New York, 1958.

Gupta, S.P., and Ramachandran, K.S. (ed.), *Aspects of Indian History and Archaeology*, Delhi, 1977.

Gyani, S.D., *Agni Purāṇa: A Study,* Vārāṇasī, 1964.

Hinduqui, K.K., *Yaśastilakachampu and Indian Culture,* Sholapur, 1949.

Hopkins, E.W., *Great Epic of India*, New York, 1901, rept. Calcutta, 1969.

Hutchison, J. and Vogel, J. ph., *History of the Panjab Hill States,* vol. I, Lahore, 1933, rept. Shimla, 1982.

Jain, G.C., *Yaśastilaka Kā Sāṁskṛtika Adhyayana*, Amritsar, 1967.

Jain, J.C., *Life in Ancient India as Depicted in the Jaina Canon and Commentaries* (*6th century* BC *to 17th century* AD), Delhi 1984.

Jain, J.P., *The Jaina Sources of the History of Ancient India (100 BC-AD 900)*, Delhi, 1964.

Jain, R.C., *Ethnology of Ancient Bhārat,* Vārāṇasī, 1970.

Jayaswal, K.P., *Hindu Polity*, Bangalore, 1981.

———, *History of India (AD 150 350)*, Lahore, 1933.

———, "Chronology and History of Nepal, 600 BC-AD 800", *JBORS*, vol XXII, pt. III, 1936, pp. 157-264.

Jones, W., "On the Chronlogy of the Hindus", *As. Res.,* vol. 2, 1st pub. 1799, rept. Delhi, 1979, pp, 107-13.

Kaegi, A., *Life in Ancient India (Studies in Rig Vedic India)*, trans. from the German by R. Arrowsmith, Calcutta, 1950.

Keith, A.B., *History of Sanskrit Literature*, Oxford, 1920, rept. Delhi, 1973.

———, *The Religion and Philosophy of the Veda and Upanishads*, HOS, vol. XXXI, pt. I, Cambridge, Mass, 1925. rept. Delhi, 1976.

Kennedy, J., "The Purāṇic Histories of the Early Aryas", *JRAS*, 1915.

Kosambi, D.D., *The Culture and Civilisation of Ancient India in Historical Outline*, Delhi, 1972.

———, *An Introduction to the Study of Indian History*, Bombay, 1975.

Krishnamacharias, M., *History of Classical Sanskrit Literature*, 3rd edn., Delhi, 1974.

Kumar, V., *Tilakamañjarī kā Ālocanātamaka Adhyayana*, Ujjain, 1978.

Law, B.C., *A History of Pali Literature*, 2 vols., Delhi, 1983.

———, *Geographical Essays Relating to Ancient Geography of India*, Delhi, 1976.

Macdonell, A.A., *History of Sanskrit Literature*, 1st edn. Oxford, 1899, 3rd Indian edn., Delhi, 1972.

Macdonell, A.A. and A.B. Keith, *Vedic Index of Names and Subjects*, 2 vols., 1st edn., London, 1912, rept. 3rd edn., *Indian Texts Series*, Delhi, 1967.

Majumdar, A.K., *Early Hindu India: A Dynastic Study,* vol. I, 1st edn. Dhākā, 1917, rept. Delhi, 1981.

Majumdar, R.C. (ed.), *The Vedic Age*, Bombay, 1965.

———, *Ancient India*, Delhi, 1977.

Mankad, D.R., "Studies in Purāṇic History, Genealogies and Chronology in Modern Times", in *Purāṇa*, IV, I, 1962, pp. 3-22.

———, *Purāṇic Chronology*, Vallabh Vidyānagar, 1951.

Masson-Oursel, P. & C., *Ancient India and Indian Civilisation*, London, 1951.

Max Müller, F., *A History of Ancient Sanskrit Literature*, 1st edn., London, 1859, revd. and ed. by S.N. Śāstrī, Vārāṇasī, 1968.

———, *The Vedas* (Collections of lectures and writings of Max Müller pub. in his various books), Vārāṇasī, 1969.

———, *India — What Can it teach us*, London, 1883, 1899.

Mirashi, V.V., "Some Purāṇic Passages corroborated by Inscriptional and Numismatic Evidence", in *Purāṇa*, vol. I, pt. I pp. 31-38.

Mishra, B.B., *Polity in the Agni Purāṇa*, Calcutta, 1965.

Mishra, B.P., *Nepal Kā Itihāsa*, Bombay, 1904.

Mitra, R.L., *Sanskrit Buddhist Literature of Nepal,* Calcutta, 1882.

Mookerji, R. Kumud, *Ancient India*, Allahabad, 1956.

Muir, J., *Original Sanskrit Texts on the Origin and History of the People of India, their Religion and Institutions,* vol. II, 2nd edn., London, 1871.

Mukerjee, R. Kamal, *The Culture and Art of India,* London, 1959.

Mukhtar, J.K., *Varṇi Volume*, Sāgar, 1949.

Murthy, H.V.S., "Historical Biography in Kannada Literature", in S.P. Sen (ed.), *Historical Biography in Indian Literature*, pp. 342-44.

Nehru, J.L., *The Discovery of India*, Delhi, 1974.

Padmanabhan, S.N., "Historical Biographies in Tamil Literatue", in S.P. Sen (ed.), *Historical Biography in Indian Literature,* pp. 315-26.

Pande, S.N., *Geographical Horizon of the Mahābhārata*, Vārāṇasī, 1980.

Pargiter, F.E., *Ancient Indian Historical Tradition*, 1st edn. London, 1922, rept. Delhi, 1972.

———, *The Purāṇa text of the Dynasties of the Kali Age,* Oxford, 1913.

———, "Ancient Indian Genealogies and Chronology", *JRAS*, 1910, pp. 1-56.

———, "Earliest Indian Traditional History", *JRAS*, 1914, pp, 267ff.

Pathak, V.S., *Ancient Historians of India,* Bombay, 1966.

Patil, D.R., *Cultural History from the Vāyu Purāṇa*, Poona, 1946, rept. Delhi, 1973.

———, "Gupta Inscriptions and Purāṇic Tradition", *BDCRI*, II, pp. 2-58.

Philips, C.H. (ed.), *Historians of India, Pakistan and Ceylon,* vol I of *Historical Writing on the Peoples of Asia,* London, 1961, rept. 1967.

Phillips, M., *The Teaching of the Vedas*, London, 1894, rept. Delhi, 1976.

Powicke, F., *Modern Historians and the Study of History*, London, 1955.

Pradhan, S.N., *Chronology of Ancient India,*Vārāṇasī, 1979.

Prakash, O., *Political Ideas in the Purāṇas*, Allahabad, *1977.*

Premi, N.R., *Jaina Sāhitya aur Itihāsa*, Bombay, 1942, revd. edn., 1956.

Pusalker, A.D., *Studies in the Epics and Purāṇas*, Bombay, 1955.

———, "Conception of History in Ancient Indian Literature", in *Our Heritage*, XII, 2, 1964, pp. 35-52.

———, "Sanskrit Histories and Chronicles", in *Cul. Her. Ind.,* vol. V, ed. by S.K. Chatterji, Calcutta, 1978, pp. 283-90.

Ragozin, Z.A., *History of Vedic India*, 1st edn., London, 1895, rept. Delhi, 1984.

Rai, R.K., *Vālmikī-Rāmāyaṇa Kośa*, Vārāṇasī, 1965.

———, *Mahābhārata Kośa*, Vārāṇasī, 1982.

Rapson, E.J. (ed.), *The Cambridge History of India,* vol. I, *Ancient India*, Cambridge, 1922, rept. Delhi, 1962.

———, *Ancient India from the Earliest Times to the first century AD,* Vārāṇasī, 1981.

Ray, S.N., *Historical and Cultural Studies in the Purāṇas,* Allahabad, 1978.

Raychaudhuri, H.C., *Political History of Ancient India,* 6th edn., Calcutta, 1953.

Regmi, D.R., *Ancient Nepal,* 3rd edn., Calcutta, 1969.

Renou, L., *Vedic India*, trans. from the French by Philip Spratt, *Classical India* vol. III, Vārāṇasī, 1971.

Reu, V.N., *Ṛgveda par ek Aitihāsik Dṛṣṭi*, Delhi, 1967.

Rowse, A.L., *The use of History*, 3rd edn., London, 1947.

Roy, B.P., *Political Ideas and Institutions in the Mahābhārata*, Calcutta, 1975.

Sarkar, J.N., *Thoughts on the Study of Indian History*, General President's Address, 37th Session, IHC, Calicut, 1976.

———, "Ideas of History in Medieval India", *QRHS*, IV, 1-2, pp. 1-21.

Śāstrī, A. Banerji, "On Ancient Indian Historical Tradition", *JBORS*, XIII, pp. 62-79.

Śāstrī, J.L., *Political Thought in the Purāṇas*, Lahore, 1944.

Śāstrī, K.A.N., *The Colas*, vol. I, Madras, 1925, vol. II, pt. I, Madras, 1937.

———, *The Pāṇḍyan Kingdom*, London, 1929.

Śāstrī, N.C., *Ādi Purāṇa mein Pratipādita Bhārat*, Vārāṇasī, 1968.

Sen, S.P. (ed.), *Historical Biography in Indian Literature*, Calcutta, 1979.

——— (ed.), *Historians and Historiography in Modern India*, Calcutta, 1973.

Sharma, R.P., *Paurāṇic Kośa*, Vārāṇasī, vs 2028.

Sharma, S.R., *The Making of Modern India*, Calcutta, 1951.

Shotwell, J.T., *Introduction to the History of History*, 2 vols., Columbia, 1939.

Sieg, E., *Die Sagenstoffe des Rgveda und die Indische Itihāsa Tradition*, Stuttgart, 1902.

———, "Itihāsa Tradition", in *ERE*, ed. J. Hastings, vol. VII, pp. 46-62.

Singh, G.P., *Early Indian Historical Tradition and Archaeology*, Delhi, 1994.

———, *Political Thought in Ancient India*, Delhi, 1993.

———, "A New Approach to the Study of Historical Data in the Epic and Purāṇic Literature Regarding Ancient India", *Proceedings of the UGC Sponsored National Seminar on History and Literature*, Sardar Patel University, Vallabh Vidyānagar, Gujarat, Feb. 1991, pp. 1-15.

———, "Was Herodotus of Greece the Father of History"? *Adhyayan*, *JBIAS*, vol. II, nos. 1 & 2, 1993, pp. 1-10.

Singh. M.G., *History of Himachal Pradesh*, Delhi, 1982.

Singh, M.R., *A Critical study of the Geographical Data in the Early Purāṇas*, Calcutta, 1972.

Sircar, D.C., *Studies in the Geography of Ancient and Medieval India*, Delhi, 1971.

Smith, P., *The Historians and History*, New York, 1964.

Smith, R.M., *Dates and Dynasties in Earliest India*, ed. by J.L. Śāstrī, Delhi, 1973.

Smith, V.A., *Early History of India*, revd. by S.M. Edwards, 4th edn., London, 1967.

Sorensen, *Index to the Names in the Mahābhārata*, 2 vols., London, 1904.

Souza, J.P. De and C.M. Kulkarni (ed.), *Historiography in Inidan Languages*, Bombay, 1972.

Stem, F. (ed.), *The Varieties of History: From Voltaire to the Present*, New York, 1957.

Temperley, H.W.V. (ed.), *Selected Essays*, Cambridge, 1930.

Thapar, R., *A History of India*, vol. I (Penguin Books), Baltimore, 1966.

———, *The Past and Prejudice*, Delhi, 1975.

———, *Ancient Indian Social History*, Hyderabad, 1984.

———, *From Lineage to State,* Bombay, 1984.

Thompson, J.W., *A History of Historical Writing*, vol. I, From the Earliest times to the end of the seventeenth century, Gloucester, 1967.

Tikekar, S.R., *On Historiography*, Bombay, 1964.

Tod, J., *Annals and Antiquities of Rajasthan,* vol. I, 1st edn., London, 1829, rept. Delhi, 1971.

Trevelyan, G.M., *Clio: A Muse and Other Essays*, London, 1930.

Tripathi, R.S., *History of Ancient India,* Delhi, 1985.

Trotter, L.J. and W.H. Hutton, *History of India from the Earliest Times to the Present Day*, Delhi, 1975.

Upādhyāya, B., *Purāṇa Vimarśa*, Vārāṇasī, 1965.

Usher, S., *The Historians of Greece and Rome,* London, 1969.

Vaidya, C.V., *The Mahābhārata: A Criticism*, Delhi, 1966.

Venkatachalam, K., *The Polt in Indian Chronology,* Vijayawada, 1953.

———, *Chronology of Ancient Hindu History*, Vijayawada, 1957.

Warder, A.K., *An Introduction to Indian Historiography,* Bombay, 1972.

Weber, A., *History of Indian Literature*, Eng. trans. from the second German edn. by J. Mann and Th. Zachariae, London, 1882, rept. Delhi, 1981.

Wheelers, J.T., *India from the Earliest Ages (Hindu, Buddhist and Brahmanical Revival)*, vol. III of *The History of India,* Delhi, 1973.

Wilford, F., "Chronology of the Hindus", *As. Res.*, V, Delhi, 1979, pp. 241-92.

Wilson, H.H., *The Hindu History of Kashmir*, Calcutta, 1960.

Winternitz, M., *History of Indian Literature,* Eng. trans. from the Original German by Mrs. S. Ketkar, vol. I, Calcutta, 1927, rept. Delhi, 1977.

Journals and Periodicals

Annals of the Bhandarkar Oriental Research Institute, Poona.

Asiatic Researches.

Bulletin of the Deccan College Research Society, Poona.

Epigraphia Indica, Delhi.

Indian Antiquary, Bombay.

Indo-Asian Culture, Delhi.

Indian Historical Quarterly, Calcutta, New rpt., Delhi.

Journal of the American Oriental Society.

Journal of the Asiatic Society of Bengal, Calcutta.

Journal of the Bombay Branch of the Royal Asiatic Society, Bombay.

Journal of the Benares Hindu University, Benares.

Journal of the Bhāratīya Itihāsa Adhyayan Saṁsthān, Allahabad.

Journal of the Bihar and Orissa Research Society, Patna.

Journal of Indian History, Trivandrum.

Journal of the Numismatic Society of India, Vārāṇasī.

Journal of the Royal Asiatic Society of Great Britain and Ireland, London.

Journal of the Royal Asiatic Society of Bengal, Letters, Calcutta.

Modern Review, Calcutta.

Our Heritage, Calcutta.

Purāṇa, Half-yearly Bulletin of the Purāṇa Department, All India Kashiraj Trust, Rāmnagar, Vārāṇasī.

Quarterly Review of Historical Studies, Calcutta.

Vienna Oriental Journal.

Proceedings and Reports

Archaeological Survey of India, Annual Reports.

G. Bühler's Rport, *Archaeological Survey of Western India,* vols. IV & V.

Problems of Historical Writing in India — Proceedings of the Seminar held at the India International Centre, New Delhi, 21-25 Jan. 1963.

Proceedings of the Indian History Congress.

Proceedings of the Oriental Conferences.

Dictionaries, Encyclopaedias and Gazetteers

Dowson, *Hindu Classical Dictionary*, London, 1888.

Encyclopaedia Britannica, London & New York.

Encyclopaedia of Religion and Ethics, New York, vol. VII, pp. 461ff.

N.L. Dey, *Geographical Dictionary of Ancient and Medieval India*, Calcutta, 1927.

Monier-Williams, *Sanskrit-English Dictionary,* Oxford, 1899, rept. Oxford, 1951.

The Imperial Gazetteer of India, vols. I-IV (Indian Empire), Oxford, 1907-09.

Index